Jacqueline Ann Butt
Cambridge Sunday

ADVANCES IN THEORY AND PRACTICE IN BEHAVIOUR THERAPY

Annual Series of
European Research in Behavior Therapy
3

Series Editors

P.M.G. Emmelkamp, I. Florin, I.M. Marks

ADVANCES IN THEORY AND PRACTICE IN BEHAVIOUR THERAPY

Editors

P.M.G. Emmelkamp, W.T.A.M. Everaerd,
F. Kraaimaat, M.J.M. van Son

SWETS & ZEITLINGER B.V. AMSTERDAM / LISSE

PUBLISHING SERVICE

CIP gegevens Koninklijke Bibliotheek Den Haag
Advances
Advances in theory and practice in behaviour therapy/
eds. P.M.G. Emmelkamp.et al.-Amsterdam [etc.]: Swets & Zeitlinger;
Berwyn: Swets North America.- Ill.- .(Annual Series of European Research in Behvior Therapy. ;3) Met lit. opg.
ISBN 90 265 0966 9 geb.
SISO 607.33 UDC 615.851 NUGI 713

Library of Congress Cataloging-in-Publication Data
Advances in theory and practice in behavior therapy/editors, P.M.G. Emmelkamp...
[et al.].
276 p..cm.--(Annual Series of European Research in behavior Therapy);3)
Includes bibliographies
ISBN 9026509669
1. Behavior therapy. I. Emmelkamp, Paul M.G., 1949-
II Series.[DNLM:1. Behavior Therapy. W1 AN78PQ v. 3/WM
425 A244]
RC489.B4A348 1988
616.89'142--dc19
DNLM/DLC
for Library of Congress 88-24946 CIP

Druk: Offsetdrukkerij Kanters B.V., Alblasserdam

ISBN 90 265 0966 9
NUGI 713

CONTENTS

Part I: Theoretical Issues

Part II: Broadening the Scope of Behaviour Therapy

Part III: Depressive Disorders

Part IV: Addictive Disorders

Part V: Behavioural Medicine

PREFACE

This third volume of the Annual Series of European Research in Behavior Therapy contains a number of selected contributions from the 17th Congress of the European Association of Behaviour Therapy.

This volume consists of 22 chapters divided into 6 parts. Part I presents some theoretical issues and deals specifically with the implications of experimental research for clinical practice. Part II focuses on rapprochement and integration with other psychotherapeutic schools. Part III to V cover significant contributions that have been made in the area of depressive disorders, addictive disorders and behavioural medicine. The three chapters in part VI describe the application of behavioural approaches in the community. No contributions in the area of anxiety disorders have been included. Volume IV of this series is dedicated exclusively to anxiety disorders.

We hope this volume will stimulate further behavioural research in Europe and will be informative to colleagues in other parts of the world.

P.M.G. Emmelkamp
W.T.A.M. Everaerd
F. Kraaimaat
M.J.M. van Son

PART 1:

THEORETICAL ISSUES

THE IMPACT OF EXPERIMENTAL RESEARCH ON CLINICAL PRACTICE

J. Teasdale

Medical Research Council, Applied Psychology Unit, Cambridge, U.K.

One of the strengths of behaviour therapy, in its early phase, was its ability to develop simple effective treatments for apparently complex clinical problems. This ability appeared to depend on a close relationship between treatment methods and existing experimental paradigms of conditioning and learning. More recent developments in behaviour therapy do not seem to have involved such a close relationship between experimental research and clinical practice.

In this paper, I shall briefly review the nature of the relationship that existed between experimental research and clinical practice in the early development of behaviour therapy, and then examine whether anything comparable exists currently. For brevity, I shall restrict discussion to only one of the more recent developments within behaviour therapy, the treatment of depression.

LEARNING PARADIGMS AND THE DEVELOPMENT OF BEHAVIOUR THERAPY

As I have discussed in detail elsewhere (Teasdale, 1982), in developing a psychological treatment for a clinical condition we need to ask a series of questions such as: 1) How should I conceptualize this problem? 2) Which of its many features should I focus on? 3) What in principle does my conceptualization of the problem suggest needs doing? 4) How in practice is this to be achieved? 5) How can I measure whether I have affected the changes I was aiming for? The answers to these questions that led to the initial development of behaviour therapy were the result of an imaginative leap which took the following simple theoretical approach: "Let us look at clinical problem X as if aspects of it were similar to the behaviour we have studied in our laboratory paradigm Y". Although this is a very simple sort of theory, it allows us to derive possible methods for treating clinical problems from the empirical generalizations already established within experimental paradigms.

So, for example, if we view phobias from the perspective of the classical conditioning paradigm we get the following answers to the questions listed above: 1) Regard the phobia as a conditioned fear. 2) Focus on the autonomic and other responses elicited by presentation of the phobic stimuli, and the passive avoidance behaviour resulting from this conditioned fear. 3) Extinguish fear conditioned to the CS by 4) repeatedly presenting the phobic stimulus in the absence of any aversive UCS's. 5) Measure autonomic and other responses to presentation of phobic stimuli, and changes in approach behaviour to phobic stimuli.

It is now a matter of history that this general approach was extremely productive in generating effective treatments for a range of conditions. What of the situation now?

THE CONTRIBUTION OF EXPERIMENTAL RESEARCH TO CLINICAL PRACTICE NOW

As far as depression and its psychological treatment are concerned, there is nothing really comparable to the close relationship that existed between basic experimental research and the development of clinical procedures in earlier phases of behaviour therapy. In this situation it is tempting to turn our backs on basic experimental research. However, I think this would be a mistake. Rather, I think we have to see basic research as one of a number of strands contributing to the total fabric of the development of new forms of treatment. Other strands would include clinical observation and intuition, the accumulated wisdom of the ages, common sense and personal experience, and evaluation of the complex packages that comprise many forms of recently developed psychological treatments. Each of these sources has its particular contribution to make. One of the most useful contributions from experimental research is to the development of applicable theory. Such theory would guide our overall attempt both to understand clinical problems and to develop treatments to change them. It has been suggested that there is actually nothing more practical then a good theory. Indeed, as I have indicated, one of the most important contributions to the development of behaviour therapy was the theoretical step of regarding clinical problems as if they were similar to the phenomena studied in experimental paradigms of learning and conditioning. At a stroke, this made a wide range of empirical findings, conceptual tools, and methods of measurement available to the clinician trying to develop clinically effective procedures.

Within clinical practice, it is of vital importance for the therapist and client to have a valid and usable shared conceptual framework both of the nature of the presenting problem and of methods for doing something about it. Such a theoretical or conceptual framework can be viewed as a map of the territory of the disorder. Providing the therapist and client with a map that shows them where they currently are and where they have to get to allows them to use their combined skill and creativity to select and devise flexible means of getting to their objective. They are able to use the methods that are most appropriate for the particular person in their particular setting, rather than having to run through, cookbook fashion, the same set of techniques for everyone.

The need for a reasonably accurate and usable conceptual framework or map of the problem seems particularly important in an area like depression. Without such a source to consult for guidance when stuck, both the therapist and client can quickly sink deeper and deeper into the swamp of hopelessness, which is so often a central feature of depression.

The need for an adequate theoretical framework is also suggested from another perspective: it could be suggested that some of the worst abuses of behaviour therapy have resulted from the superficial application of techniques without the attempt to perform an adequate functional analysis based on a valid theoretical framework.

It is not always easy to assess the extent to which experimental research has an impact on clinical practice through its contribution in shaping our working conceptual frameworks. One of the reasons for this is that we often tend to take for granted the conceptual tools and frameworks that we bring to bear when we think about how to tackle clinical problems. Often we are unaware of the sources, including experimental research, that have affected our theoretical orientations, many of which remain implicit much of the time.

So warned, that what we may be looking for may not be immediately obvious, let us now get more specific and consider some actual experimental findings, the theoretical implications that flow from them, and what this buys us for clinical practice. These are all findings that have affected my own clinical approach to depression, shaping both my current practice and the directions in which I am looking for further improvements in treatment. In the space available, I necessarily have to be selective.

DEPRESSION AND UNCONTROLLABLE AVERSIVE EVENTS

A first requirement of a theoretically informed approach to treating depression is a working hypothesis of the setting conditions that elicit or maintain the depressed state. Here, I have found experimental research investigating the effects of controllable versus uncontrollable aversive events extremely helpful (Anisman & Zacharko, 1982). Much of this work has been conducted within the well known learned helplessness paradigm. The basic experimental situation studied in this research has been the so-called *triadic design*: one group of experimental subjects receives aversive events, (such as electric shocks) which they are able to control; another group receives the same aversive events but are unable to exert any control over them; and a third control group receives no aversive events. The typical finding from research using this design has been that on a variety of dependent measures, including both behavioural and neuroendocrine variables, the group receiving uncontrollable aversive events shows considerable deficits, but these are not shown by the group that receives the same aversive events but have some control over them. The latter group typically show no deficits compared to the group receiving no aversive events (Anisman & Zacharko, 1982). While the mechanism underlying the production of deficits by uncontrollable aversive events has been a matter of dispute, there is sufficient empirical evidence to suggest that the state produced by the experience of uncontrollable aversive events can be usefully viewed as an analogue of clinical depression.

If we accept this position, then we can regard the depressed patient as being in the same position as the experimental subjects that receive uncontrollable aversive events. The therapeutic task can then be seen, at a very general level, as taking the patient from the position of a subject experiencing uncontrollable aversive events to the position of a subject in either the group receiving controllable aversive events or the group receiving no aversive events, neither of which show deficits. This could be achieved either by increasing control over the aversive events experienced, or by reducing the aversiveness of these events. Thus, basic experimental research, by singling out two dimensions of experience as critical in the production of depression, gives a general direction to our therapeutic efforts by indicating that these should be aimed at reducing the aversiveness and increasing the controllability of events experienced by depressed patients.

Further, we can expand on this basic position by drawing on other experimental work, (for example Gray (1975)) which has shown that the non-arrival of anticipated positive events (frustrative non-reward) is in many ways functionally equivalent to the administration of inherently noxious aversive events. In other words, the class of aversive events includes both the experience of inherently noxious events and experiences characterized by the failure of anticipated or desired positive events to occur. Observation suggests that, in man, the latter are in fact the more common source of aversive events.

So, from experimental research it is possible to distil the following working hypothesis describing the setting conditions under which depression will occur: *Depression occurs as a result of the experience of highly aversive outcomes perceived as uncontrollable. In man, the aversive outcomes frequently consist op the non-arrival of expected highly desired outcomes of current concern (frustrative non-reward).*

In practice, of course, the two main classes of aversive experience affecting depressed patients are the depression itself, its symptoms and effects, (Teasdale, 1985) and the non-arrival of highly desired goals such as love, happiness, material well-being, feelings of achievement, of competence, and of self-respect. The working hypothesis derived from basic experimental studies tells us that, in general terms, treatments of depression should, first, identify the major aversive events affecting patients which they perceive themselves unable to control. Having identified these, we should increase the perceived controllability of these events, wherever we can, and where we cannot we should reduce their perceived aversiveness.

What, in practice, has this working hypothesis brought me?

UNDERSTANDING THE EFFECTIVENESS OF DIVERSE PSYCHOLOGICAL TREATMENTS

A major benefit from the working hypothesis is that it helps to understand what is otherwise a somewhat bewildering situation in the current state of psychological treatments for major depression.
There is now encouraging evidence for the effectiveness of a range of psychological treatments. However, treatments that are, on average, equally effective often differ widely in their underlying theoretical assumptions. For example, some stress the importance of distorted thinking, some deficits in interpersonal functioning, other deficits in rates of positive reinforcement, and yet others deficits in self-control behaviours.

While effective treatments differ in their underlying rationales, they share a number of procedural features which would be expected to increase the perceived controllability and to reduce the aversiveness of depression and other relevant outcomes. So, they all tend to be goal-oriented problem-solving approaches focussed on change in the here and now; they have high treatment structure; and they include a credible elaborated rationale which removes blame from patients for being depressed and leads them to believe there are direct actions that can be taken to relieve symptoms of depression or the situations contributing to them. Homework assignments are usually given to implement those actions, and progress is monitored and reinforced.

From the perspective of the general working hypothesis that has been presented, it is understandable that these treatments, although differing in their stated underlying rationales, should be effective. This is because they share procedures which would be expected to increase the perceived controllability and reduce the aversiveness of depression and other related outcomes (Teasdale, 1985).

By contrast, more traditional forms of psychotherapy have been found to be relatively ineffective in producing symptomatic improvement in major depression. This is quite consistent with the position proposed because they, of course, have a much looser structure, often being more concerned with understanding the origins of difficulties rather than with changing the perception of the here and now and going out and doing something about it. We gain more than a sense of intellectual tidiness from this suggestion for understanding the way in which a range of structured psychological treatments may be effective in reducing depression. The suggestion offers us a way forward beyond the plateau of therapeutic effectiveness that seems to have been reached in this area. A range of structured treatments have now been shown to be moderately effective in treating major depression. However, none of them is so clearly superior to the others that it provides clear guidelines for the direction to take in developing the next generation of more effective and efficient treatments. Experience with the treatment of phobias suggests that an important step in increasing the effectiveness and efficiency of treatments is the identification of the central therapeutic components shared by a range of treatments. These components can then be built in to a new treatment which embodies them as effectively and efficiently as possible. So, one of the most productive ways of moving off the present plateau in psychological treatments of depression is to construct a working hypothesis of the general requirements of these treatments, in the way that I have attempted, and then to operationalize these more effectively and efficiently in new treatments. I have found the experimentally derived working hypothesis that I have outlined very helpful in guiding my thinking on this issue.

I can illustrate the way in which the working hypothesis could guide the development of better treatment by describing the way it has affected my own practice of Beck's cognitive therapy. As is well known, this treatment is directed at the identification and modification of negative depressed cognitions which, it is assumed, are responsible for the maintenance of depression. Several specific techniques are available for this purpose, for example, helping patients to generate less negative alternative interpretations of situations. These techniques are not difficult to learn. What is difficult is learning to recognize to which of the profusion of negative thoughts shown by depressed patients these techniques are most fruitfully applied. When I was learning this treatment approach, I had a tendency to try to deal with almost every negative thought that came up, a tendency I have noticed in other novice therapists. At this stage, I tended to regard the application of the technique as the goal or aim of therapy, ignoring, or being unable to discern, the distinction between centrally relevant and peripherally relevant thoughts. In contrast to this almost reflexive application of technique, experienced and effective therapists appear to operate from a wider conceptualization and functional analysis of patients' problems. They regard dealing with negative thoughts as a means to an end, rather than an end in itself. The end they are pursuing might be symptomatic relief or it might be more effective problem-solving.

I have found the working hypothesis I have outlined very helpful in providing a guiding general framework within which to come to a broad problem-oriented conceptualization of a patient's difficulties. Within this framework I can regard specific techniques as means, not ends. The working hypothesis tells me that I have to identify the major aversive events affecting the patient which they perceive as uncontrollable and about which they are hopeless about affecting change. The hypothesis tells me that some of these will be inherently unpleasant events, such as the symptoms of depression themselves, but others will consist of frustrated positive goals. Thus treatment, in addition to aiming for symptomatic relief from depression, is likely to also include goals such as feeling loved or respected, having better accommodation, reducing friction in a marriage, having friends, or having a more satisfying job. Having identified the major desired goals which the patient is hopeless about achieving, I know that my task is then to implement problem-solving activity which uses the correction of negative thinking, and other cognitive and behavioural techniques, as a means to achieve those goals rather than as ends in themselves.

Simple as it sounds, this shift in approach which follows from the working hypothesis can have a profound effect on the way treatment is conducted and on its effectiveness. It provides an illustration of the way in which the working hypothesis, if applied for depression, could provide both a unifying conceptual framework and lead to increments in effectiveness and efficiency.

So far, I have illustrated the use of experimental results as one of a number of threads in weaving a working hypothesis at a fairly general level. This is a very important and necessary exercise, but it is one in which the links between experiment, theory, and action can get rather loose. This does not do justice to the way in which the high quality evidence derived from experimental studies can be used to provide a very secure foundation from which to derive theory and clinical practice.

DO NEGATIVE THOUGHTS MAINTAIN DEPRESSION?

It is implicit in what I have said so far that psychological treatments for depression can be effective even though the theories on which they are based may not be wholly accurate. A central assumption underlying my own preferred approach to treating depression, Beck's cognitive therapy, is that the stream of negative thoughts which depressed patients experience is an important factor maintaining their depression. From this assumption it follows that if, by suitable therapeutic procedures, these thoughts can be reduced in frequency or intensity then depression should be reduced. One way to examine the validity of this assumption is to test it experimentally. If the assumption can be supported by the high quality evidence that carefully controlled experiments can yield, then at least one relatively secure foundation for the theoretical position underlying my clinical practice could be established. There are good practical reasons for doing this: being fully aware of therapists' ability to persuade themselves of the truth of their preferred theories even when these are false, it is very helpful, in a treatment which often puts the therapist at risk of sinking into hopelessness with their patients, to have at least a few solidly established foundations on which to stand.

Fennell, Teasdale, Jones and Damlé (1987) reported the most recent of a series of experiments that have examined the effects on patient's depression of reducing the frequency of their spontaneously occurring depressing thoughts. As well as illustrating the way in which the validity of a clinical theory can be supported by high quality experimental data, this study also demonstrates two further bonuses of experimental approaches. The first is their ability to produce unexpected, serendipitous findings. The second is the way in which, having acquired good quality data for one purpose it is there to come back to, again and again, to raise, and sometimes answer, further questions.

Patients with major depressive disorders each received brief periods of two interventions. In the first, they simply sat doing nothing for a brief period. In the second, they described to themselves in great detail what they could see in a series of slides projected on a wall for the same period. The purpose of the latter distraction procedure was, by having patients direct their attention and information processing resources to dealing with stimuli from an external source, to reduce the processing of information from internal sources that led to the production of the stream of depressive ruminations.

Distraction was effective in reducing the frequency of spontaneously occurring depressive thoughts, as measured by a thought sampling technique. In patients with a clinical picture of neurotic depression, as indicated by a low score on the Newcastle Diagnosis Scale (see below), the reduction in thought frequency by the distraction procedure produced an appreciable reduction in depressed mood. This, of course, is just what the cognitive model of depression would predict. Similar results were obtained for measures of psychomotor function. As this was the third time we had confirmed this prediction in this type of experiment, and as we had taken care to deal with some of the possible interpretative difficulties of our earlier studies, we were very confident in the validity of these results. These experiments were actually very important in increasing my confidence that the theory on which my clinical practice was based had some solid foundation, rather than the mere plausibility which, unfortunately, is often all many clinical theories possess.

At the time, this was the main effect this study had on my thinking. However, I have recently reflected on it further, and have come to the conclusion that it has some very important further implications. The time scale of the experiment was very brief, only five minutes of each intervention. Nonetheless, substantial changes in patient's mood were achieved simply by preventing the occurrence of thoughts that might otherwise have occurred. Not only does this suggest that, in general, affective state may be very powerfully influenced by what, from moment to moment, is in consciousness. It also suggests that of the many cognitive processes that might be involved in the production of the stream of negative depressive thoughts, and thereby in the maintenance of depressed mood, at least one stage in the process involves a step which shares limited resources in common with the processes involved in the distraction task. This must be so if allocating those resources to the distraction task, simply by the redirection of attention, can so effectively cut in to the processes maintaining depressed mood. I believe this has important implications. First, it considerably narrows the area in which to conduct further experiments aimed at yielding a more detailed understanding of the process involved. Second, it suggests that therapeutic procedures that use the redirection of attention as a way of controlling the pattern of activity of the information processing system may be extremely valuable.

What of the serendipitous aspect of this line of experimental enquiry? In earlier studies we had noticed, although we were not making it an explicit focus of our investigation, that the extent to which distraction was successful in reducing the frequency of depressing thoughts was related to patients' scores on the Newcastle Diagnosis Scale (Carney, Roth & Garside, 1965). This is a measure of the extent to which patients' depression conforms to a neurotic or endogenous picture. There appeared to be a trend for control of thought and mood to be easier in patients with more neurotic forms of depression. So, in the Fennell, Teasdale, Jones and Damlé (1987) study we explicitly set out to explore this patient variable. For patients with more neurotic forms of depression, distraction was extremely effective in reducing both the frequency of negative thoughts, and depressed mood, as already described. By contrast, for patients presenting a more endogenous picture, distraction was less effective in reducing thought frequency, and such reduction as was achieved had very little effect on mood. Even when pairs of neurotic and endogenous patients were matched for the extent of thought reduction, the endogenous patients still showed much less reduction in depressed mood than their more neurotic match-mates. This leads to the very important suggestion that thinking and affect appear to have a different functional relationship to each other in the two types of patients. In the more neurotic patients the situation is as Beck's model suggests: the stream of negative thoughts seems to contribute substantially to depressed mood from moment to moment, and reducing the frequency of such thoughts leads to rapid improvement in mood. In the more endogenous patients, however, the moment to moment contents of consciousness appear to play a much less important role in maintaining depressed mood. Reducing the frequency of depressing thoughts in such patients has little immediate effect on their mood, at least over the brief time intervals studied. Clearly, this originally serendipitous finding has substantial implications for the way we should think about applying cognitive therapeutic procedures to patients that score towards the more endogenous end of the Newcastle Diagnosis Scale.

MOOD, MEMORY AND THE MODIFICATION OF SELF-EVALUATION

The next example of the way that basic experimental research can have an impact on clinical practice illustrates the interplay of experimental findings, theory and clinical observation. It also demonstrates one of the greatest virtues of experimental research: its ability to tell you that you are wrong, and in doing so to open up a whole range of new possibilities.

The starting point here was the question: why is it that depressed people's thinking seems to be so biased in a negative direction? One possibility that was experimentally testable was the hypothesis that depressed mood in some way increases the accessibility of negative cognitions. That is, in depressed mood, negative information is just that much easier to get access to and is more likely to come to mind and to be used to interpret current experience, the converse being true for more positive information. We have investigated this accessibility hypothesis in a series of experiments which examined the effects of induced and naturally occurring mood states on the ease and probability of recall of positive and negative memories, particularly of events from subjects' lives (Clark and Teasdale, 1982; Teasdale, 1983). In a typical experiment, students were put into either an elated or depressed mood and then presented with a series of neutral cues to which they had to recall related autobiographical memories. Subsequently, in neutral mood, these memories were rated and categorized as being of originally happy or unhappy experiences. The typical result of such an experiment, which both we and other investigators have reported (Bower, 1981), is that people are more likely to recall happy memories in elated than depressed mood, whereas unhappy memories are more likely to be recalled in depressed mood than in elated mood.

This type of experiment confirmed the accessibility hypothesis. On the basis of this and related types of experiments, Gordon Bower proposed an associative network theory of mood and memory (Bower, 1981). This theory, while based on memory experiments, proposed that mood would have effects on a wide range of cognitive processes. Specifically, it suggested that in addition to the effects of mood increasing the accessibility of memories of experiences congruent with the mood, there would also be effects of mood on the activation of interpretative concepts, evaluations and inference rules. Consequently, the way experience is interpreted and evaluated could be powerfully affected by mood: evaluations and interpretations will tend to be congruous in tone with the prevailing mood. It was suggested that memories, concepts, evaluations, and inference rules that had previously been associated with a given mood state would be reactivated quite automatically and unconsciously when that mood state was subsequently re-instituted.

So, although this theory was originally based on memory experiments, it was extended to the effects of mood on a wider range of phenomena, including ones that are of much more obvious clinical relevance. For example, it suggested that the negative self-evaluation or low self-esteem shown by depressed people is, at least in part, a result of depressed mood reactivating self-devaluative patterns of thinking that had previously been associated with, or caused, depressed mood. Alternatively, it was suggested that in forming some evaluation of oneself one might quickly scan memory for relevant information. If, as a result of the effects of mood on the relative accessibility of memories, this data base is negatively biased, then, again, one might come to the conclusion that one is inadequate and inferior. In either case, the theory suggested that these effects of mood would occur automatically and unconsciously as a result of direct activation of negative cognitive processes by depressed mood state. Further, according to the theory, these effects should occur more or less independently of the source of the mood (Teasdale, 1983).

THE MODIFICATION OF CHRONIC NEGATIVE SELF-EVALUATION

Now, if there is this powerful automatic effect of mood on one's evaluation of one's self or one's life in general, the question naturally arises whether, in treatment, we can use alternations in mood or affective state to change the patterns of negative self-evaluative thinking in depressed patients. If low self-esteem is the result of reactivation of negative self-evaluations in depressed mood, can we, by inducing a mood previously associated with more acceptant, non-evaluative patterns of thinking, change these negative self-evaluations?

The particular clinical problem I had in mind was attempting, within cognitive therapy, to change the negative self-evaluation of patients for whom this has been a very long-standing feature of their view of themselves, often related to a history of childhood rejection or deprivation. My impression was that the usual cognitive therapy procedures, such as having patients review all the positive aspects of themselves and their lives, which are often effective in dealing with negative self-evaluation in other patients, tend to be relatively ineffective in changing the more enduring belief of these patients that they are basically no good and worthless. What seemed to be required was a way of suspending their chronic negative self-devaluative activity to provide them with direct experiential evidence of feeling acceptable to themselves and worthwhile, just as they were. According to the theory I have just outlined, in order to provide this experience I would need to induce an affective state in which the cognitive operations related to self-evaluation, particularly negative self-evaluation, were suspended or reduced. In other words, could I change patterns of self-evaluation by inducing a change in affective state? The theory clearly suggested I could.

A suspension of evaluative cognitive operations appears to be a feature of the states associated with certain types of meditation and with naturally occurring mystical-like states. In such states, it appears that people simply cease to make evaluative judgments of themselves and others, and this is associated with feelings of acceptance and forgiveness. Thus, it seemed worthwhile to explore the use of these states clinically in the treatment of the type of patient with persistent negative self-evaluation that I have described.

A LIFE TRANSFORMED

By good chance, the first patient with whom I began this exploration produced results that were so dramatic that they convinced me that something very important was happening, even if I might not fully understand what it was.

This patient was a woman, Mrs. C., who had been chronically and severely depressed for at least 12 years, during which time she had been in and out of hospital with virtually no lasting improvement. She had a very low self-esteem and a sense of worthlessness which dated from early childhood, and was related to experiences of rejection by her parents. When I asked if there had been any time that she had felt peaceful and accepting of herself and of the world, she identified a time at the age of 18. She had gone down to the sea shore intending to kill herself. The day had been a very stormy one and the waves were so dramatic in their fury that they captured her attention. She did not throw herself into the sea as she had intended, but, instead, sat for some hours just looking at the waves. She came away no longer wanting to kill herself but feeling quite calm and peaceful.

That feeling rapidly passed. However, similar states had reappeared quite spontaneously on a number of occasions. She had dismissed the importance of these states, viewing them as transient oddities without any real significance for her view of herself.

As a first step towards making more effective therapeutic use of these states, I gave Mrs C. a book that described methods of meditation and the states that were produced. She immediately recognised that her own experiences conformed to relatively well established and highly valued states. By using a combination of trips back to the seaside and sitting quietly in a sound-proof room we were able to reinduce these states. From the experience of these states, and the associated patterns of cognitive processing, we were able to re-establish a very firm sense in which Mrs C. felt that, although she might have difficulties and problems, she was basically all right, and could be acceptant and forgiving towards herself. From this firm basis she was able to take steps, including leaving her husband, which over a very short period produced a dramatic and remarkable improvement. She ceased to be depressed, and to people who had known her for the previous 12 years appeared to be a radically transformed person. Indeed, she had made one of the most dramatic changes that I have seen clinically.

Inevitably, when I came to try a similar approach on the next patient or two the results were by no means as dramatic. However, experiences of this kind are so striking that I was convinced that something very important was going on, but that the deliberately simple-minded approach that I had taken to the problem was probably not sufficient. Perhaps not surprisingly, something more than merely getting people into a relaxed frame of mind which would then produce an automatic unconscious shift in their self-evaluative processes seemed to be necessary.

While I was puzzling over these clinical observations, the experimental basis of Bower's associative network theory, on which my simple-minded approach had been based, was itself coming under attack. Although the basic findings of experiments investigating mood congruous memory, of the type I described above, continued to be replicated, attempts to replicate experiments more directly related to the foundations of Bower's theory had often failed, even when conducted by Bower and his colleagues themselves (Bower, 1986). Further, experiments testing key predictions from the theory on the effects of mood on perception were beginning to be reported and these had also produced mainly negative results.

It was clear that some re-examination of the whole basis of thinking in this area was necessary. It was at this point that I became aware of the importance of the work of Gerry Clore and Norbert Schwarz on the role of feelings as information.

FEELINGS AS INFORMATION

Schwarz and Clore (in press) have proposed a different approach to understanding the way in which affective state modifies judgments and evaluations. They suggest that feelings themselves are a source of information, and that individuals may use their perceived affective reactions as relevant information when making evaluative judgments. In other words, when I am trying to evaluate myself, or another person, or the quality of my life in general, or a piece of poetry, a crucial item of information is my actual momentary feeling state when I consider the object to be evaluated. On this view, the effects of mood on evaluation occur because people mistakenly interpret feelings due to a pre-existing state as a reaction to the target stimulus.

The notion that feelings have informational value is, of course, by no means novel. In Howard Leventhall's perceptual-motor theory of emotion (Leventhal, 1984), for example, it is clearly suggested that emotional states convey a form of implicit meaning.

Clore and Schwarz's "feelings as information" hypothesis offers a perspective on the way that depressed mood may affect evaluations of oneself or one's whole life that is very different from that suggested by Bower's mood congruity hypothesis. A crucial difference between the two positions is that, according to Clore and Schwarz, the impact of affective states on evaluative judgments is a function of their perceived informational value. If indidivuals attribute their current feelings to a source that is irrelevant to the evaluation of the target stimulus, then the informational value of their affective state should be discredited and their feelings should not influence evaluative judgments. According to models of mood congruent retrieval, on the other hand, the impact of affective state should depend only on the cognitive processes activated by the mood rather than on the information provided by the affective states themselves. Clearly, these two positions are going to have different implications for the clinical problem that we have been considering.

Schwarz and Clore (in press), have mustered an impressive body of evidence that lends considerable support to their account of the way in which feelings affect judgments. Space only allows presentation of one example of the studies they have conducted. Schwarz and Clore (1983) investigated the effects of mood on subjects' general evaluation and satisfaction with their lives. In one condition, no attempt was made to alter the way in which subjects could use their feeling state as a basis on which to make their judgments. In the second condition, an attempt was made to discredit the informational value of the feeling state by bringing the true source of subject's feeling state into awareness. It was predicted that in this condition the effects of mood on global evaluations of life satisfaction would be reduced or eliminated. To get subjects in different states of happiness, some subjects were telephoned on sunny days, and others on rainy days. It was made to appear that the call came from some distance away so that it was plausible to ask about the weather. In one condition, subjects were simply telephoned and asked to rate how happy they were feeling at that moment and then to rate their general satisfaction with life. In the other condition, the interviewer, prior to asking for these ratings, asked "By the way, how's the weather down there?" This was to bring to the subject's awareness the factor assumed to be actually affecting their mood so that less weight would be attached to feeling state when subjects computed their judgement of general life satisfaction.

Subjects called on fine days did indeed feel significantly happier than those called on wet days. Most importantly, these differences in feeling state were the same whether or not attention was drawn to the weather. When weather was not mentioned, there was a significant and substantial effect of mood on ratings of general life satisfaction, satisfaction being less on the wet days. However, simply by briefly mentioning the weather, the effect of mood on judgement was entirely eliminated. It should be noted that this occurred in the absence of any effect of mentioning the weather on actual mood state. Mentioning the weather affected the use made of mood as a source of information as far as general life satisfaction was concerned, without affecting the state itself.These findings were exactly as predicted by the feelings as information hypothesis. However, it is difficult for the mood congruity or accessibility hypothesis to explain this result. This is only one of a series of findings which has lent considerable support to the hypothesis that at least some of the effects of feelings on judgments are best viewed in terms of feeling state being used as one of a number of sources of information that have to be integrated in making judgments.

The feelings as information hypothesis has sufficient support to make it worthwhile examining its clinical implications. What guidance can it offer?

As far as the specific clinical problem we have been considering is concerned, this hypothesis suggests that altering feeling state could be effectively used as a way to alter global negative evaluative judgments of oneself, one's life, or the future, but only if this is done within an informational context that discredits the informational value of negative feelings and increases the credibility of positive feelings. Interestingly, this fits quite precisely the clinical example presented above; it was only when the patient was provided with information which suggested that her experiences in spontaneously altered states of consciousness were highly valued by others, and generally regarded as revealing one's true and basic state, that she was able to make use of these experiences. Therapy with this patient had also included working out with her a plausible explanation of how she had come to the erroneous conclusion that she was of little self worth, and of why she should continue to feel depressed. In this way the information value of her normal depressed feeling state was discredited, at the same time as the informational value of the positive state was increased. The feelings as information hypothesis also explains clearly why, in the absence of detailed and subtle attention to these factors, merely training people in relaxation or meditation may have only limited effects.

The feelings as information hypothesis offers a way of looking at the importance of providing patients, as part of treatment, with a credible explanation for why they are depressed. Directing subjects' attention to the weather as the true source of their low mood eliminated the effects of mood on evaluations of life in general. In the same way, providing patients with information that points to alternative sources for their depression may reduce the effects of depressed mood on patients' evaluations of themselves, their life and the future.

More generally, the feeling as information hypothesis, when used in conjunction with other experimentally derived theoretical accounts of emotion (eg. Leventhal, 1984), provides a framework within which experimentally-oriented clinicians can begin to explore the range of constructive uses of emotion and feeling state that have been developed by more experientially-oriented therapists. For example, Gendlin (1986) has developed a very clearly described systematic procedure, called focusing, which is explicitly designed to help clients access the often surprising informational content of feelings, by attending to the so-called "felt sense" of a problem. It appears that something similar may lie at the heart of effective psychotherapeutic process in a variety of approaches. Now that experimentally anchored theories are becoming available within which such experientially-oriented procedures can be conceptualized, the exciting prospect of behaviour therapists incorporating these approaches into their research and practice becomes a realistic possibility.

CONCLUSION

Let me conclude by summarizing what I see as the potential power of the link between experimental research and clinical practice.

I have suggested, with others, that clinical practice needs good applicable theories of some generality, and that experimental research is one of the best ways of developing such theories. It is clearly not the only way to generate theory - the field of psychological treatment is not short of somewhat fuzzy, loosely articulated, clinically derived theories. The importance of theories linked to experimental research is that they have to be articulated in sufficient detail for them to be experimentally investigated. This operation itself is invaluable in clarifying theory to a point where it can be clearly articulated, and specific clinical applications and implications derived. Equally, or more importantly, the precision with which such theories are stated enables them to be tested against alternatives and shown to be wrong. Nobody enjoys being wrong, and it is possible to maintain our loose clinical theories quite effectively by a range of cognitive tricks on ourselves. However, the power of experiments is that they force us to acknowledge that we may be wrong, and in that way open us up to explore new possibilities, which, in turn, will give us better clinically applicable theories. This may not be a recipe for the knowledge without difficulties, truth without falsehood, attainment without effort, and progress without sacrifice that we all, at some level, seek. However, it does provide us with a route to follow that may avoid some of the pitfalls that might otherwise hinder our progress in improving psychological treatments.

REFERENCES

Anisman, H. & Zacharko, R.M. (1982) Depression: the predisposing influencing of stress. *Behavioural and Brain Sciences, 5*, 89-137.

Bower, G.H. (1981) Mood and Memory. *American Psychologist, 36*, 129-148.

Bower, G.H. (1986) Personal Communication, November 3, 1986.

Carney, M.W.P. Roth, M. & Garside, R.F. (1965) The diagnosis of depressive symptoms and the prediction of ECT response. *British Journal of Psychiatry, 111*, 659-674.

Clark, D.M. & Teasdale, J.D. (1982) Diurnal variation in clinical depression and accessibility of memories of positive and negative experiences. *Journal of Abnormal Psychology, 91*, 87-95.

Fennell, M.J.V., Teasdale, J.D., Jones, S. & Damlé, A. (1987) Distraction in neurotic and endogenous depression: an investigation of negative thinking in major depressive disorder. *Psychological Medicine, 17*, 441-452.

Gendlin, E.T. (1986) What comes after traditional psychotherapy research? *American Psychologist, 41*, 131-136.

Gray, J.A. (1975) *Elements of a two-process theory of learning*. London: Academic Press.

Leventhal, H. (1984) A perceptual-motor theory of emotion. *Advances in Experimental Social Psychology, 17*, 117-182.

Schwarz, N. & Clore, G.L. (1983) Mood, misattribution and judgments of well-being: informative and directive functions of affective states. *Journal of Personality and Social Psychology, 45*, 513-523.

Schwarz, N. & Clore, G.L. (in press) How do I feel about it? The informative function of affective states. In K. Fiedler & J. Forgas (Eds.) *Affect, Cognition and Social Behaviour*. Toronto: Hogrefe International.

Teasdale, J.D. (1982) What kind of theory will improve psychological treatment? In J. Boulougouris (Ed.) *Learning theory approaches to psychiatry*. Chichester: John Wiley.

Teasdale, J.D. (1983) Negative thinking in depression: cause, effect or reciprocal relationship? *Advances in Behaviour Research and Therapy, 5*, 3-26.

Teasdale, J.D. (1985) Psychological Treatments for depression: how do they work? *Behaviour Research and Therapy, 23*, 157-165.

COMMON-SENSE THEORY AND THE PRACTICE OF HEALTH PSYCHOLOGY

H. Leventhal

University of Wisconsin, Madison, U.S.A.

INTRODUCTION

When I began to outline this paper I felt myself a masochist for agreeing to speak to practitioners about the importance of theory for practice. I felt that way as I suspect that the astute practitioner may do a better job than the academician in elaborating a richly differentiated theory of behavior. I also believe that careful observation of individual cases allows the practitioner to obtain the clearest view of the way situations constraint underlying process and overt action. In short, the practitioner may have the richest conceptual model of the dynamic interplay among the many factors shaping behavior.

There are, however, at least two good reasons for talking about theory. One is to see if my ideas are palatable to you who are in practice. The second is more complex. I believe, as may many of you, that there is yet a third theoretician at work in developing explanations for behavior: specifically, the patients you see and the subjects serving in my studies. If we accept the premise that patients and subjects are theoreticians, it is essential to ask how we should regard their theories. My goal therefore, is to see if I can convince you that self generated theories are not irrelevant oddities, but conceptual systems that must be incorporated into the theories devised by the practitioner and the academic observer.

To understand how the concepts of the layperson impinge upon the theory making of the academician and clinician, it is important to distinguish between the *pragmatic* and the *explanatory* use of concepts. Concepts play a pragmatic role when used to describe and communicate what we see and hear, and when used to predict the future occurrence of an event on the basis of its occurrence in the past. Description, communication and prediction are consequences of using words to categorize events.

For example, if we are conducting a smoking cessation program, we may categorize participants as Heavy Smokers or Addicts, versus Occasional Smokers or Chippers and we may describe our treatments as behavioral rather than psychotherapeutic. These categories clearly ignore many attributes both of our clients and our treatments, but they can communicate information essential for understanding how patients respond to treatment. For example, you have a fair idea of what transpired when I tell you that Tim Baker obtained a 50% quit rate for a group of pack-a-day smokers two years after the termination of a treatment that combined rapid smoking and counseling to enhance coping skills (Tiffany, Martin & Baker, 1986).

Labelling, however, ignores many attributes of our patients and many aspects of our intervention, and the choice of label may imply understanding of causal processes where such understanding is lacking. For example, if we called Baker's pack-a-day smokers addicts, the label would imply a pharmacological process of nicotine addiction and suggest that smoking was used to eliminate withdrawal signs caused by drops in nicotine level. This label ignores learning and positive, or appetitive motivation in the smoking dependence process and it fails to explain why the bulk of quitting failures occurs months after the end of treatment when withdrawal signs have disappeared.

Explanatory concepts may lack a simple, one-to-one relationship with the surface or descriptive level of behavior. We do not explain observable behaviors such as depression, chronic symptom concern, seeking health care, or smoking, by attributing them to underlying traits of depression, hypochondriasis, propensity to seek health care, or need to smoke. The psychological explanation of observed behaviors, lies in specifying a *set of underlying, process variables* which identify the situational stimuli that are necessary and sufficient to evoke the behavior and the internal operations that transform and enrich the stimulus into a perceptual experience with a specific valence that directs the behavior. The advantage of concepts that explain behavior relative to those that merely describe it are two-fold: 1. They allow us to understand *how the behavior is generated and maintained over time*, and 2. They allow us to understand *how to change or modify it.*

For example, to explain illness behavior, or seeking health care, we need concepts that tell us what types of stimuli generate the behavior, e.g., body sensations, and how these stimuli are processed or interpreted to form a *working representation* or model of illness in conscious experience. The model would also tell us how specific behavioral options or *coping plans*, such as seeking health care are generated by the representation, and how the response is *appraised* or evaluated for success in reducing the health threat. As can be seen in figure 1 which depicts this model, the stimulus and its interpretation may generate an *emotional response* which leads to a separate line of *coping* and *appraisal*. Thus, the representation of a health problem may lead to different coping reactions than those provoked by the emotional reaction elicited by the threat of the disease and different appraisal rules may be used to evaluate the adequacy of each.

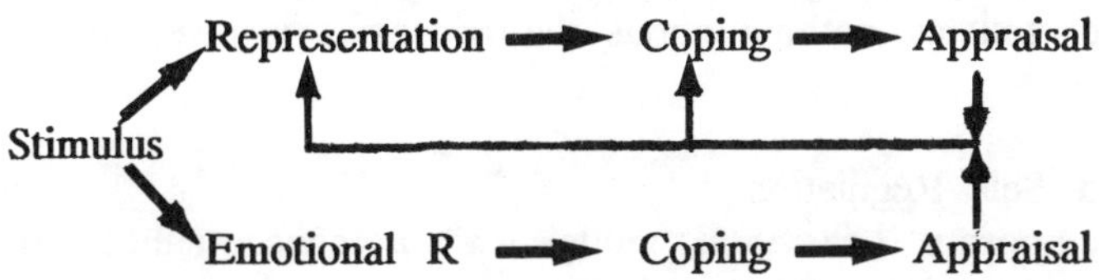

Fig. 1 Parallel processing in self regulation.

Understanding the factors that generate and maintain a behavior, should enhance our ability to intervene and change it. Thus, we should be abie to generate new stimuli, create new interpretations, teach new coping reactions, and alter appraisals of behavior so that the processing system generates a new reaction to the existent stimulus setting.

TWO SOURCES OF THEORY: SUBJECT AND OBSERVER

The theories of the practitioner and the academic investigator are generated from the perspective of external observers; those of the actor are generated by self observation. How should we treat these self generated, actor theories? Are they simply irrelevant noise which tells us nothing about how information is processed, i.e., do they lack explanatory value? Or, are they part of observer theories and critical for adequate explanation? Are they simply descriptive or pragmatic or are they explanatory? In short, should we take these third party models seriously?

Common Sense Models

I have referred to self-generated, actor models, as *common-sense theory* of behavior (Leventhal, Meyer & Nerentz, 1980). The decision to ignore or use common-sense theories depends in part upon our own, theoretical predilection. Behaviorally oriented social and personality psychologists have generally viewed common-sense models in the most denigrating way imaginable. For example, many behaviorists (Bem, 1967) believe that conscious, self descriptions are epi-phenomenon, or after the fact descriptions of what has happened rather than statements about the stimulus processes that determine behavior. Social psychologists studying cognitive biases offer an equally bleak picture of the value of self explanations: they suggest that people are ignorant both of the causes of their behavior, and of what they have done (Nisbett and Wilson, 1977). Each of these critical points of view could suggest that self descriptions are, at best, pragmatic: that is they may describe an observed action but tell us nothing about the processes involved in its occurrence.

Common-Sense and Self Regulation

By contrast, contemporary behavioral models which conceptualize the individual as a *constructive*, self regulatory system appear more hospitable to common sense models. Self regulatory models view the individual as a collection of regulatory or homeostatic components which maintain a state of biological and psychological balance in both the internal environment and between the individual and her physical and social environment (See Carver and Scheier, 1981). The same perspective can be found in clinical models which treat the patient as an active, if not always successful, problem solver (Lazarus and Folkman, 1984). But unlike physical control systems where set points or goals are fixed and the regulatory machinery limited, human goals and regulatory machinery are virtually infinite in diversity and must be generated or constructed in each behavioral episode. And because human beings can observe themselves and others acting upon their physical and social worlds, and formulate common-sense theories about themselves, their worlds, and their fit to the world they use their common-sense to construct goals and select regulatory actions. In short, human beings can introduce changes in the regulatory system, altering their goals and selecting different types of machinery for self regulation.

FOUR USES OF COMMON-SENSE IN THEORY CONSTRUCTION

There are at least four ways in which common-sense theories identify the determinants of behavior, and must, therefore, be incorporated into OBSERVER theory. First, the self observations included in common-sense theory can reveal the way a person interprets his world, i.e., the meaning he gives to stimuli. These meanings are critical as guides to action. Second, common-sense may reveal the processes by which stimuli are interpreted. Third, common-sense can uncover the individual's behavioral plans and decisions. And fourth, an issue of special interest to health psychology, the individual's common sense models may give insight into and help explain how behavioral events regulate biological processes. Let me elaborate briefly on each of these four points.

Common-Sense and Stimulus Interpretation

We have uncovered a number of instances where people's common-sense explanations of their environment must be included in the observer's theoretical model if he is to explain and influence their behavior. The first example appeared in our study of hypertension (Meyer, Leventhal & Gutmann, 1985). Patients who had been in continuous treatment for hypertension (they had no history of dropping out) had been told that hypertension is asymptomatic; it was no surprise, therefore, that the great majority, 80%, agreed with statements such as. "People can't tell their blood pressure is elevated". Yet 88% of the very same group of patients stated that they could tell when their own blood pressure was up: they did so by monitoring cues such as headaches, warm face, heart beating, etc. More important, the number of patients who reported failures in taking medication and who were in fair or poor blood pressure control, was significantly higher among patients who thought their medication had no effect on the symptoms they were monitoring. We traced the development of this belief in a group of patients new to treatment, and found that while 71% thought they could tell when their blood pressure was elevated at the first treatment session, this proportion increased to 92% six months later. Those who monitored symptoms were also more likely to drop out of treatment. In short, symptoms were interpreted as indicators of the disorder and used to guide medication taking. The patients common-sense model, his or her representation of hypertension, guided the coping strategies (medication taking) used to regulate the disease: it and the patient's appraisal of outcomes, needs to be incorporated in an observer theory designed to explain the patients behavior.

Our studies of the development of smoking provide another illustration of the way common-sense can reveal interpretations that affect behavior. Virtually all children (85% to 95%) try at least one cigarette, but only about a third of those who try one take a second (Hirschman, Leventhal and Glynn, 1984). The noxious side effects are perceived as signs of damage to the body, and coughing among them, appears to be a barrier to further experimentation. Youngsters also believe they will adapt to these noxious side effects and that adaptation means they are no longer being injured. Not surprisingly, youngsters who continue to smoke are more likely to believe that adaptation means they are not subjects to injury (Leventhal, Glynn, Fleming & Ershler, in press).

Descriptions of Process

That common-sense models can reveal the meaning that individual's assign to body sensations and that these meanings can affect future behavior is perhaps the easiest to accept of my four points. Limiting common-sense models to stimulus interpretation, however, severely limits both theory and practice. If, for example, we know a hypertensive patient is using symptoms to monitor her condition and regulate her treatment, but we do not understand how she arrived at and justifies this practice, we will be limited in our ability to educate and convince her that her blood pressure is elevated even when she is asymptomatic, and that she is at risk when she reduces or stops taking her medication. It may help to tell the patient we know she is monitoring symptoms, but such an intervention is unlikely to be sufficient to develop new and more effective behavioral strategies. Knowledge about process, i.e., how individuals go about constructing their illness representations, could be helpful for developing effective "therapies".

Contemporary models of cognitive processes suggest that illness representations are formed when body sensations are matched to prior perceptual memory schemata (Leventhal, 1987; 1984; 1984; Pennebaker, 1982): much as we interpret the features of letters and words while reading, so too are body sensations "read" or interpreted by body and illness schemata which convert sensations to symptoms; e.g., a pain becomes angina. As much of this processing is pre-attentive or non-conscious, we can expect the patient's self observations and their resultant common-sense models to provide only limited insight into the process by which illness representations are constructed.

We can, however, look at the matching process in two ways: 1. As a *bottom-up* sensory-perceptual process, or 2. As a *top-down*, conceptual process. The *bottom-up* view emphasizes the sensory events eliciting and matching to perceptual schemata: it is unlikely this common-sense model will reveal much about this perspective on the matching process. The *top-down* view refers to the pre-existent schemas or categories and hypotheses that organize the input, and the patient's common sense model can tell us a good deal about the top portion of this hierarchical process. For instance, a patient might identify prior experiences responsible for the content of his interpretations: e.g., he might tell us that a symptom, "Feels just like the last time I had food poisoning". This interpretation, means he is prepared to interpret a wide range of thoracic sensations as gastrointestinal in origin, though the pain may be caused by an injured heart muscle: actions that reflect such interpretations could be fatal.

While people may have crude and poorly articulate ideas about illness, we can often make shrewd judgments about the way they are likely to interpret body sensations. For example, given that most people have had a series of acute, short term illnesses during their lives, we can anticipate they may deal with illnesses, chronic or acute, as though they were acute. And an astute observer can probe for specific, prior acute experiences which are likely to be used in categorizing new experiences and shaping adaptive behavior. For example, in our study of hypertensives, we discovered that at the beginning of treatment, patients were likely to assume hypertension was an acute disorder: the same was true of cancer patients in chemotherapy treatment (Leventhal et al., 1986). While we anticipated the patient's conceptualization of the illness would move toward a chronic view over time, we also expected and found that patients who conceptualized hypertension as an acute disorder were much more likely to drop out of treatment than those who conceptualized it as a chronic condition.

There is, however, another aspect to the constructive process. Body sensations are inherently ambiguous: we usually cannot identify their precise source and they change over time. As a consequence, the interpretive process is extended in time and is often externalized. The patient's hypothesis about the source of a symptom is likely to initiate a search process for an immediate, environmental precipitant, and this search (resting, taking aspirin, etc.) will usually be consistent with a common-sense view of the problem as acute and curable; i.e., a symptom is expected to last a short period of time and go away with, or without, treatment. And because symptoms change, new appraisal responses will be needed to evaluate potential shifts in their meaning. The degree to which a person can report on and say what his appraisal responses have been depends upon many factors including his/her verbal facility and the degree to which the appraisal processes are active, extended over time, and open to self observation. Some appraisal response, e.g., touching, looking, probing, etc., may take place quickly and with little deployment of attention, and be unreported or even unreportable.

On the other hand a number of patients spontaneously provided detailed reports of their appraisal procedures. For example, a nurse mentioned that she always had headaches when her blood pressure is elevated: she had tested and confirmed this hypothesis by taking her pressure whenever she had headaches. We may also discover that she fails to check her pressure when she does not have a headache, and never learns, therefore, that her pressure is elevated chronically. Knowledge of this common-sense procedure allows us to formulate a self-education strategy designed to disconfirm the incorrect hypothesis (that pressure is elevated only when I have a headache) and construct a new hypothesis, "My pressure is elevated both when I have a headache and when I do NOT have a headache". The need to take medication on a stable basis could be tied to this new hypothesis.

If we remain ignorant of the procedures by which patients test hypotheses and confirm or disconfirm the value of specific treatments, we may fail to develop interventions that are effective in enhancing the common-sense models they use to guide their preventive and therapeutic actions, particularly over the longer term.

Generation of Ongoing and Future Behavioral Decisions

As our prior discussion has made clear, the attributes of illness representations establish targets or goals for ongoing self regulation and have a continuing impact on behavior. Thus, representations can affect a wide range of a health actions including compliance with treatment and acceptance and ongoing performance of health promotive action.

Common-sense models, however, include more than the representation of health threat: they also include views of the individual's resources for controlling the threat. These resources include the adequacy of specific behaviors for cure and/or prevention, the appraisals of ones-self with regard to knowledge and ability to control one's own behavior and emotional feelings, and the appraisal of one's interpersonal resources, e.g. physicians, family, etc., to assist or eliminate health dangers. The individual's common-sense views of her resources are a second key area of beliefs which can impact upon current and future decisions to begin, continue, or stop engaging in specific curative and preventive health actions.

It is relatively easy to find illustrative examples of the impact of common-sense appraisals of the environment and the self on both plans and performance of health relevant action when we examine behaviors that require difficult to achieve, long term, self regulation. An example of an environmental perception is the adolescent's gross overestimation of the number of persons who smoke: they believe that virtually all adults smoke (90% versus 27% who actually do smoke) and that a majority of their peers smoke when only 10% to 15% actually do (Leventhal, Glynn, Fleming & Ershler, 1987). The combination of these misperceptions and the awareness that few people are dying of lung cancer, suggests that smoking is indeed safe. These misperceptions are stronger both in adolescents who expect to smoke and those who already do so. Indeed adolescents seem to think that only adults are at risk for the health effects of smoking.

Beliefs about the self can also have important effects on decisions not to undertake healthful action. For example, virtually all youngsters who begin to smoke at 16 to 17 years of age will try to quit (Ershler, Leventhal, Fleming & Glynn, in press). Many, however, fail at this first attempt and it is not unlikely that failure leads them to define themselves as smokers dependent upon cigarettes and unable to control their behavior. Common-sense ideas regarding the nature of addiction also may play an important role in the development of risk behaviors such as smoking. Adolescents may believe that smoking does not harm them because they adapt to many of the noxious side effects such as coughing, burning throat, etc., that are prominent in their early smoking experience. They may also believe they can tell when they are becoming addicted, and because they have no clues for their dependence until they try to stop and fail, they are likely to experiment until they become nicotine dependent (Leventhal, Fleming & Glynn, in press). These beliefs are very likely to be barriers to quitting. In sum an individual's evaluation of his or her competence at controlling smoking, dieting, and other risk behaviors, can have a substantial influence on initiating and maintaining such efforts.

Changes in self appraisal are also likely with advancing age, and these appraisals can affect both the way people interpret symptoms and the way they choose to cope with symptoms once they occur. For example, it is commonly believed (by people of all ages) that chronic conditions are inevitable with advancing age. Parallel with this belief we find increased performance of protective and health promotive actions (Prohaska, Leventhal, E. & Leventhal, H., 1985). On the other hand, as people age they are also more likely to attribute symptoms to aging rather than to illness, and when this attribution is made, these symptoms are less likely to be given swift, medical attention (Prohaska, Keller, Leventhal, E. & Leventhal, H., 1987).

It is clear, therefore, that common sense of illness, the environment and the self, influence both ongoing and future behavioral decision models ranging from simple decisions to undertake a specific protective action through the maintenance of action over time, to the ability to continue a normal life in the face of serious disease and noxious treatment.

Common Sense and the Regulation of Biological Processes

To this point we have treated common-sense models as a set of psychological mechanisms that affect the regulation of behavior through the construction in consciousness and active memory of: 1. representations of diseases, environments and self; 2. procedures for acting or regulating these situations; and 3. criteria for evaluation. Collectively, these mechanisms represent the psychological algorithms or computational rules and procedures that describe the construction or generation of behavior.

Cognitive scientists draw a distinction between these psychological processes and the medium in which they are represented: the former are variously labelled software, computational models, etc., and the latter the hardware or central nervous system. On occasions theoreticians in these areas state that the nature of the medium, whether it is physical or physiological, is of little consequence: they are primarily concerned with the differential equations and programs that comprise the computational model. The nature of this medium is of great concern, however, to health psychologists in at least two ways: 1. It is the matrix in which we observe disease, a key endpoint that may be a consequence of maladaptive activity at the computational level; and 2. The physical and physiological matrix (the body system) sets limits upon, constrains and helps us define the make up of mental processes, i.e., the psychological algorithms. Whereas cognitive science places the mind in the brain and is motivated by analogies between the brain and the computer, the Health Psychologist places the mind in the body, thus recognizing many distinctions between the computer with its single source of power and transmission along a common medium on the one hand, and the body with its multiple organs and multiple hormonal and neurotransmitter systems for communication. The question before us now is whether common-sense affects biological processes, and if so, "How?"

The links between self-regulated behavior and disease

the first step toward answering the question as to how common-sense affects biological changes such as those seen in hypertension, cancer, and so on, is to recognize that we need to divide the question into sub-questions. As a beginning I will attempt to define the various ways in which behavior might impact on biological processes, and to then consider how common-sense ideas would impact on each of these behavior to disease relationships. The following three dimensions and the eight sub-sets of questions they generated seemed a useful starting point for this very preliminary analysis: 1. Do the behaviors have *extrinsic* and/or *intrinsic* linkages to disease (or both); 2. Is the behavior health motivated; and 3. Does the behavior reflect monitoring of body cues? Common-sense models might affect behavior-body relationships in different ways in each of the eight types of linkages of behavior and body formed by these three dimensions.

1. *Extrinsic and Intrinsic Links to Disease*. Behavior can be said to have *extrinsic* effects on bodily processes when it establishes the conditions by which some other agent produces the bodily change but the behavior itself is neither sufficient nor necessary for the outcome. By contrast, behavior is *intrinsically* linked to a body process when the behavior itself generates physiological events that can lead to the

disease outcome. Examples of extrinsic effects include outcomes such as serious injuries in car accidents or becoming ill after eating a contaminated food in a restaurant. While each of the behaviors established a context in which disease may arise, neither, driving cars nor eating in restaurants, has any direct or necessary connection to injury or illness. But even when the link between action and disease is extrinsic, common-sense models of illness may dictate more or less sensible actions in these areas. For example, one may avoid restaurants in unclean areas of a city and reduce the probability of illness. On the other hand, one may avoid going out on rainy days which has no effect on the probability of illness.

Because many examples of extrinsic effects seem uninteresting we run the risk of ignoring those that are. Among these are cases where common-sense suggests a behavior to enhance health when it actually poses a health risk. For example, the common-sense belief that sunlight and fresh air can insure good health and cure illness can lead to risk of skin cancer when extrapolated as a dose-response rule, i.e., "If some fresh air and sun is good, more is better".

We can identify intrinsic effects that parallel that of excess sunshine given above: the common-sense view that exercise is the key to good health and a cure for all that ails us can be generalized to the belief that more exercise is always better than less. Unfortunately, women who exercise to excess can disrupt estrogen production and increase the risk of osteoporosis. The effect is intrinsic because estrogen suppression, which increases the risk of osteoporosis, is a direct consequence of excessive exercise.

2. *Health or non-health motivated.* If an individual sees no relationship between a behavior and disease, it is unlikely that his or her common-sense views of illness will have any effect on the initiation, maintenance or cessation of that action. Indeed, many actions, both health promotive and risk inducing, are performed for non-health reasons, e.g., health promotive acts such as exercise and tooth brushing may be performed for enjoyment and social reasons, and risk inducing behaviors such as excessive dieting and smoking may be performed to present a socially acceptable self image.

It is difficult to predict how common-sense notions will affect performance of an action that has not been linked to a health threat when that link is drawn. For example, following the publication of the first surgeon general's report on smoking (1964), people who smoked to relax were clearly in a dissonant condition: i.e., a pleasurable action was officially designated as dangerous. For many individuals common-sense ideals about the cause of hypertension and cardiovascular disease justified continuation of smoking if they reasoned that both smoke and stress induced coronary risk, and they believed that the increased risk from smoke was counter-balanced by the reduction of stress by smoking.

If you have ever interviewed smokers suffering from chronic, obstructive, lung disease, you are undoubtedly aware of the astonishing array of justifications they can give for continuing to smoke and the equally astonishing array of explanations they give for their illness. One of the 50 patients Bob Hirschman and I interviewed came up with a rather extraordinary accounting for his emphysema. When asked what caused his condition, he replied, "A broken leg?" Astonished by this assertion, we asked how that was so and whether his past and current smoking might have contributed to his illness. The reply was simple: Smoking had indeed contributed to his illness, but would not have done so if he had not broken his leg and been unable to exercise! The patient's common-sense reasoning posited a trade off between a protective factor and a risk factor.

Effects involving body cues.

At least four questions must be addressed to investigate whether common sense models that encourage the use of body cues for self regulation have physiological consequences that induce or reduce disease processes: 1. Does the body provide accurate (veridical) information about physiological processes and what is the nature of this information? 2. Are responses available to the individual which can regulate these biological process? 3. Does common-sense identify the appropriate cues, i.e. those which actually reflect physiological processes? and 4. Does common-sense select the responses which can regulate these processes? In short, common-sense orients attention and affects the interpretation of body sensations and affects the selection and performance of specific self-regulatory actions.

1. *Monitoring invalid cues as a source of risk.* The study by Meyer, Leventhal and Gutman (1985) described before, found that common-sense monitoring of body sensations reduced compliance with medication taking and increased dropping out of treatment. A study by Linda Baumann and I (Baumann and Leventhal, 1985) made clear how common-sense monitoring increases risk. We asked 43 employees of an insurance company to complete symptom and mood check lists and to predict their blood pressure readings (as low, average, or high) twice a day for 10 days and also recorded their actual blood pressures. The data showed that our subjects used symptoms to make judgments of their blood pressure though neither symptoms nor their judgments of blood pressure estimates were correlated significantly with their systolic (or diastolic) blood pressure. In short, the common-sense choice óf cues to estimate blood pressure was invalid, at least in the work setting. These findings have been replicated at least twice in a study by Pennebaker and Watson (in press) with an important variation: when vigorous exercise was included among the situations in which

predictions and measures of symptoms and blood pressure were taken, people did a much better job predicting their pressure. Accuracy improved because judgments and pressure were assessed across multiple situations one of which induce increases in both blood pressure and the symptomatic cues used in common-sense predictions!

2. *Ignoring cues and risks*. On the other hand, studies also suggest that ignoring body cues can increase the likelihood of disease. Type A's have been found to ignore body signs of fatigue and distress in competitive situations. This may put these individuals at risk for cardiac disease because it precludes taking time-outs to reduce stress and lower stress related physiological processes such as elevated catecholamines and blood lipids. A study by Matthews and her colleagues (1983) shows that type A's run a high risk of death during coronary attacks because they ignore the early warning signs of heart attacks and, therefore, delay in seeking medical care.

3. *Specificity of feedback and response selection*. The lack of specificity of most body signals creates a good deal of uncertainty for the use of body cues in the regulation of physiological processes. Somatosensory feedback is often general rather than specific, i.e., the body signals physiological upset with generic signals such as fatigue and "feeling ill", rather than providing detailed information from specific organ systems, perhaps because our conscious system would be overloaded if detailed inputs were received from each of our separate internal organs. Our conscious system is kept busy enough monitoring the external environment. Hence, a wide variety of bodily mishaps may generate the very same sense of tiredness or "sickness" making it especially difficult to decide how to regulate and modify these feelings. Responses capable of direct impact on the ailing physiology may well be available to the individual: the trick is to discover them. And it is clear the process of discovery will be greatly abetted by guidance from the social environment. But from whence will this come? Because vague feelings of tiredness and/or sickness lack specificity, they may be of little interest to the diagnostically oriented physician, though they are of considerable concern and cause considerable distress for patients, their families and friends. Social comparison and interpersonal influence will play a substantial role in establishing common-sense interpretations of body sensations and suggesting tactics for their management.

4. *Traits versus common-sense models*. Substantial amounts of data have been reported in the bio-feedback literature showing that individuals differ in the way they make use of internal information in self regulation in particular settings. In general, effects of this sort have been attributed to stable characteristics of the subjects; i.e., whether they are sensitizers or repressors, individuals who monitor their

bodies or individuals who distract and actively avoid attending to threat cues and body stress. A detailed, meta-analysis by Suls and Fletcher (1985) reinforces the conclusion that cognitive or defensive styles to monitor or ignore body information effect adjustment to a wide variety of health crises. Specifically, they found that defensive avoidance facilitates adaptation to stressful settings for the short term, (it may allow one to "catch one's wind" or ignore minor, short lasting stresses) but has negative effects over the long term. Monitoring body sensations, on the other hand, improves the chances for effective adaptation over the long term because it allows for careful attention to environmental and body cues needed to guide adaptation.

Individual differences in ability to self regulate during stressful episodes are usually described, as a product of interactions between stress situations and the psychological style of the individual subjects. I believe these individual differences can be reconceptualized as the operation of common-sense models respecting the stressors, (illnesses and treatments) and the individual's common sense view on how to manage or remain emotionally controlled during stressful exposures. Rather than measuring a fixed disposition, tests of cognitive or defensive styles may actually be indirect measures of the individual's theory about how he or she can best manage stressful situations. Direct assessment of common-sense beliefs may provide situationally specific measures of response and better explanations for adaptive successes and failures. Studies of pain control are congruent with this idea. For example, while most people believe it best to avoid and distract when exposed to a noxious stimulus (cold pressor pain) for a 5 or 6 minute interval, others believe (know?) that pain will disappear subsequent to monitoring the noxious stimulus, a belief that is correct as monitoring facilitates habituation and reduction of pain to such stimuli (Ahles, Blanchard & Leventhal, 1983; Leventhal et al., 1979).

CONCLUSION

The big issue upon which I have focussed, is that people have theories about the causes of their own behavior. I have argued that we must pay attention to and use these theories in generating our own theoretical explanations of behavior. As others before (such as Kelly, 1955), I have rejected the position that common-sense models are merely pragmatic descriptions of prior events and believe these theories reveal an important set of factors that shape and direct ongoing and future behaviors. Common-sense models of the world and illness, of coping and the appraisal of outcomes, cause and explain behavior in at least four ways:

1. By defining stimulus situations; 2. By influencing the process of interpreting and appraising body sensations; 3. By affecting ongoing and future behavioral strategies and decisions; and 4. By altering biological mechanisms.

In discussing the impact of common sense models on biological mechanisms, I outlined three dimensions for organizing the effects of behavior on the biological processes that cause disease: 1. The extrinsic-intrinsic connection between behavior and disease process; 2. The presence of a health motive for the behavior; and 3. The dependence of the behavior on monitoring information from the body. Common sense models could influence each of the eight sub-sets formed by the intersection of the three dimensions. I gave most attention to the use of body information, and raised key questions such as; 1. Is there a computational algorithm which allows people to monitor the physiological processes that generate a disease risk? 2. How are these physiological processes manifested in consciousness? 3. How do individuals interpret these cues once aware of them? 4. Can people modify their behavior so as to reduce the risk entailed in these physiological changes? 5. Can they make these changes "on-line" or can they only be done so as to later future or prospective action? 6. Do their models lead to good or poor choices of behaviors for self control? 7. Do variation in models or variation in "stable" individual traits account for individual differences in strategies for adapting to stressful situations?

These questions suggest that subjective feelings of distress, sickness and pain, function as clues to our physical states and as guides to self-regulation for self protective action. In short, common-sense suggests that distress has the important, positive function of telling us to take the time needed to restore and replenish our resources before attempting to leap life's next hurdle.

In short, we have much to learn by listening to people's reports of their common-sense representations of illness, their coping strategies and tactics to adapt to and control illness, and the varied appraisals they make of the adequacy of specific tactics, strategies, and social resources during self regulative episodes. These third party theories are the essential declarative and procedural knowledge guiding health and illness behavior. The study of common-sense models is not, however, an easy task as we are faced with modelling an active and moving system. At the very least it is a challenge to our capacity for representing the principles shaping health and illness behavior in which familiar and expected outcomes are punctuated by unexpected surprises.

ACKNOWLEDGEMENTS

Preparation of this talk was made possible by grants from NIA AG03501 and NIDA 2RO1DA03530-04.

REFERENCES

Ahles, T., Blanchard, E. & Leventhal, H. (1983). Cognitive control of pain: Attention to the sensory aspects of the cold pressor stimulus. *Cognitive Therapy and Research, 7*, 159-178.

Baumann, L.J. & Leventhal, H. (1985). "I can tell when my blood pressure is up: Can't I?" *Health Psychology*, 4, 203-218.

Bem, D.J. (1967). Self perception: An alternative interpretation of cognitive dissonance phenomena. *Psychological Review, 74*, 183-200

Carver, C.S. & Scheier, M.F. (1981). *Attention and self-regulation: A controll-theory approach to human behavior*. New York: Springer-Verlag.

Ershler, J., Leventhal, H., Fleming, R. & Glynn, K. The quitting experience for smokers in sixth through twelfth grades. *Addictive Behaviors (in press)*.

Hirschman, R., Leventhal, H. & Glynn, K. (1984). The development of smoking behavior: Conceptualization and supportive cross-sectional survey data. *Journal of Applied Social Psychology, 14*, 184-206.

Kelly, G. (1955). *The psychology of personal constructs*. (Vol. 2). New York: Norton.

Lazarus, R.S. & Folkman, S. (1984). *Stress, appraisal, & coping*. New York: Springer.

Leventhal, H. (1982). The integration of emotion and cognition: A view from the perceptual motor theory of emotion. In M. Clark & S. Fiske (Eds.), *Affect and cognition: The 17th annual Carnegie Symposium on Cognition*, (pp.121-156). Hillsdale, N.J.: Erlbaum.

Leventhal, H. (1984). A perceptual-motor theory of emotion. In: L. Berkowitz (Ed.), *Advances in Experimental Social Psychology, 17*, 117-182.

Leventhal, H. (1987). Symptom reporting: A focus. In: S. McHugh & M.T. Vallis (Eds.), *Illness behavior, a multidisciplinary model: Proceedings of the second international conference*, (pp.219-237). New York: Plenum Press.

Leventhal, H., Brown, D., Schacham, S. & Engquist, G. (1979). Effects of preparatory information about sensations, threat of pain, and attention on cold pressor distress. *Journal of Personality and Social Psychology, 37*, 688-714.

Leventhal, H., Easterling, D.V., Coons, H., Luchterhand, C. & Love, R.R. (1986). Adaptation to chemotherapy treatment. In: B. Andersen (Ed.), *Women with cancer*, (pp.172-203). N.Y.: Springer-Verlag.

Leventhal, H., Fleming, R. & Glynn, K. (in press) A cognitive-developmental approach to smoking intervention. In: S. Maes (Ed.), *Proceedings of the First Annual Expert Conference in Health Psychology*. New York: John Wiley.

Leventhal, H., Glynn, K., Fleming, R. & Ershler, J. Is the smoking decision an "informed choice"?: Effects of smoking risk factors on smoking beliefs. *Journal of the American Medical Association, 257* (24), 3373-3376.

Leventhal, H., Meyer, D. & Nerenz, D. (1980). The common sense representation of illness danger. In: S. Rachman (Ed.), *Medical Psychology*, Vol. II (pp.7-30). New York: Pergamon Press.

Matthews, K.A., Sigel, J.M., Kuller, L.H., Thompson, M. & Varat, M. (1983). Determinants of decisions to seek medical treatment by patients with acute myocardial infarction symptoms. *Journal of Personality and Social Psychology, 44* (6), 1144-1156.

Meyer, D., Leventhal, H. & Gutman, M. (1985). Common Sense Models of Illness: The example of hypertension. *Health Psychology, 4*, 115-135.

Nisbett, R.E. & Wilson, T.D. (1977). Telling More than we can know. Verbal reports on mental processes. *Psychological Review, 84*, 231-259.

Pennebaker, J.W. (1982). *The psychology of physical symptoms*. New York: Springer-Verlag.

Pennebaker, J.W. & Watson, D. (in press). Blood pressure estimation and beliefs among normotensives and hypertensives. *Health Psychology*.

Prohaska, T.R., Keller, M.L., Leventhal, E.A. & Leventhal, H. (1987). Impact of Symptoms and Aging Attribution on Emotions and Coping. *Health Psychology, 6*, 495-514.

Prohaska, T.R., Leventhal, E.A. & Leventhal, H. (1985). Health practices and illness cognition in young, middle-aged, and elderly adults. *Journal of Gerontology, 40*, 569-578.

Suls, J. & Fletcher, B. (1985). The relative efficacy of avoidant and non-avoidant coping strategies: A meta-analysis. *Health Psychology, 4* (3), 249-288.

Tiffany, S.T., Martin, E.M., Baker, T.B. (1986). Treatment for cigarette smoking: An evaluation of the contributions of aversion and counseling procedure. *Behaviour Research and Therapy, 24*, 437-452.

U.S. Public Health Service (1964). Smoking and Health. Report of the Advisory Committee to the Surgeon General of the Public Health Service. U.S. Department of Health, Education, and Welfare, Public Health Service, Center for Disease Control, PHS Publication No. 1103.

INTEGRATING CONTEMPORARY MODELS OF ANIMAL AND HUMAN CONDITIONING: IMPLICATIONS FOR BEHAVIOUR THERAPY

G.C.L. Davey

The City University, London, U.K.

Traditionally, conditioning models were used extensively in an attempt to explain a variety of clinically-based problems such as phobias and other anxiety problems. The fact that these problems appeared to be acquired through conditioning processes was also one of the important reasons for the development of behavior therapies. However, in the last ten to twenty years, conditioning accounts of anxiety-based problems have been getting an increasingly bad press, and are usually given short shrift in contemporary clinical texts. The criticisms ranged at the conditioning model are numerous and varied, but, by and large, reflect the feeling that the conditions which generate and maintain pathological problems such as anxiety-based reactions rarely comply with the necessary and sufficient conditions known to generate and maintain conditioned responding.

Now, while the list of criticism of the conditioning model superficially appears formidable (see Marks, 1976, for example), I wish to argue that a conditioning model of anxiety-based problems can be salvaged and indeed, can form the central core of a theory of acquired fears. At the very least, since a majority of anxiety-based problems appear to be acquired it seems reasonable to assume that some learning processes should be identifiable in the mechanism which underlies anxiety reactions. What needs to be specified is the nature of this learning - in terms of environmental conditions which give rise to it, the changes in cognitive structures which occur as a result of it, and the performance mechanism which translates this learning into the fear or anxiety response observed by the clinician. I believe that contemporary conditioning theory can take adequate account of all three of these questions, and in this chapter I will attempt to address the first two.

Criticisms of conditioning models largely stem from the conception of

Pavlovian conditioning as a contiguity-based associative mechanism which differs considerably from contemporary views of conditioning as a complex information processing task, and the demise of the conditioning model as an explanation of anxiety-based problems appears to have stemmed largely from a failure to appreciate the significant developments that have occurred in the animal conditioning literature of the last 10-15 years. At this stage it is worth summarizing the important features of contemporary animal conditioning theory.

CONTEMPORARY ANIMAL CONDITIONING THEORY

The most impressive developments in animal conditioning have involved the use of inferential techniques which tell us a considerable amount about the unobservable facets of the conditioning mechanism. The two most important developments have concerned (i) the kinds of associations that are formed during different types of Pavlovian conditioning, and (ii) the nature of the cognitive representations that are formed to mediate the conditioned response. One simple technique - known as post-conditioning stimulus revaluation - will illustrate these developments. In the prototypical example of Pavlov's salivating dog, the dog can learn one of two possible associations: it may learn to associate the bell CS with the food UCS (a stimulus-stimulus, S-S association), or it may learn to associate the bell CS with salivating (a stimulus-response, S-R association); either possibility leads the dog to eventually salivate during the bell. However, these associations are not directly observable and have to be inferred. The nature of the learnt association can be inferred by altering the animal's evaluation of the UCS after conditioning has been concluded; if the CR is mediated by the animal's evaluation of the UCS (an S-S association) then altering the animal's evaluation of the UCS will also affect the strength of the CR. Revaluation of the UCS can be carried out in a variety of ways. For instance, the dog can be made averse to the food by pairing it with a substance that makes the animal sick; however, if an aversive UCS is used, the animal can be habituated to the UCS so that it seems less aversive. In both cases if the CR is mediated by S-S associations, the animal should exhibit a much weakened CR after UCS revaluation. If the CR is mediated by S-R associations, then UCS revaluation should have no effect, because the animal's evaluation of the UCS plays no part in mediating the CR.

In nearly all first-order Pavlovian studies where UCS revaluation has been attempted, the strength of the CR has been immediately weakened or eliminated entirely as a result of this manipulation, suggesting that the subjects have learnt a CS-UCS association and the strength of the CR is mediated by the subject's evaluation of the UCS (cf. Dickinson, 1980; Rescorla, 1980; Davey, 1987 b). To put it anthropomorphically, when Pavlov's dog hears the bell ring, this stimulus elicits a cognitive representation of the food that is to follow; via this representation the dog evaluates the food as being palatable and as a result salivates. When the food is paired with sickness, the bell still elicits a representation of the food, but this time the dog evaluates it as sickness-inducing or unpalatable and does not salivate. These procedures tell us two things about Pavlovian conditioning: First they tell us that a CS-UCS association has been formed, and that the CR is mediated by the animal's evaluation of the UCS; Secondly, they tell us that any factor which affects the subject's evaluation of the UCS will also affect CR strength. In certain other situations, such as some second-order conditioning procedures, S-R associations may be formed (cf. Rescorla, 1977, 1980), but, by and large, the above two conclusions hold for the majority of first-order preparations that have been studied.

I have argued elsewhere that the two major findings from UCS revaluation studies have important implications for an understanding of conditioning in humans (Davey, 1983, 1987a). What is more, they are partially important in understanding some of the phenomena which are unique to conditioning in humans. These phenomena include instruction and information effects, and attribution effects.

ASSOCIATION IN HUMAN CONDITIONING

The nature of the associations formed during human Pavlovian conditioning are extremely important in determining which kinds of manipulations will eventually modulate response strength and which will not. For instance, only if subjects have learnt a CS-UCS association will information about the UCS be able to modulate performance. If the subject has learnt a reflexive S-R association then information about the UCS should have no effect on response strength (since the CR is not mediated by cognitions associated with the UCS). In a UCS revaluation study with human subjects, we were able to demonstrate that in a second-order electrodermal conditioning procedure, subjects learnt an association between the second-order CS (CS2) and the UCS (Davey & McKenna, 1983). When subjects were habituated to the UCS after conditioning, the response to the second-order CR was immediately lost. This implies that CR2 was mediated by the subject's evaluation of the UCS: when habituation rendered it less aversive to the subjects this also weakened the CR. What is perhaps more important with human subjects is that this UCS revaluation can be achieved not just by experience with the UCS, but also by providing information about the UCS. When subjects in this study were told that there would be no more UCS presentations, it had exactly the same effect on CR2 as the habituation procedure; the response to CS2 was immediately lost.

We can see from the above study that revaluation of the UCS can directly affect response strength when CS-UCS associations have been formed during conditioning, and that instructions are an important means of achieving UCS revaluation. This has a number of implications for both an understanding of anxiety-based problems and behavior therapy methods: (i) If an anxiety-based response is mediated by associations formed between the anxiety-provoking stimulus or event and some traumatic UCS, then this reaction can be modulated by revaluation of the traumatic UCS. This modulation may occur as a result of experience with the UCS that causes the UCS to be revalued as less aversive, or it might be produced by socially or verbally transmitted information that leads the individual to believe either that the UCS is not as aversive as originally believed or is unlikely to occur again in the future. Note that under these circumstances the anxiety-based CR can be reduced in strength or even eliminated without any changes occurring in the strength of the association between the anxiety-provoking CS and the UCS. The CS-UCS association does not necessarily have to be extinguished for the CR to be suppressed or eliminated. At least some instances of spontaneous remission might result from UCS revaluation of this kind; (ii) Although they have yet to be detected in human conditioning studies, there is no reason to suppose that under certain circumstances an anxiety-based response might not be mediated by more reflexive S-R associations, and that evaluation of the UCS may play little if any role in determining response strength (cf. Davey, 1987a). Reflexive S-R associations have been detected in second-order aversive conditioning in animals (Holland & Rescorla, 1975; Rescorla, 1977, 1980), where the second-order CS (CS2) becomes directly associated with a generalized aversive motivational state. Under these circumstances no amount of UCS revaluation will reduce or modulate the strength of the CR; only extinction of the CS2-CR association will achieve this. Thus, if an anxiety-based response is mediated by S-R associations, this response will be relatively unaffected by cognitive restructuring therapies which attempt to alter the individual's evaluation of the events surrounding the disorder. In such circumstances, a more effective therapy would be one which attempts to extinguish directly the association between the anxiety-provoking CS and the response. Most traditional behavior therapy methods which attempt to either block the occurrence of the CR in the presence of the CR or to destroy the contingency relationship between CS and the CR/UCS complex should prove more successful than cognitive restructuring.

THE EFFECT OF FACTORS WHICH REVALUE THE UCS

In the first section of the chapter I have attempted to persuade the reader that mediation of an anxiety-based response may occur through one of two associative routes: either CS-UCS associations or CS-CR associations. In what little literature there is currently available on the subject, it appears that in human conditioning, mediation by CS-UCS associations is much more commonplace than by CS-CR associations (cf. Davey, 1983, 1987a). This being the case, it is therefore much more likely that the modulation of response strength will occur not through the strengthening of weakening of the association between CS and UCS, but through factors which affect the individual's evaluation of the UCS. It is worth discussing some of the ways in which UCS revaluation might occur for human subjects - especially in relation to anxiety-based problems.

I have already discussed two methods by which the UCS might be revalued. First, by direct experience with the UCS alone, which leads the individual to reassess an aversive UCS more favourable. Thus, on future encounters with the CS, a much weakened CR is elicited; and secondly, by socially or verbally transmitted information which leads the individual to revalue more favourably the UCS or believe that it is unlikely to occur again in the future. A third method is one that we have investigated in some detail in our laboratory, and alludes to processes of response attribution.

Whenever a response (CR) is salient enough for the individual to discriminate both its occurrence and to some extent its strength, this must provide that individual with some information that needs to be put into a relative context. For example, when an anxiety or fear reaction occurs, individuals will usually attempt to locate the causes of this reaction (the process of response attribution). If the cause of the anxiety is attributed to a particular stimulus or event, this may result in the event being revalued as more aversive than it was before. In a simple electrodermal conditioning and extinction procedure we found that allowing subjects to discriminate their CRs during extinction by providing auditory feedback of response levels resulted in a significant resistance to instructed extinction when compared with appropriate controls (cf. Davey, 1987a). Further analysis of this effect suggested that, although subjects were fully informed of the extinction stage of the experiment, those subjects who received response feedback took considerably longer to extinguish because, being able to observe their responses on early extinction trials, this led them to believe that the aversive UCS was still likely to occur. That is, observing themselves still appearing fearful to the CS overrode the UCS devaluing effects that the extinction instructions should have had. Indeed, most subjects who received response feedback reported after the experiment that they did not fully believe the extinction instructions. In this situation, we attempted to devalue the UCS through instructions (i.e. the UCS will no longer occur), but this failed because some other source of information (the subject's discrimination of their own reaction to the CS) led the UCS to be evaluated differently.

The attribution of the causes of discriminable responses probably has an important role in anxiety-based reactions. What our studies have suggested is that if the fear response is salient enough to be easily discriminated, then the event that the subject believes causes that response is likely to be negatively evaluated. Thus, when representations of that event are evoked in the future (either through conditioned associations or other means), the fear response associated with it will also be evoked. In many natural situations this attribution process may override any attempted UCS devaluation through cognitive restructuring. In this case, a more sensible approach might be to intervene directly at the attribution stage, either to redirect the individual's attributions in a more desirable way, or to deceive the individual with false response which indicated that no fearful reactions are occurring (in a similar way to the false feedback studies of Valins, 1966, and Valins & Ray, 1967).

SUMMARY

In this chapter I have attempted to argue that human conditioning is a much more complex phenomenon than anyone who has read Hilgard & Marquis's historic tome on conditioning might be led to believe. In particular, an understanding of the associations that mediate human conditioning is important, as well as an understanding of the nature of the cognitive representations that generate the response. Much of human conditioning appears to be mediated by CS-UCS associations, and thus the strength of the CR will to a large extent be determined by the subject's evaluation of the UCS. What this means is that the strength of the association between CS and UCS is not the only factor that will affect response strength. What are arguably more important are those factors which affect the individual's evaluation of the UCS, and in doing so affect the strength of the response. Some of these latter factors include experience with the UCS alone, socially and verbally transmitted information about the UCS, and response attributions. All of these factors need to be included in a model of human conditioning which permits accurate prediction of response strength. Furthermore, they help to account for some of the anomalies within conditioning models of anxiety-based responses. These anomalies all allude to the fact that certain phenomena cannot be explained easily in terms of modulation of associative strength between stimuli. However, an extended model of human conditioning of the kind outlined in this chapter does permit variation in response strength without changes in associative strength, and many important paradoxical features of anxiety-based disorders may be interpreted in terms of UCS-revaluation phenomena.

REFERENCES

Davey, G.C.L. (1983) An associative view of human classical conditioning. In G.C.L. Davey (Ed.) *Animal Models of Human Behaviour*, John Wiley: Chichester.

Davey, G.C.L. (1987a) An integration of human and animal models of Pavlovian conditioning: Associations, cognitions, and attributions. In G.C.L. Davey (Ed.) *Cognitive Processes and Pavlovian Conditioning in Humans*, John Wiley: Chichester.

Davey, G.C.L. (1987b) *Ecological learning theory*, Methuen: London.

Davey, G.C.L. & McKenna, I. (1983) The effect of post-conditioning revaluation of CS and UCS following Pavlovian second-order electrodermal conditioning in humans. *Quarterly Journal of Experimental Psychology*, 35B, 125-33.

Dickinson, A. (1980) *Contemporary animal learning theory*, Cambridge University Press: Cambridge.

Holland, P.C. & Rescorla, R.A. (1975) The effects of two ways of devaluing the unconditioned stimulus after first- and second-order appetitive conditioning. *Journal of Experimental Psychology: Animal Behavior Processes*, 5, 355-363.

Rescorla, R.A. (1977) Pavlovian second-order conditioning: Some implications for instrumental behavior. In H. Davis & H.M.B. Hurwitz (Eds.) *Operant-Pavlovian interactions*, Lawrence Erlbaum Associates: Hillsdale, N.J.

Rescorla, R.A. (1980) *Pavlovian second-order conditioning: Studies in associative learning*, Lawrence Erlbaum Associates: Hillsdale, N.J.

Valins, S. (1966) Cognitive effects of false heart-rate feedback, *Journal of Personality and Social Psychology*, 4, 400-408.

Valins, S. & Ray, A.A. (1967) Effects of cognitive desensitization on avoidance behavior. *Journal of Personality and Social Psychology*, 7, 345-350.

PART II:

BROADENING THE SCOPE OF BEHAVIOUR THERAPY

TOWARDS A SCIENTIFICALLY ORIENTED ECLECTICISM

S.L. Garfield

Washington University, St. Louis, Missouri, U.S.A.

The topic of my presentation reflects a value system that we hold in common - namely, that a scientifically oriented and empirically based psychotherapy is a goal worth striving for and not just an autistic fantasy. Furthermore, such a goal in no way contradicts the importance of the therapist or of the role of the therapist-patient relationship in the process and outcome of psychotherapy, be it behavioral or otherwise. I do not distinguish between psychotherapy and behavior therapy as some have done. I consider behavior therapy to be a significant movement within the broad field of psychotherapy that shares with other approaches the common goal of ameliorating human suffering by psychological means.

In looking back at the history of psychotherapy it is clear that psychotherapeutic approaches for the most part developed with little apparent concern for the usual requirements associated with scientific pursuits. From the time of Freud to the present day we have witnessed the development of numerous schools of psychotherapy with their gurus, special institutes, and the like. What has always impressed me about most of these schools is the unquestioned loyalty of the leader's followers, the adherence to dogma, and the absence of any real demand for empirical verification. In fact, for many years, the field seemed unconcerned about any needs to verify theoretical assumptions or to demonstrate empirically that the therapeutic approaches were in fact efficacious. I can remember clearly one earlier experience of mine which illustrates this pattern and I will recount it briefly.

In 1949 I was working in a psychiatric outpatient clinic where the main modality of treatment was psychotherapy. After working there for a few months I was rather surprised to note that no attempts had been made to evaluate the work being done and that no one considered this to be a problem. I then decided to broach this issue at a staff meeting and to suggest an outcome study in which we could all participate. I told my colleagues that on the basis of my observations all of us functioned on the basis of one hypothesis, namely, that every contact we had with a patient was therapeutic for the patient. However, I went on to state that in the absence of data to support this hypothesis two other hypotheses were equally tenable. One was that any contact we had with a patient had no effect on the patient whatsoever. At this point, I began to note some frowns of disapproval on the faces of some of my colleagues. Bravely, I went on to say that in the absence of data to substantiate either of these first two hypotheses, a third hypothesis was equally tenable, namely, that any contact we had with a patient was detrimental to the patient's welfare! Well, that seemed to end the meeting with one of my psychiatric colleagues saying, "Sol, how could you say that? You know we help all the patients."

The view expressed by my colleague appeared to me to be the modal view of psychotherapists and it consisted of several components. As already indicated, most therapists saw little need to support their efforts with empirical data for the truth of efficacy was self-evident. Another facet was the emphasis on internal personality dynamics which defied systematic or quantitative appraisal. And, thirdly, was the view that psychotherapy was an art, and could never be a science. These views haven't all disappeared by any means, but some changes began to take place in the following years that have had a significant impact. Let me now make some references to these events and influences.

POST-WAR DEVELOPMENTS

A number of events have taken place in the post World War II years that appear to have had an influence on the development of psychotherapy. One was the setting up of Ph.D. programs in clinical psychology in the U.S. and elsewhere to meet expanding mental health needs. Although I may be biased, I strongly believe that psychologists, because of their research training in academic departments of psychology, have contributed a scientific-research emphasis to the psychotherapeutic enterprise that was not in evidence previously. Stimulated by Hans Eysenck's critical appraisals of psychotherapy outcome, there was evident gradually both a greater awareness of the need for research and a greater interest in conducting such research. Although progress at first was slow, it began to increase at a more rapid pace. Prior to 1940, there was hardly any published research on psychotherapy and in Eysenck's 1952 paper reference was made to 24 reports. By the 1960's, however, an increase in research production was apparent and in the 1970 volume by Meltzoff and Kornreich, reference was made to 101 studies of outcome in psychotherapy. I am referring to numbers here, and not necessarily to quality. Another item of importance, if you'll forgive a personal reference, was the appearance the next year, 1971, of the first edition of the Bergin-Garfield *Handbook of psychotherapy and behavior change*. This volume very specifically emphasized the importance of an empirical approach to psychotherapy and was also eclectic in its orientation.

There were some other developments that also were noteworthy. One was the very slow acceptance of a behavioral approach prior to the appearance of Wolpe's (1958) *Psychotherapy by means of reciprocal inhibition* and the rather rapid development afterward. Although behavior therapists constitute only a relatively small minority of psychotherapists, in our survey of clinical psychologists they made up only about 10% of the sample (Garfield & Kirtz, 1976), nevertheless, they have been a very energetic, articulate and even vociferous group who have had a very decided impact on the field of psychotherapy over the past 20-25 years. Of particular significance has been the behavioral emphasis on empirical validation of specific therapeutic procedures. This general emphasis, which appears to be the common thread tying together the many diverse techniques developed by behavior therapists, has been evident in the vast output of research reports produced by these therapists. Bergin (1971), for example, pointed out the significant increase in behavioral therapy research studies published in the *Journal of Abnormal Psychology* and the *Journal of Consulting Psychology* in the period 1965-1969, and as you people know better than I, the appearance of new behavioral journals is enough to cause neurotic behavior among those who try to keep up with the research literature.

At the same time as these important developments were taking place, other developments of interest were also discernable. Two are of especial interest. One is the spectacular increase in the number of different approaches to psychotherapy. Although the rate of inflation has decreased significantly, al least in the U.S., the increase in the number of psychotherapeutic schools continues at an astonishing rate. Although I have not really computed the exponential curve for the next twenty years, on the basis of Herink's (1980) report of over 200 varieties of psychotherapy in 1980 and Kazdin's report of over 400 varieties in 1986, I am inclined to predict that sometime in the next century there will be one form of psychotherapy for every adult in the Western World! Unfortunately, I do not expect to be around to check on the accuracy of my prediction, but I've asked Paul Emmelkamp, a much younger man, to check it out for me.

This proliferation of psychotherapeutic systems is actually a serious problem for the field and for society generally. When you have literally hundreds of supposedly different treatments for comparable problems, not only is public confidence in the efficacy of the treatments threatened, but there is also some basis for scientific concern. Most of these systems of psychotherapy have never been evaluated in some systematic fashion and their actual efficacy is thus unknown. Another concern springs from medical history:

> "There are at least two generalizations substantiated by the history of medical therapeutics. The first is that the greater the number and variety of treatments employed for a given illness, the greater the likelihood that none of them is definitive or completely effective. The second is that it is not at all unusual to find empirical practice to be totally unrelated to existing theories of disease (e.g., foxglove was used for the treatment of dropsy long before the etiology of edema with heart failure was recognized" (Group for the Advancement of Psychiatry, 1975, p.271).

Both of these generalizations, I believe, have implications for the current status of psychotherapy and I will elaborate a bit on this later. However, there is another recent development that I want to discuss before moving on. Here, I refer to the less obvious but potentially more important trend toward rapprochement and integration. As some of you know, this particular trend or development has tended in the U.S. to feature a conciliatory movement among some behavioral and cognitive therapists on the one hand and analytically oriented therapists on the other, although some old-fashioned eclectics like me have also been included.

Although not everyone responds positively to this development, it does offer one possible means of bringing some degree of order out of the bewildering diversity that characterizes the field of psychotherapy today. Furthermore, such a view also underlines the fact that current approaches have not yet reached the limits of improvement that may be obtainable by more effective psychotherapeutic procedures. Current approaches tend to be limited to particular theories and particular techniques derived from the theories with the implication that these are necessary and sufficient. Since the latter supposition is not fully valid, a broadening of perspective as exemplified in the move for integration in psychotherapy, and in the formation of the Society for the Exploration of Psychotherapy Integration (SEPI) constitutes an important development.

One other fairly recent occurrence is also worth mentioning here. I refer to what has been called in the U.S., "the current climate of accountability", a trend that apparently is not limited solely to the U.S. Surprisingly, in the past there was little demand on the part of the public or governmental agencies for evidence to support the claims for the efficacy of psychotherapy. I would guess that back of this benign attitude was the view that psychotherapy, "the talking cure", couldn't really hurt anyone, so why get concerned about it? It was strictly an individual matter until governmental concerns and insurance costs became an issue. Now the situation has changed and there has been a fair amount of attention devoted to the issue of efficacy. It is no longer just Hans Eysenck who is raising questions about whether or not "psychotherapy works", as some journalists have phrased it. Accounts from governmental agencies, news reports, and articles in popular magazines have all attested to the recent interest in the efficacy of psychotherapy. A spotlight has been focused on psychotherapy which is not particularly to the liking of its practitioners.

In this connection, it is interesting to compare the official treatment accorded food and drugs in the U.S. with that accorded psychotherapy. In 1908 the Food and Drug Act was passed which primarily emphasized honesty in the labeling of such products. In 1938 new legislation was passed emphasizing the safety and non-noxious elements of drugs. However, in 1962 concerns had shifted from safety to matters of efficacy and 10 years later regulations were developed by the Food and Drug Administration to evaluate efficacy. Psychotherapy has been spared such regulatory concerns thus far but the situation may be changing.

A SCIENTIFICALLY-ORIENTED ECLECTICISM

Now that I have sketched out developments in the field of psychotherapy that I believe are important, let me discuss more directly some possibilities for an empirically based and scientifically oriented eclectic psychotherapy. For a number of reasons some of which have already been alluded to, the time may be propitious for such a development. We have made considerable progress in moving away from a relatively subjective-intuitive model of psychotherapy and toward a more objective and scientifically oriented perspective. However, much remains to be done before such an objective perspective can be attained.

As long as we are willing to adhere to objective verification of our therapeutic theories and techniques we start from a solid base. As I have indicated, this has been a significant unifying theme for practically all behavioral therapists. At the same time, it is important for behavior therapists to recognize that they are not the only ones who have this value system nor have they cornered the market on truth. With over 400 different approaches to psychotherapy it should be apparent that no one approach has found the single true path to therapeutic effectiveness. This should make us humble instead of boastful. Ideally, also, it should motivate us to strive harder to expand and improve our therapeutic procedures. To remain locked in to one view or set of procedures is to limit seriously one's effectiveness.

Psychoanalysis in my view overemphasized intra-psychic and past events at the expense of overt behavior and the patient's current situation. The role of the therapist as a passive screen for the patient's free associations also tended to increase the length of therapy. The emphasis on changing behavior and on a rather active and directive role of the therapist were significant antidotes offered by behavior therapists. In contrast to traditional psychodynamic emphases, these new emphases stressed behavioral change, the evaluation of such change, and the resultant efficiency of therapy. Specific procedures for specific problems, dismantling strategies, and the formation of treatment packages were all new contributions made by behavior therapists. What has been very encouraging about such developments is that they have been recognized as positive by non-behaviorists, particularly individuals referred to as eclectics and integrationists.

Despite such contributions from behavior therapists, however, psychotherapists have not yet reached the promised land. There are a number of factors that indicate more change and innovation are required in order to increase the current levels of psychotherapeutic effectiveness. Included here are research evaluations of the efficacy of psychotherapy, the possible existence of common therapeutic variables among the different forms of psychotherapy, and the importance of patient and therapist variability in relation to outcome. Despite an awareness of the uniformity myth formulated by Kiesler (1966, 1971) some years ago, and the emphasis by Gordon Paul (1967) on the individuality of treatment, problem, patient, therapist and setting, not a great deal has actually been accomplished along these lines. As pointed out recently by Stiles, Shapiro, and Elliot (1986), this matrix-like paradigm is a very difficult one to apply and test in practice. Thus, there are many aspects currently that need to be considered thoughtfully in assessing where we are and what paths are potentially available for exploration and appraisal.
Having said this, let me go ahead now to discuss first the issue of differential therapeutic efficacy.

DIFFERENTIAL THERAPEUTIC EFFICACY

I have speculated that psychotherapists develop new schools or approaches to psychotherapy or become eclectics because of dissatisfaction with the approach they had been taught or used previously. It seems reasonable to assume that satisfaction with a therapeutic approach would not lead to the abandonment or modification of that approach. The implication from this is that some therapeutic systems are more effective than others. Since not all of the different psychotherapies have been evaluated or compared in some systematic manner, it is impossible to give a definitive answer to the issue of differential therapeutic efficacy. However, there is some research available in which a relatively small number of therapeutic approaches have been compared and I will make only a brief reference to this research here. Most of it is familiar to most of you.

Since the earlier reviews by Eysenck (1952, 1961, 1966) where psychotherapy, excluding behavior therapy, was found wanting, most of the more recent reviews have not only tended to find some degree of superiority of psychotherapy over no psychotherapy, but generally, few significant differences have been secured between the therapies evaluated. This has been the overall finding in the reviews of Meltzoff and Kornreich (1970), Bergin (1971), and Bergin and Lambert (1978) as well as in the famous study by Sloane et al. (1975) comparing behavior therapy and psychoanalytically oriented psychotherapy. The meta-analysis of Smith, Glass, and Miller (1980) also found relatively little difference among the orientations evaluated. The review by Rachman and Wilson (1980), perhaps not surprisingly, favored the behavioral therapies. The most recent review by Lambert, Shapiro, and Bergin (1986) in the third edition of the *Handbook of Psychotherapy and Behavior Change* offers an interesting conclusion which differs somewhat from earlier conclusions and which I now want to quote:

> "Although research continues to support the efficacy of those therapies that have been rigorously tested, differences in outcome between various forms of therapy are not as pronounced as might have been expected. Behavior therapy, cognitive therapy, and eclectic mixtures of these show superior outcomes to traditional verbal therapies in several studies on specific disorders, although this is by no means the general case. When this superiority is in evidence, the results have been attributed to the bias of researchers and the selectivity in criteria of change; however, the critics can be biased and selective too. Although there is little evidence of clinically meaningful superiority of one form of psychotherapy over another with respect to moderate outpatient disorders, behavioral and cognitive methods appear to add a significant increment of efficacy with respect to a number of difficult problems (e.g., phobias and compulsions) and to provide useful methods with a number of nonneurotic problems with which traditional therapies have shown little effectiveness (e.g., childhood aggression,

psychotic behavior, stuttering).

Given the growing evidence that there are probably some specific technique effects, as well as large common effects across treatments, the vast majority of therapists have become eclectic in orientation. This appears to reflect a healthy response to empirical evidence and a rejection of previous trends toward rigid allegiances to schools of treatment." (pp. 201-202).

Three items in this excerpt are of particular significance to me. These are "specific technique effects, large common effects across treatments," and a possible trend toward empirical eclecticism. I shall return to these topics. However, before concluding this section, I want to refer to the NIHM Collaborative Study of Depression so ably coordinated by Irene Elkin (1985). As some of you may know, this large scale study conducted at three separate centers by highly trained and selected therapists compare Beck's Cognitive-Behavioral Therapy, the Interpersonal Therapy developed by Klerman, Weissman and their colleagues, the Tricyclic Imipramine, and a pill placebo plus clinical management condition. The overall preliminary results at the end of treatment indicated no significant differences between either of the psychotherapies and imipramine, or between the two forms of psychotherapy in reduction of depressive symptoms or in overall functioning. All of the treatments as well as the pill-placebo plus clinical management condition secured a significant reduction in depressive symptomatology. Furthermore, although patients in the three treatment conditions showed consistently better outcome at termination of treatment than did those in the placebo group, the differences often were not statistically significant. It is important that I emphasize in this regard the fact that the placebo patients were seen weekly by experienced psychiatrists who provided support and encouragement as well as a pill.

When the patients were divided into severely depressed (20 or more on the Hamilton Rating Scale for Depression) and less severely depressed groups, some additional findings of interest were secured. For the less severely depressed patients, no significant differences were obtained between the four groups. For the more severely depressed group of patients, who made up 44% of the total sample, some differences did emerge. Patients in the Interpersonal Psychotherapy and Imipramine groups secured significantly lower scores than the placebo group on the Hamilton Scale. This was not true for the severely depressed patients who received the cognitive behavior therapy. This finding is somewhat at variance with one of the conclusions from the review by Lambert, Shapiro, and Bergin that I quoted earlier. However, it is too early to draw any final or definitive conclusions about the effectiveness of Beck's Cognitive Behavior Therapy with severely depressed patients. The results (for this treatment) were quite variable across the three research centers participating in the collaborative study and final follow-up data are not yet available.

It was hypothesized also that some types of differential outcomes might be secured (e.g. greater improvement in social adjustment for the patients receiving Interpersonal Psychotherapy and a comparable advantage in cognitive functioning for those patients in the Cognitive Behavioral group). Thus, scales to measure such specific areas of functioning were included in the study in addition to the general measures of depression and overall functioning. However, such differential effects generally were not obtained. Instead, improvement appeared to take place for all groups across a wide range of outcome measures. These findings appear congruent with those reported by Simons, Garfield, and Kelly (1984) in a study comparing cognitive behavior therapy and pharmacotherapy in terms of cognitive changes during the process of therapy. In that study, there were no differences secured in outcome between the two treatment groups; however, patients who improved in both groups in terms of depression also showed comparable patterns of significant positive change in cognitive functioning.

A study by Zeiss, Lewinsohn, and Munoz (1979) also secured similar results in comparing outcome in cognitive therapy, pleasant activities, and social skills training. Although all three treatments were equally effective in reducing the level of depression, changes on the hypothesized intervening dependent measures were not specific to the treatment.

In a very recent and carefully conducted study of elderly depressed patients by Thompson, Gallagher, and Breckenridge (1987), ninety-one patients with a major depressive disorder were treated with either behavioral, cognitive, or brief psychodynamic psychotherapy. Overall, at termination, 52% of the treatment sample were judged to be in remission and another 18% showed significant improvement. The different psychotherapies, however, did not differ significantly among themselves in effectiveness. Furthermore a one-year follow-up has been completed and the results are quite comparable (Gallagher, Thompson & Breckenridge, 1986).

Well, what sort of conclusions can we draw from this multitude of findings? First, a considerable portion of the studies carried out to evaluate and compare the efficacy of psychotherapy has failed to find truly significant differences among the forms of psychotherapy compared. This is a finding that has led me to emphasize the potential importance of common factors and to list such possible factors in my book, *Psychotherapy: An Eclectic Approach* (Garfield, 1980). Even in the review by Lambert et al., (1986) where behavior therapy, cognitive therapy, and mixtures of these two were reported as superior for certain disorders, reference also was made to the importance of factors common to most forms of psychotherapy. In fact, the comparability of results among cognitive and behavioral therapies also suggests the possibility of common therapeutic factors. The meta-analysis reported by Berman, Miller, and Massman (1985), for example, showed essentially no differences between cognitive and desensitization therapies, and combinations of the two therapies did not increase the level of improvement. As Lambert et al. (1986) remark, "These results suggest that there may be important common factors in these two modes of treatment that account for the equal outcomes, and that the common factor problem is not limited to comparisons with verbal expressive therapies" (p.167).

The potential importance of common therapeutic factors thus should be recognized and research planned to evaluate them in some systematic fashion. Even cognitive-behavioral therapists have noted the possibility of common therapeutic factors (Kazdin, 1986b) as well as the desirability of possible integration among therapeutic orientations (Goldfried, 1982). The former has been clearly mentioned by Lewinsohn and Hoberman (1982) in a review of behavioral and cognitive approaches to depression:

> " It is clear that cognitive-behavioral approaches and conceptualizations are characterized by great diversity but that empirical support for the therapeutic efficacy of each has been provided. Since all are theoretically derived, i.e., they are specifically designed to modify the specific cognitions and/or behaviours assumed by the theory to be a critical antecedent for depression, the question needs to be raised, how could they all be effective?" (p.344).

This is indeed the question that not only needs to be raised, but needs to be answered.

Several well-known behavioral psychologists were critical of the findings of the Sloane et al. (1975) study because a variety of patients were used and the behavior therapists were not restricted to specific behavioral techniques (Garfield, 1983). In the NIMH Collaborative Study referred to earlier, however, all of the subjects were carefully screened and met explicit criteria for uni-polar non-psychotic depression. Manuals were developed for each of the therapies and the therapists trained and monitored to insure that the specific therapies were actually administered. Thus, some of the criticisms made of the Sloane study do not apply to the NIMH Study. Nevertheless, roughly similar overall results were obtained at post-treatment for the two psychotherapies studied, and of even more interest was the lack of differences found when aspects emphasized by the two different psychotherapies were evaluated. I think we have a responsibility to try to explain this lack of difference.

There is also another matter that deserves mention here. This is the matter of optimum improvement, both in terms of the percentage of patients improved as a result of treatment and in terms of the degree of improvement reached by most patients. As I have indicated elsewhere, only a relatively small percentage of patients are truly "cured", secure the maximum improvement theoretically possible, or function at what might be termed a "normal" level of adjustment (Garfield, 1981). Even leading behavior therapists acknowledge this situation. In the research conference on "Behavioral approaches to Anxiety Disorders" held in Albany, New York, a few years ago, "It was acknowledged, however, with regard to both (agoraphobia and obsessive-compulsive) disorders, that the extent of the improvement is not always optimal, and that a significant minority of patients relapse" (Barlow & Wolfe, 1981, p.449). Although realistically we may never cure everyone who undergoes psychotherapy, I believe that we can probably improve the efficacy and efficiency of psychotherapy by trying to ferret out the variables that make for change. In this process, we shall have to identify and operationalize clearly the common factors involved as well as indicating the specific factors that are important for particular kinds or problems. I am heartened by the fact that increased attention is being given to common factors, including the book recently published in the Netherlands by van Kalmthout, Schaap, and Wojciechowski (1985). Recognizing and attempting to identify common therapeutic factors in no way demeans or limits the potential significance of specific factors that may be highly therapeutic for specific disorders or problems.

Although I have emphasized common factors in psychotherapy, I want to acknowledge again that behavioral therapies have secured the best results with cases of phobias, compulsions, and autism. I certainly believe that behavior therapists should be justly proud of their accomplishments in these areas. I would think that most patients with phobias, for example, would rather be rid of their phobias in a reasonable period of time by means of behavior therapy, even if they do not attain full insight into why they developed a phobia, than to spend years in some kind of treatment where they learn all about the possible early childhood causes of their phobias, but somehow are unable to be rid of them. Clearly, performance is an important component of psychological treatment and this emphasis has been a significant contribution of behavior therapists.

At the same time, we need to keep in mind that how the therapist administers the treatment, how he/she is perceived by the client, what rationale is provided, and the like, are also important parts of a performance based treatment. Clients differ and so do therapists an although techniques are important, they do not constitute all there is to psychotherapy. Behavior therapy, for example, has been influenced by social learning theories and cognitive emphases. I regard the newer emphasis on cognitive-behavior therapy as an advance over pure behavior therapy or pure cognitive therapy if such therapies actually exist in reality. Certainly the human animal thinks as well as behaves and hopefully the behavior is influenced by constructive thought. However, we humans also feel, and it is disturbed feelings that most frequently lead people to seek psychotherapeutic help. Thus, we cannot neglect feelings and affects in our therapeutic work. Furthermore, relationships between individuals and significant others play an exceedingly important role in the feelings and emotions we experience. Consequently, all such aspects of the clients we see in therapy are of importance.

How the client feels about the therapist and how the relationship develops in therapy appear to be of some consequence in therapeutic outcome, and this has been stressed by such leading behavior therapists as Goldfried and Davison (1976), Wilson and Evans (1977) and Emmelkamp (1986). If we pay attention to the post-therapy reports of patients, we find that successful patients tend to emphasize certain features as responsible for their improvements that are common to most successful forms of psychotherapy. Mentioned in such reports are the following: the personality of the therapist; being understood; the therapist's confidence in the client; and being encouraged to face one's problems. Although I do not want to overemphasize or mystify the importance of the therapeutic relationship, it is a non-technique variable of some consequence. Various process scales developed by analytically-oriented psychotherapists have indicated a consistent relationship between a variable called "Patient Involvement" and outcome, and in one study this variable was the best predictor of outcome for three different groups of therapists (Gomes-Schwarz, 1978). Seemingly, it is a variable that cuts across orientations. I have hypothesized that the so-called therapeutic alliance may actually reflect the patient's subjective feeling early in therapy that progress is being made and that this is the important feature in both behavioral and psychodynamic therapy (Garfield, 1986).

Whatever the case may be, we should not restrict our approach in a narrow fashion. Rather, it is important to consider other contributions where they are supported by valid empirical data. At the same time, we have to investigate more thoroughly the processes of therapy realizing that many different explanations have been offered to account for the outcomes secured. When a simpler explanation seems just as congruent as the more complex one we have been using, we should be eclectic enough to use the simpler one. As we take a more flexible and less rigid stance, I believe we shall progress to a more scientifically oriented eclectic psychotherapy, and one in which behavioral procedures play an important part.

NOTE:
Part of this paper will also be published in the Nordisk tidskrift för beteendeterapi.

REFERENCES

Barlow, D.H. & Wolfe, B.E. (1981). Behavioral approaches to anxiety disorders: A report on the NIMH-SUNY, Albany research conference. *Journal of Consulting and Clinical Psychology, 49*, 448-459.

Bergin, A.E. (1971). The evaluation of therapeutic outcomes. In A.E. Bergin, & S.F. Garfield (Eds.) *(1986) Handbook of psychotherapy and behavior change*. New York: Wiley.

Bergin, A.E. & Garfield, S.L. (Eds.) (1971). *Handbook of psychotherapy and behavior change*. New York: Wiley.

Bergin, A.E. & Lambert, M.H. (1978). The evaluation of therapeutic outcomes. In S.L. Garfield & A.E. Bergin (Eds.), *Handbook of psychotherapy and behavior change* (2nd ed.). New York: Wiley.

Bergman, J.S., Miller, R.C. & Massman, P.J. (1985). Cognitive therapy versus systematic desensitization: Is one treatment superior? *Psychological Bulletin, 97*, 451-461.

Emmelkamp, P.M.G. (1986). Behavior therapy with adults. In: S.L. Garfield & A.E. Bergin (Eds.), *Handbook of psychotherapy and behavior change* (3rd ed.), pp.385-442. New York: Wiley.

Elkin, I. Parloff, M.B., Hadley, S.W. & Autry, J.H. (1985). NIMH treatment of depression collaborative research program. *Archives of General Psychiatry, 42*, 305-316.

Eysenck, H.J. (1952). The effects of psychotherapy: An evaluation. *Journal of Consulting Psychology, 16*, 319-324.

Eysenck, H.J. (1961). The effects of psychotherapy. In H.J. Eysenck (Ed.), *Handbook of Abnormal Psychology* (pp. 697-725). New York: Basic Books.

Eysenck, H.J. (1966). *The effects of psychotherapy*. New York: International Science Press.

Gallagher, D., Thompson, L.W. & Breckenridge, J.S. (1986, August). *Maintenance of gains versus relapse following brief psychotherapy for depression*. Paper presented at the annual meeting of the American Psychological Association, Washington D.C.

Garfield, S.L. (1980). *Psychotherapy: An eclectic approach*. New York: Wiley.

Garfield, S.L. (1981). Evaluating the psychotherapies. *Behavior Therapy, 12*, 295-307

Garfield, S.L. (1983). The effectiveness of psychotherapy: The perennial

controversy. *Professional Psychology, 14*, 35-43.
Garfield, S.L. & Kurtz, R. (1976). Clinical psychologists in the 1970s. *American Psychologist, 31*, 1-9.
Goldfried, M.R. (Ed.) (1982). Converging themes in psychotherapy. *Trends in psychodynamic, humanistic, and behavioral practice*. New York: Springer.
Goldfried, M.R. & Davison, G.C. (1976). *Clinical behavior therapy*. New York: Holt, Rinehart and Winston.
Gomes-Schwarz, B. (1978). Effective ingredients in psychotherapy: Predictions of outcome from process variables. *Journal of Consulting and Clinical Psychology, 46*, 1023-1035.
Group for the Advancement of Psychiatry (1975). *Pharmacotherapy and psychotherapy: Paradoxes, problems, and progress*. New York: Author.
Herink, R. (Ed.) (1980). *The psychotherapy handbook. The A to Z guide to more than 250 different therapies in use today*. New York: New American Library.
Kazdin, A.E. (1986a). Comparative outcome studies of psychotherapy: Methodological issues and strategies. *Journal of Consulting and Clinical Psychology, 54*, 95-105.
Kazdin, A.E. (1986b). Research designs and methodology. In: S.L. Garfield & A.E. Bergin (Eds.), *Handbook of psychotherapy and behavior change* (3rd ed.) (pp.23-68). New York: Wiley.
Kiesler, D.J. (1966). Some myths of psychotherapy research and the search for a paradigm. *Psychological Bulletin, 65*, 110-136.
Kiesler, D.J. (1971). Experimental design in psychotherapy research. In: A.E. Bergin & S.L. Garfield (Eds.), *Handbook of psychotherapy and behavior change: An empirical analysis*. New York: Wiley (pp.36-74).
Lambert, M.J., Shapiro, D.A. & Bergin, A.E. (1986). The effectiveness of psychotherapy. In: S.L. Garfield & A.E. Bergin (Eds.), *Handbook of psychotherapy and behavior change* (3rd ed.) (pp.157-212). New York: Wiley.
Lewinsohn, P.M. & Hoberman, H.M. (1982). Behavioral and cognitive approaches. In: E.S. Paykel (Ed.), *Handbook of affective disorders*. Edinbugh: Churchill Livingstone.
Meltzoff, J. & Kornreich, M. (1970). *Research in psychotherapy*. New York: Atherton Press.
Paul, G.L. (1967). Strategy of outcome research in psychotherapy. *Journal of Consulting Psychology, 31*, 109-118.
Rachman, S.J. & Wilson, G.T. (1980). *The effects of psychological therapy* (2nd ed.). New York: Pergamon Press.
Simons, A.D., Garfield, S.L. & Murphy, G.E. (1984). The process of change in cognitive therapy and pharmacotherapy for depression. *Archives of General Psychiatry, 41*, 45-51.

Sloane, R.B., Staples, F.R., Cristol, A.H., Yorkston, N.J. & Whipple, K. (1975). *Psychotherapy versus behavior therapy*. Cambridge, MA: Harvard University Press.

Smith, M.L., Glass, G.V. & Miller, T.I. (1980). *The benefits of psychotherapy*. Baltimore: The John Hopkins University Press.

Stiles, W.B., Shapiro, D.A. & Elliott, R. (1986). Are all psychotherapies equivalent? *American Psychologist, 41*, 165-180.

Thompson, L.W., Gallagher, D. & Breckenridge, J.S. (1987). Comparative effectiveness of psychotherapies for depressed elders. *Journal of Consulting and Clinical Psychology, 55*, 385-390.

van Kalmthout, M.A., Schaap, C. & Wojciechowski, F.L. (1985). *Common factors in psychotherapy*. Lisse: Swets & Zeitlinger.

Wilson, G.T. & Evans, I.M. (1977). The therapist-client relationship in behavior therapy. In: A.S. Gurman & A.M. Razdin (Eds.), *Effective psychotherapy. A handbook of research*. New York: Pergamon (pp.544-565).

Wolpe, J. (1958). *Psychotherapy by reciprocal inhibition*. Stanford, CA: Stanford University Press.

Zeiss, A., Lewinsohn, P. & Munoz, R. (1979). Nonspecific improvement effects in depression using interpersonal skills training, pleasant activities schedules, or cognitive training. *Journal of Consulting and Clinical Psychology, 47*, 427-439.

ECLECTICISM IN BEHAVIOUR THERAPY

A.A. Lazarus

Graduate School of Applied and Professional Psychology, Rutgers University Piscataway, New Jersey, U.S.A.

THE VARIETIES OF ECLECTICISM

Eclecticism is not a single edifice or a unitary construct. The *Handbook of Eclectic Psychotherapy* (Norcorss, 1986) clearly shows that eclecticism is a complex set of structures and conceptions, comprising, among others, an atheoretical position, a transtheoretical stance, a synthetic integration, a structural-phenomenological approach, and one that is governed by a preferred theory but also borrows techniques from other theoretical orientations (technical eclecticism). Yet there is a widespread and persistent tendency to refer to an treat "eclecticism" as a single entity. Thus, Eysenck (1986, p.378) writes that "an eclectic point of view by definition means an anti-scientific point of view: eclecticism has always been the enemy of scientific understanding." This misguided view stems from the refusal to recognize that rapprochement, convergence, and unification can all rest on the bedrock of rigorous scientific inquiry.

Systematic eclecticism is the product of years of painstaking research and clinical work; it should not be bracketed with haphazard, idiosyncratic eclecticism. The enemies of science are those "eclectic" psychotherapists who experiment indiscriminately with new "fads" and require neither a proper rationale nor empirical validation for the methods they employ. Unsystematic eclecticism is a jumble of untested ideas, an unscientific approach to therapy that spells chaos and subjective bias. But systematic eclectics are interested in achieving a comprehensive psychotherapy based on a unified and empirical body of information. These practitioners do not simply choose "whatever feels right". Systematic prescriptive eclecticism is a scientific endeavor to measure the threefold impact of patient qualities, clinical skills, and specific techniques. It is essential to note that a systematic, technical eclecticism does not foster an overemphasis upon techniques at the cost of theoretical, conceptual, and scientific understanding (cf. Franks, 1984).

It may be helpful to separate *eclecticism* from *fusionism* and *integrationism*.

Fusionists tend to blend what they regard as the most helpful notions and ingredients from two seemingly disparate orientations. Starting with a paper by French (1933), the proposed fusion that has received the greatest attention is the attempted consolidation of psychoanalysis and behaviour therapy (e.g., Arkowitz & Messer, 1984; Goldfried, 1982; Marmor & Woods, 1980; Wachtel, 1977). More recent fusionists propose to integrate cognitive behaviour therapy and Gestalt therapy (Fodor, 1987), and systems and psychodynamic methods (Kirschner & Kirschner, 1986). Any bimodal intermingling strikes me as arbitrary and capricious. If this trend proliferates, we can anticipate any number of strange bedfellows-Primal/Existential; Adlerian/Morita; Jungian/Rational-Emotive (the list is almost endless).

Integrationists are opposed to ideological rigidity, and try to meld disparate ideas and conflicting schools into a cooperative and harmonious whole. While the field of psychotherapy is in need of a unified theory, a superordinate umbrella that will reconcile divergent points of emphasis and blend multiple concepts and techniques within a coherent framework, the preparadigmatic level at which we presently function is far from this ideal. Meanwhile, to my way of thinking, it is a mistake to blend seemingly compatible theories from different schools in the hopes of harnessing greater energy from each. The main problem here is that, upon close scrutiny, what seems to be interchangeable between different theories, often turns out to be totally irreconcilable. As Messer and Winokur (1981) have shown, "in many instances what appears at first glance as commonality becomes, on closer inspectation, so basic a difference that we wonder on what grounds therapists of different theoretical persuasions can meet" (p.1547).

Hence my emphasis on *technical eclecticism* (Lazarus, 1967, 1971, 1981), which looks mainly to social and cognitive learning theory (Bandura, 1986) for explanatory constructs, since all of its tenets are grounded in research and are open to verification and disproof. By operating from a consistent, testable, theoretical base and then drawing on useful techniques from any discipline without necessarily subscribing to the theoretical tenets that gave rise to the techniques in question, one avoids the jumble, the melange, and the subjective bias of theoretical eclecticism or integrationism. It is most important to bear in mind that one remains theoretically consistent when practicing technical eclecticism (cfr. Dryden, 1987). Moreover, it is imperative not to overemphasize technique to the detriment of a conceptual and theoretical appreciation of the issues at stake. Technical eclecticism, as many have erroneously assumed, is not anti-theoretical or atheoretical. Unfortunately, some who call themselves technical eclectics have tended to select methods and styles that *they* individually consider appropriate, based on guiding principles that are at best questionable.

Having emphasized that eclecticism is not a unitary entity, and having pointed out some of the diversities, as well as the differences between various forms of eclecticism, fusionism, and integrationism - and especially the virtues of a theoretically consistent systematic technical eclecticism - we may now ask why it is necessary to introduce any form of eclecticism into behaviour therapy. But first let us consider the main ingredients of "behaviour therapy".

THE ESSENCE OF BEHAVIOUR THERAPY

Behaviour therapy is a set of assumptions, beliefs, and hypotheses about human beings and the nature of their problems; a methodology for evaluating and assessing these problems; and a technology for intervening. A large armamentarium of techniques has been made available so that clinicians can approach a sizable number of psychiatric problems in a focused and highly specific manner (Lazarus & Fay, 1984). Behaviour therapy is closely linked to experimental psychology, especially to learning theory; its main intent is the development of effective psychological treatment. Wherever possible, clinical phenomena are operationally defined, and priority is given to those factors that are amenable to experimental investigation. Behaviour, instead of being regarded as necessarily reflective of deeper processes within the psyche, is often viewed as significant in its own right.

The behavioural approach has evolved from a naive, rigid, symptom-centered, and rather mechanistic set of ideas and procedures, to a sophisticated and flexible system that is marked by a diversity of views and continues to spawn a broad range of assessment and treatment strategies (Wilson, Franks, Kendall & Foreyt, 1987). While there is now a high degree of diversification among behaviour therapists, there are several central notions to which the vast majority subscribe. Great value is placed on meticulous observation, careful testing of hypotheses and continual self-correction on the basis of empirically derived data. Furthermore, behaviour therapists display extreme caution in the face of conjecture and speculation, and show due regard for scientific objectivity. They favor a rigorous process of deduction from testable theories and show a fitting indifference toward persuasion and hearsay. In essence, behaviour therapy addresses psychiatric problems using (a) a testable conceptual framework, (b) treatment methods that can be objectively measured and replicated, (c) outcome criteria that can be validated, and (d) evaluative procedures for determining the effectiveness of specific methods applied to particular problems. This has resulted in a degree of precision that has been lacking in other psychological (nonbiological) orientations.

WHY IS THERE A NEED FOR ECLECTICISM IN BEHAVIOUR THERAPY?

One of the first behaviour therapy texts (Wolpe & Lazarus, 1966) described 18 different techniques - mainly within the context of assertion training, systematic desensitization, and the use of sexual responses. Also described were several ancillary procedures such as "thought stopping", "flooding", "emotive imagery", "feeding response", "anxiety-relief responses", and "aversive conditioning". The Wolpe-Lazarus volume regarded cognitive methods or "rational corrections" as "in most instances, merely a background to the specific reconditioning of reactions that usually belong to the autonomic nervous system" (p.131). Yet in 1987, at the 21st National Convention of the Association for Advancement of Behavior Therapy held in Boston, Massachusetts, many presentations stressed that cognitive influences within behaviour therapy have now played a significant role for more than a decade. Likewise, at the 17th Congress of the European Association for Behaviour Therapy held in Amsterdam, Holland during August, 1987, cognitive-behavioural workshops, symposia, lectures and posters were clearly presented.

My book *Behavior Therapy and Beyond* (Lazarus, 1971) argued for a "broad-spectrum" approach after follow-ups on clients who received traditional behaviour therapy showed a disappointingly high relapse rate. Unlike the Wolpe & Lazarus (1966) volume, the Lazarus (1971) book included an entire chapter on "cognitive restructuring". While the interrelatedness of thought and action is now espoused by all but a minority of diehard radical behaviorists, most "behaviour therapists" during the 1970s responded negatively to the introduction of cognitive structuring, fearing a return to mentalism, the superfluous Freudian superstructure, and Cartesian dualism. It has since become evident that it is absurd to draw a dichotomy between pure cognitive and pure behavioural interventions. It would be extremely difficult to find a behavioural method that had zero cognitive input, or a cognitive technique that was devoid of any elements of performance. But as we enter the final decade of the 20th Century, the field of behaviour therapy has already transcended the mere addition of cognitive appraisal to behavioural performance. As Kendall (1987, p.118) stated: "Perhaps we can avoid the hyphenated hybrid, "cognitive-behavioral-affective-social-developmental therapy", but we need not be avoidant of the underlying multifaceted approach to treatment."

The reasons for expanding behaviour therapy are entirely pragmatic. The vagaries of human conduct call for methods that go beyond those explicated by Wolpe and Lazarus (1966). Therapists are confronted by a complex and changing array of information during treatment sessions. Too narrow a lens will miss the crucial factors that call for scrutiny and correction. Wide open eclecticism will plummet the therapist into the familiar errors of faulty judgment, illusory correlation, and confirmatory bias. As Turk and Salovey (1985, p.31) have stated: "The time has come for the clinician to stop defensively avoiding these issues and the researcher to stop wagging a condescending finger at the hapless clinician."

As a whole, the field of psychotherapy needs greater experimental rigor (especially in nonbiological research areas), more rational and empirical theoretical bases in place of purely notional and speculative conceptualizations, more clearly operationalized and concretized therapist-decision-making processes, and a systematic, prescriptive (technical) eclecticism that encourages the individual practitioner to draw from many sources without falling prey to subjective whims. We need complete treatment plans that attend to each patient's idiosyncrasies and carefully assess such issues as orientation, choice of treatment setting, format, frequency and duration of sessions, choice of somatic treatments, and ways of combining treatments. The more coping responses a person learns in therapy, the less likely he or she is to relapse. This often calls for the correction of maladaptive and deviant behaviours, unpleasant feelings, negative sensations, intrusive fantasies, dysfunctional beliefs, stressful relationships, and possible biochemical imbalance. To the extent that diagnosis (problem identification) examines each of these modalities, whereupon treatment remedies the salient deficits and maladaptive patterns, treatment outcomes will be positive and long-lasting (Lazarus, 1976, 1981, 1987).

Here are two specific examples of technical eclecticism within behaviour therapy.

Jourard (1964), a humanistic psychologist, had expounded on the virtues of "self-disclosure". Whereas psychoanalysts studiously avoid self-disclosure with their patients and remain distant and detached, there are no reasons for behaviour therapists to adopt a similar stance. (Interestingly, Wolpe, 1984, objected to the use of self-disclosure, and stressed that it is "not a behaviour therapy technique", p.1326). After reading Jourard's book, the *act* of selective self-disclosure (but not the theories that Jourard had put forth) seemed like a worthwhile technique to incorporate into a behavioural repertoire. It fitted very well into the framework of teaching-showing-sharing-modeling. As Rimm and Masters (1979) emphasized, selective self-disclosure often enhances the therapeutic relationship and proves valuable when using modeling and behaviour rehearsal techniques. When a therapist tells an anxious client, "I used to do X,Y, and Z", we have the hallmarks of good behaviour therapy - rapport, empathy, identification, specificity, and practice.

The second example is the "empty chair technique", a method of pretending that a significant other is sitting in an empty chair, whereupon a dialogue is enacted. The client expresses thoughts and feelings to the imagined person in the empty chair, and then changes places, now occupying the formerly empty chair and acting as that other person. This technique owes its origins to Gestalt therapy and psychodrama, but it is used in behaviour therapy quite differently. In the behavioural context, the empty chair technique is seen as a variant of behavioural rehearsal, role-playing, and role-reversal. When used by psychodramatists and Gestalt therapists, the empty chair technique is often aimed at resolving historical events and "unfinished business". In behaviour therapy it is employed primarily to modify current maladaptive patterns of behaviour.

The corner has been turned. Kendall (1987, p.117) writing in the *Review of Behavior Therapy* states: "It is my belief that eclecticism can be a good thing, but only when the ingredients within the eclectic approach are each the recipient of careful evaluation and empirical scrutiny". I rest my case.

REFERENCES

Arkowitz, H. & Messer, S.B. (Eds.) (1984). *Psychoanalytic therapy and behavior therapy: Is integration possible?* New York: Plenum Press.

Bandura, A. (1986). *Social foundations of thought and action: A social cognitive theory*. Englewood Cliffs, N.J.: Prentice-Hall.

Dryden, W. (1987). Theoretically consistent eclecticism: Humanizing a computer "addict"." In: J.C. Norcross (Ed.) (1987). *Casebook of eclectic psychotherapy*. New York: Brunner/Mazel (pp.221-226).

Eysenck, H.J. (1986). Consensus and controvery: Two types of science. In: S. Modgil & C. Modgil (Eds.). *Hans Eysenck: Consensus and controversy*. London: Falmer Press (pp.275-398).

Fodor, I.G. (1987). Moving beyond cognitive-behavior therapy: Integrating Gestalt therapy to facilitate personal and interpersonal awareness.

In: N.S. Jacobson (Ed.) *Psychotherapists in clinical practice*. New York: Guilford Press (pp.190-231).

Franks, C.M. (1984). On conceptual and technical integrity in psychoanalysis and behavior therapy: Two fundamentally incompatible systems. In: H. Arkowitz & S.B. Messer (Eds.). *Psychoanalytic and behavior therapy: Is integration possible?* New York: Plenum Press (pp.223-248).

French, T.M. (1933). Interrelations between psychoanalysis and the experimental work of Pavlov. *American Journal of Psychiatry, 89*, 1165-1203.

Goldfried, M.R. (1982). *Converging themes in psychotherapy*. New York: Springer Publishers.

Jourard, S.M. (1964). *The transparent self*. Princeton, N.J.: Van Nostrand.

Kendall, P.C. (1987). Cognitive processes and procedures in behavior therapy. In: G.T. Wilson, C.M. Franks, P.C. Kendall & J.P. Foreyt. *Review of behavior therapy: Theory and practice*. Vol. 11, New York: Guilford Press (pp.114-153).

Kirschner, D.A. & Kirschner, S. (1986). *Comprehensive family therapy: An integration of systemic and psychodynamic treatment models*. New York: Brunner/Mazel.

Lazarus, A.A. (1967). In support of technical eclecticism. *Psychological reports, 21*, 415-416.

Lazarus, A.A. (1971). *Behavior therapy and beyond*. New York: McGraw-Hill.

Lazarus, A.A. (1976). *Multimodal behavior therapy*. New York: Springer Publishers.

Lazarus, A.A. (1981). *The practice of multimodal therapy*. New York: McGraw-Hill.

Lazarus, A.A. (1987). The multimodal approach with adult outpatients. In: N.S. Jacobson (Ed.), *Psychotherapists in clinical practice*. New York: Guilford Press (pp.286-326).

Lazarus, A.A. & Fay, A. (1984). Behavior therapy. In: T.B. Karasu (Ed.), *The psychiatric therapies*. Washington, D.C.: American Psychiatric Association (pp.483-538).

Marmor, J. & Woods, S.M. (Eds.) (1980). *The interface between the psychodynamic and behavioral therapies*. New York: Plenum Press.

Messer, S.B. & Winokur, M. (1981). Therapeutic change principles: Are commonalities more apparent than real? *American Psychologist, 36*, 1547-1548.

Norcorss, J.C. (Ed.) (1986). *Handbook of eclectic psychotherapy*. New York: Brunner/Mazel.

Rimm, D.C. & Masters, J.C. (1979). *Behavior therapy: Techniques and empirical findings*. 2nd ed. New York: Academic Press.

Turk, D.C. & Salovey, P. (1985). Cognitive structures, cognitive processes, and cognitive-behavior modification: II. Judgments and inferences of the clinician. *Cognitive Therapy and Research, 9*, 19-34.

Wachtel, P.L. (1977). *Psychoanalysis and behavior therapy: Toward an integration*. New York: Basic Books.

Wilson, G.T., Franks, C.M., Kendall, P.C. & Foreyt, J.P. (1987). *Review of behavior therapy: Theory and Practice*. New York: Guilford Press.

Wolpe, J. (1984). Behavior therapy according to Lazarus. *American Psychologist, 39*, 1326-1327.

Wolpe, J. & Lazarus, A.A. (1966). *Behavior therapy techniques*. Oxford: Pergamon Press.

THE THERAPEUTIC RELATIONSHIP IN BEHAVIOR THERAPY: ENHANCING THE QUALITY OF THE BOND

C. Schaap, & C.A.L. Hoogduin

Catholic University Nijmegen, Department of Clinical Psychology, The Netherlands

THE THERAPEUTIC RELATIONSHIP

The importance of non-specific or common factors in therapeutic effectiveness has been established in different fields of research. It has, for instance, been shown in the comparison of different schools of psychotherapy (Garfield, 1981; Smith, Glass & Miller, 1981). Also, improvement rates in the treatment of a wide range of conditions by practitioners of the so-called alternative healing methods are impressive and in many ways comparable to those of the established forms of psychotherapy, suggesting the importance of these factors (Van Kalmthout, Schaap & Wojciechowski, 1985; Krippner, 1975; Vahia, 1973; Van Dijk, 1979). Non-Western healing practices are also in many ways comparable to the different forms of Western psychotherapies, both in process as well as outcome (Jilek, 1974; Nawas, Pluk & Wojciechowski, 1985; Prince, 1964; Pluk & Wojciechowski, 1985; Torrey, 1972). Finally, the comparison of the effectiveness of experimental versus placebo conditions in psychotherapy research, particularly if controlled for credibility of the rationale, suggests that the same processes are at work in these settings (Nawas et al., 1985; Prioleau, Murdock & Brody, 1983; Rosenthal, 1980; Shapiro, 1985; Wilson & Evans, 1977). The fact that these figures, again, are comparable to those for treatments by paraprofessionals (Durlak, 1979; Hattie, Sharpley & Rogers, 1984; Strupp, 1978), is also proof of the impact of theoretically unspecified and common factors in a variety of healing settings.

A crucial ingredient of these common (i.e. common to the different healing practices) or non-specific factors (i.e. not considered to be an essential ingredient of treatment in the theory of the healers) is the establishment of an intense relationship, characterized by such complementary features as: trust and trustworthiness, dependency and dependability, emotional arousal and directness, disclosure and responsivity (Frank, 1961; Nawas, Pluk & Wojciechowski, 1985; Pope, 1979). For the interested reader, we refer to Gurman (1977) and, more recently, Orlinsky and Howard (1986) who extensively review the available evidence for the impact of the therapeutic relationship on outcome.

In the behavioral literature these factors have traditionally been considered to be nonspecific, which was caused by the fact that they were until recently hard to operationalize in learning theory and behavioral terms. Moreover, the development of effective techniques received, understandably, all the attention (Wilson & Evans, 1977). Nevertheless, a survey by Swan and MacDonald (1978) indicated that relationship enhancement procedures were used routinely by sixty percent of the behavior therapists polled.

From a behavioral point of view the client-therapist relationship can be looked at in two ways (Hoorens, 1986): (a) as a catalyst and (b) as a therapeutic ingredient. The therapeutic relationship can have a positive or negative impact on the effectiveness of the diverse activities on the road towards change. In this regard it is important to provide the client with explanations that raise the plausibility of therapy. Effectiveness of therapy is increased if activities are judged credible, relevant to the person's needs, and acceptable in terms of response costs (Rosenthal, 1980). Moreover, it is important to create favorable outcome expectancies (Kirsch & Henry, 1977; McGlynn, Kinjo & Doherty, 1978; Catanese, Rosenthal & Kelley, 1979) and to maintain healer credibility (Rosen, 1975). The client-therapist relationship may also play an important role as an essential ingredient of the learning process. The therapist is an important model for the client in function of similarity, attraction and available rewards. Furthermore, the therapist may reinforce desired behaviors and ignore or punish ineffective behaviors of the client. Finally, the therapist constitutes an important source of discriminative stimuli, that may even be enhanced by an increase in attractiveness and prestige (Wilson & Evans, 1977). The catalyst and therapeutic ingredient role of the therapeutic relationship, moreover, do influence each other mutually. To the extent that the therapist evokes more positive emotional responses, he will be a stronger source of social reinforcement and discriminative stimuli and will, by the same token, be more attractive as a role model, which will in turn help the client to change. Rosenthal (1980), although in a somewhat different terminology, arrives at a similar conclusion. Based on the evidence presented in his article he concludes that if a distressed client is given a summary of the proposed treatment that gives reason for its value and relates its aim to some coherent formulation of the client's problems, which are depicted in soluble, hopeful terms, this will have an important impact.

We will now present some empirical evidence for the impact of the therapeutic relationship as a source of variance in outcome. We will focus mainly on research on exposure and response prevention with obsessive-compulsives (Emmelkamp, 1982), since it is in this area that the impact is systematically and well documented. After a short literature survey, we will present the results of two empirical studies on the predictive value of the therapeutic relationship. After this presentation we will focus on strategies to improve the therapeutic relationship.

THE THERAPEUTIC RELATIONSHIP AND OBSESSIVE-COMPULSIVE DISORDER

Rabavilas, Boulougouris and Perissaki (1979) asked patients suffering from phobic and obsessive-compulsive disorders, who were treated using exposure in vivo, to judge their therapists on 16 variables regarding their attitude and their style of treatment. Respect, understanding and interest were significantly related in a positive direction with outcome. So were the style variables encouragement, challenge and explicitness. Satisfaction of dependency needs and permissiveness were negatively related. Emmelkamp and Van der Hout (1983) also report a significant correlation between outcome and the therapeutic relationship in a group treatment for agoraphobic patients.

We will now present a study on the predictive value of the therapeutic relationship. In the first part of this study, 60 obsessive-compulsive patients were treated using exposure and response prevention in an out-patient clinic. The patient-therapist relationship was measured after the tenth session using the Dutch version of the Barrett-Lennard Relationship Inventory (Lietaer, 1976). The relation between the therapeutic relationship and outcome was assessed. In the second part of this study, the Relationship Inventory was used with 25 patients after both the second and the tenth sessions, in order to assess the predictive value of the quality of the patient-therapist relationship in a earlier phase of treatment.

Method

To be included in the study, patients had to meet the DSM-III criteria for obsessive-compulsive neurosis. Patients were randomly assigned to one of three therapists. After ten sessions, approximately twenty weeks after the start of therapy, the out-patient treatment, using exposure and response prevention, was terminated and the posttest was held. Sixty patients took part in the first part of this study and 25 patients in the second part.

When patients suffer from an obsessive-compulsive neurosis consisting of obsessional thoughts only, the only way to measure these is by self-registration. In this study, therefore, self-registration was used. The patient recorded the frequency and/or the duration of the main obsessive-compulsive phenomena. Emmelkamp (1982), Emmelkamp et al. (1983), and Foa et al. (1983), in their studies of success and failure in the treatment of patients with obsessive-compulsive neurosis, defined failed treatment as an improvement of 30% or less. In this study, this criterion was also applied.

The first part of the study formed part of a much larger study, described elsewhere (Hoogduin & Duivenvoorden, 1988). After the tenth session the patient-therapist relationship was measured using the Barrett-Lennard Relationship Inventory. In the second part of this study, the scores on the Barrett-Lennard Relationship Inventory were recorded after both the second and the tenth session.

Results

Twenty-two percent of the 60 patients taking part in the first part of this study showed an improvement equal to or less than 30% (failure group). Seventy-eight percent, therefore, benefitted from treatment (success group). Significant differences, using the Mann-Whitney U-Test, in the patient-therapist relationship were found between the failure group and the success group. These differences were seen on both the patient form and the therapist form. The results of these tests and the mean scores are shown in Table 1.

Table 1: **Patient-therapist relationship in failure (F) and success (S) group. Part I; 60 patients.**

	F-group	S-Group	Significance (U-Test)
Relationship Inventory Therapist-form (Mean)	127	139	$p < .05$
Relationship Inventory Patient-form (Mean)	111	124	$p < .005$

The results of the second part of this study are presented in table 2. Twenty-five patients were taking part in this study. There was no significant correlation between treatment outcome and the quality of the therapeutic relationship as assessed by the patient after the second session (.02; n.s.). There was a significant correlation between treatment outcome and the quality of the therapeutic relationship as assessed by the therapist after the session. (.44; $p < .05$). The predictive value of the Relationship Inventory after the second session was then compared to its value after the tenth session. Both the patient and the therapist assessment of the quality of their relationship were significantly correlated with treatment outcome. To be more precise, the results were as follows: After the tenth session, there was a significant correlation between treatment outcome and the quality of the therapeutic relationship as assessed by the patient (.43; $p < .05$). As after the second session, there was a significant correlation between treatment outcome and the quality of the therapeutic relationship as assessed by the therapist (.42; $p < .05$). A significant correlation was also found between patient assessment after the second session and that after the tenth (.48; $p < .05$). Finally, there was also a significant correlation between therapist assessment after the second session and after the tenth (.76; $p < .001$).

Table 2: **Outcome and therapeutic relationship Part II; 25 patients.**

	Mean	s.d.	Correlations with outcome	Significance
Relationship Inventory Patient-form				
2nd session	133	25	.02	n.s.
10th session	131	18	.44	$p < .05$
Relationship Inventory Therapist-form				
2nd session	126	14	.43	$p < .05$
10th session	126	16	.42	$p < .05$
Success (%)	26	18		

Conclusions

The results of the first part of this study show a distinct connection between a good therapeutic relationship and positive outcome. In a study by Emmelkamp and Van der Hout (1983) phobic patients, undergoing group treatment by exposure in vivo, were asked to fill out the Dutch version of the Relationship Inventory. A significantly positive correlation between outcome and post-treatment score on the Relationship Inventory was established for the combined scores of patient and therapist ($p < .05$). In the study presented here, the relation between outcome and score on the R.I. was even more substantial. The problem is, however, that the correlation was found after the tenth session. The second part of the study was therefore carried out and the quality of the therapeutic relationship was measured after the second and the tenth session. Again a significant correlation was found between the patient's and the therapist's assessment of the quality of their relationship after the tenth session and treatment outcome. The quality of the relationship after the second session from the point of view of the patient had no predictive value with regard to treatment outcome. The assessment of the relationship by the therapist after the second session, however, had predictive value with regard to treatment outcome. This leads to the conclusion that the therapist's assessment of the quality of the therapeutic relationship can be useful in determining the prediction of outcome in an early phase of treatment. This study also emphasizes again the importance of the therapeutic relationship for outcome of treatment. This, in turn, leads us to the issue of enhancing this relationship.

ENHANCING THE THERAPEUTIC BOND

Much has been written about strategies to motivate people to accept something or to buy something (e.g. Van der Velden, 1977, 1980). It is obviously impossible to cover this whole area. We therefore limited ourselves to the most important literature on directive behavioural therapy, the literature on compliance, and on motivation for therapy. This literature is critically reviewed in Dhaenens and Schaap (1987) and Kersten, Hoogduin and Schaap (1988). Based on literature of common factors, partly referred to above, we were able to cluster these strategies in the categories that will be given below. Examples of the strategies are added each time.

Therapist accepts the client unconditionally

We all recognize in this category of motivating strategies one of the

Rogerian conditions. The therapist warmly confirms the client as a person and takes the client seriously. This will instill security, a necessary ingredient for therapeutic change to take place.

The following strategies were encountered in treating specific clients. The client *who has not finished his homework assignments*: Negative and clearly punishing responses should be avoided. Take a neutral, analyzing stance. Even go as far as to take the blame. Apologize for not having explained the assignments well enough.

Therapist is courteous

The therapist treats the client according to general etiquette, with due respect and courteousness. The therapist should, for instance, be patient and wait with a problem until the client starts. He should also be friendly, back-channel, smile and make positive statements.

We also encountered some client-specific strategies. The following is an example from the clinical literature on motivating the *unfriendly* client: His unfriendliness is part of his front towards others. Remain interested and friendly but don't be submissive and don't try to cheer him up. A helpful person will be a real discovery for him.

Therapist instills confidence in himself as a competent expert

The competent and self-assured behavior of the therapist will given the client faith that the therapist will be able to help him to solve his problems. A number of factors will determine the client's faith: His expectations, information about the therapist and/or treatment, and the therapist's behaviour. Strategies from this category may focus on any of these factors. The therapist should, for instance, show self-confidence and prestige. But he should also be dependable.

Therapist stays in the client's frame of reference

The therapist is empathic, interested in the client and begone with the client. This is expressed in his attentive listening as well as in his pacing and mimicry. He should listen attentively and maintain an average level of eye-contact; too much eye-contact is invasive, too little shows desinterest.

Among the client-specific strategies is the following: The *indifferent* client is hard to serve. He doesn't say anything about what he likes or dislikes. He is not going to negotiate. Be patient and try to become his partner. Take him in exactly, it will give you some hint about his real interest.

Therapist sells the treatment procedures

The therapist tunes his plans and the presentation of his plans in with the preferences and needs of his client. The therapist should, for instance, emphasize the client's strong points, and match interventions with client characteristics.

Not surprisingly, strategies have been developed for specific clients that fit well under this heading, for instance, *the client that has been sent by others*. The client has not come out of his own motivation. He will be aloof and careful. Therefore, be patient and show him your interest. Be concerned about his complaints. If the complaints are somatic, tell the client that somatic complaints lead to psychological stress. Not the other way around. Agree with the client's ideas in that he has a somatic disorder. The doctors disagree with him. In contrast, you agree and tell him that the psychological complaints possibly are the result of somatic complaints.

Therapist offers support

The strategies in this category are used by the therapist to make the client stronger and more self-confident. He will have more faith in himself that he will be able to solve his problems. The therapist, for instance, should label positively, compliment the client, and ask for his positive qualities. He will make the client feel at ease and encourage him. Also some client-specific strategies were encountered. For instance, the *inhibited* client: Praise him for the fact that he will take the necessary time to think before saying something. Compliment him for his seriousness.

Therapist offers help

In contrast to the foregoing category where the main emphasis was on increasing the client's self-confidence directly, in this category his problems are emphasized. The therapist will help the client to be specific in the description of his trials and tribulations and let him verbalize his feelings and responses.

Also under this category fall a number of client-specific strategies, for instance, for the *vacillating* client. Help this client by showing him a number of solutions, by talking about them and comparing them. Emphasize that you would hate it if he accepted an advice that he afterwards wouldn't like.

Therapist instills faith in the treatment

The therapist gives a credible rationale for the problems of the client and a logically compelling explanation for the effective ingredients of the therapeutic treatment. Moreover, he will conscientiously employ ritualistic, catharsis-like techniques.

Therapist gives information

In the beginning of treatment the therapist should give the client information about the treatment, about the procedures and about the client and therapist roles.

Therapist stimulates client towards participation

In the literature, a strong relationship is reported between therapy outcome and active participation by the client. It is, therefore, important that the therapist explicitly requests his participation and makes use of homework assignments such as: monitoring and self-observations.

Therapist utilizes resistance

The therapist responds towards uncooperative behavior of the client in such a way that the behavior pattern can be used to achieve reduction in complaints. This implies that he, for instance, accepts the resistance and suggests that the client is not ready yet for this assignment. Moreover, a number of strategies were encountered that were considered specific to a particular type of client. For instance, regarding the *dominating* client the following strategy was amongst those suggested: ask the client about his own strategies applied to his complaints and choose an appropriate one. Prescribe it in a more consistent way. In contrast, a client that *cannot be helped* (doctor shopping) could be tackled with the following strategy: listen with awe to the incompetence of your predecessors and be modest about your own talents; remain empathic but passive and let the client suggest solutions.

Therapist puts pressure on the client

The therapist sometimes puts pressure on the client to make him do something or he creates, by the use of a deal, a situation where the client feels obliged to keep up the appointment. The therapist could, for instance, use contingency contracting and make use of sanctions.

Therapist gets a third party involved

The client is motivated towards a positive or participating attitude towards treatment or towards specific assignments because the spouse or other person is involved to assist the client or perhaps simply check on him.

CONCLUDING REMARKS

We have presented evidence for the impact of the client-therapist relationship on outcome in behavior therapy. Hoogduin and Duivenvoorden (1988) show that on the basis of seven psychological variables, considered together, namely depression, anxiety, overvalued ideation of the contents of obsessional thoughts, motivation, anger, intelligence and interactional problem solving capability, a correct prediction of therapeutic outcome was possible for 80% of the patients involved. Many patients of the 20% that could not correctly be predicted reported a positive therapeutic relationship. This means that a good therapeutic relationship can overcome the negative effects of other factors. The presumption, on the basis of the study reported here, is that an even better prediction will be obtained by adding the assessment of the quality of the therapeutic relationship. It is also implied that improving the therapeutic relationship might be very important, particularly in those cases where other negative factors are at work.

We have also presented some strategies, developed in different settings of interpersonal influence, that may be of use to the therapist. They constitute just a sample of interpersonal options, developed in different spheres of human endeavors, that the therapist may apply. What is needed next is a decision tree that specifies what needs to be done at different phases in the treatment process and with what type of clients. We have recently started an explorative study in a large out-patient clinic to assess the extent to which the therapeutic relationship can be improved. The decision about what motivating strategy to choose is based on (1) the process model of behavior therapy as described by Kanfer and Griamm (1980), (2) interpersonal typologies, such as the one described by Kiesler (1982), and (3) the personality disorders and traits as described in the Diagnostic and Statistical Manual III-R (Axis II).

REFERENCES

Catanese, R.A., Rosenthal, T.L. & Kelley, J.E. (1979). Strange bedfellows:Reward, punishment, and impersonal distraction strategies in treating dysphoria. *Cognitive Theory and Research, 3*, 229-305.

Dhaenens, R. & Schaap, C. (1987). Compliance en Essentiële Hypertensie (Compliance and Essential Hypertension). *Internal Report*, Catholic University Nijmegen.

Dijk, P. van (1979). *Geneeswijzen in Nederland*. Deventer: Ankh-Hermes.

Durlak, J.A. (1979). Comparative effectiveness of paraprofessionals and professional helpers. *Psychological Bulletin, 86*, 80-92.

Emmelkamp, P.M.G. (1982). *Phobic and obsessive-compulsive disorders*. New York: Plenum Press.

Emmelkamp, P.M.G. & Van der Hout, A. (1983). Failure in treating

agoraphobia. In: E.B. Foa & P.M.G. Emmelkamp (Eds.), *Failures in behavior therapy* (pp.58-81), New York: Wiley.
Foa, E.B. & Emmelkamp, P.M.G. (1983) (Eds.). *Failures in behavior therapy.* New York: Wiley.
Frank, J. (1961). *Persuasion and healing.* Baltimore: John Hopkins.
Garfield, S.L. (1980). *Psychotherapy: An eclectic approach.* New York: Wiley.
Gurman, A.S. (1977). The patient's perception of the therapeutic relationship. In: A.S. Gurman & A. Razin (Eds.), *Effective psychotherapy: A Handbook of research* (pp.503-543). New York: Pergamon Press.
Hattie, J.A., Sharpley, C.F. & Rogers, H.J. (1984). Comparative effectiveness of professional and paraprofessional helpers. *Psychological Bulletin, 95*, 534-541.
Hoogduin, C.A.L. & Duivenvoorden, H. (1988). A decision model in the treatment of obsessive-compulsive neurosis. *British Journal of Psychiatry* (accepted).
Hoorens, V. (1986). De kliënt-therapeut relatie in gedragstherapie. *Gedragstherapie, 19*, 263-278.
Jilek, W.G. (1974). *Salish Indians mental health and culture change.* Toronto: Holt.
Kalmthout, M. van, Schaap, C. & Wojciechowski, F.L. (1985). *Common factors in psychotherapy.* Lisse: Swets & Zeitlinger (194 pp).
Kanfer, F.H. & Grimm, L.G. (1980). Managing clinical change: A process model of therapy. *Behavior Modification, 4*, 419-444.
Kersten, T., Hoogduin, C.A.L. & Schaap, C. (1988). Instrumenten om motivatie voor psychotherapie te meten: Een overzicht (Instruments to measure motivation for psychotherapy: A review). *Internal Report*, Catholic University Nijmegen.
Kiesler, D.J. (1982). Confronting the client-therapist relationship in psychotherapy. In: J.C. Anchin & D.J. Kiesler (Eds.). *Handbook of interpersonal psychotherapy.* New York: Pergamon.
Kirsch, I. & Henry, D. (1977). Extinction versus credibility in the desensitization of text anxiety. *Journal of Counseling and Clinical Psychology, 45*, 1052-1059.
Krippner, S. (1975). *Song of the siren: A parapsychological odyssey.* New York: Harper.
Lietaer, G. (1976). Nederlandstalige revisie van Barrett-Lennard's Relationship Inventory voor individueel-therapeutische relaties. *Psychologica Belgica, 16* (1), 73-94.
McGlynn, F.D., Kinjo, K. & Doherty, G. (1978). Effects of cue-controlled relaxation, a placebo treatment, and no treatment on changes in self-reported test anxiety among college students. *Journal of Clinical*

Psychology, 34, 707-714.
Nawas, M.M., Pluk, P. & Wojciechowski, F.L. (1985). In search of the nonspecific factors in psychotherpy: A speculative essay. In: M. van Kalmthout, C. Schaap & F. Wojciechowski (Eds.), *Common factors in psychotherapy*. Lisse: Swets & Zeitlinger.
Orlinsky, D.E. & Howard, K.I. (1987). Process and outcome in psychotherapy. In: S. Carfield & E. Bergin (Eds.), *Handbook of psychotherapy and behavior change*. New York: Pergamon.
Pope, B. (1979). *The mental health interview: Research and application*. New York: Pergamon.
Prince, R.H. (1964). Indigenous Yoruba psychiatry. In: A Kiev (Ed.), *Magic, faith and healing*. New York: Free Press.
Prioleau, L., Murdock, M. & Brody, N. (1983). An analysis of psychotherapy versus placebo studies. *The Behavioural and Brain Sciences, 2*, 275-285.
Rabavilas, A.D., Boulougouris, J.C. & Perissaki, C. (1979). Therapist qualities related to outcome with exposure in vivo in neurotic patients. *Journal of Behavior Therapy and Experimental psychiatry, 10*, 293-294.
Rosen, G.M. (1975). Subjects' initial therapeutic expectancies toward systematic desensitization as a function of varied instructional sets. *Behavior Therapy, 6*, 230-237.
Rosenthal, T.L. (1980). Social cueing processes. *Progress in Behavior Modification, 10*, 111-146.
Smith, M.L., Glass, G.V. & Miller, T.I. (1980). *The benefits of psychotherapy*. Baltimore: John Hopkins
Strupp, H.H. (1978). Psychotherapy research and practice: An overview. In: S. Garfield & A.E. Bergin (Eds.), *Handbook of psychotherapy and behavior change: An empirical analysis*. New York: Wiley.
Swan, G. & MacDonald, M.L. (1978). Behavior therapy in practice: A national survey of behavior therapists. *Behavior Therapy, 9*, 799-807.
Torrey, E.F. (1972). What Western psychotherapists can learn from witchdoctors. *American Journal of Orthopsychiatry, 42*, 69-76.
Vahia, N.S. (1973). Psychophysiologic therapy based on the concept of Tatanjali. *American Journal of Psychotherapy, 27*, 557-565.
Velden, K. van der (1977) (Red.). *Directieve therapie I*. Deventer: Van Loghum Slaterus.
Velden, K. van der (1980) (Red.). *Directieve therapie II*. Deventer: Van Loghum Slaterus.
Wilson, G.T. & Evans, W.I.M. (1977). The therapist-client relationship in behavior therapy. In: A.S. Gurman & A. Razin (Eds.), *Effective psychotherapy: A handbook of research*. (pp.544-565). New York: Pergamon.

CLIENT-THERAPIST INTERACTION AND THERAPEUTIC CHANGE

L. Schindler

Max Planck Institute of Psychiatry, Psychological Department, Munich, West Germany

INTRODUCTION

During therapy the client and therapist are involved in some kind of non-technical interaction comprising approximately 50% of their joint activity. During these phases the therapist tries to enhance motivation, to introduce the therapeutic model or to prepare for the use of techniques. This kind of client/therapist interaction has been described by social psychologists as a process of social influence (e.g. Maddux, Stoltenberg & Rosenwein, 1987; Strong & Claiborn, 1982). Until recently research in behavior therapy has centered only on technical aspects. Thus empirical knowledge about appropriate strategies of social influence is limited up to now. We know we have to build up sufficient motivation in the client for example, but we know little about the tactics necessary to establish it. If we want to specify which therapist behavior is indicated in a certain situation with a certain client to achieve a positive client reaction, then we have to investigate the ongoing client-therapist interaction within the therapy session. This means we have to analyze the process of therapy on a behavioral level.

In this approach the interaction of client and therapist is recorded, then divided into speech acts and then coded according to behavioral categories. It is then possible to study either the frequency of certain classes of behavior in relation to the client's experience or to analyze the contingent effects of certain behaviors of one participant on the other. There are a few studies on this topic described in the literature (see Russel & Stiles, 1979 and Russel & Trull, 1986, for an overview), but only one within the framework of behavior therapy (Chamberlain, Patterson, Reid, Kavanagh & Forgatch, 1984).

Therefore our research aims at exploring the significance of the therapist-client interaction in behavior therapy. This chapter is meant to give a description of our research methods, as well as of some selected results from our studies.

CODING SYSTEM FOR INTERACTION IN PSYCHOTHERAPY (CIP)

For the kind of systematic behavioral observation mentioned above we developed a category system which includes categories for client and therapist behaviors. The categories are mutually exclusive and are derived from theoretical assumptions about beneficial and detrimental within-session behaviors of the therapist and client. They are also derived from other category systems described in the literature (for further description see Schindler, Hohenberger-Sieber & Hahlweg, 1988). The complete system contains 19 categories for therapist behavior which are subsumed under the 6 dimensions (or primary categories) of "empathy", "support", "exploration", "explanation", "directiveness" and "classification". The 20 categories for client behavior are clustered into the 7 dimensions of "self-disclosure", "problem description", "short answers", "change attempts", "cooperation", "information seeking" and "resistant behavior".

We used this coding system in a process-outcome study which was designed to analyze the in-session behavior of client and therapist. The aim was to investigate the interaction between client and therapist during the therapy sessions in order to identify mechanisms of social influence and their impact on therapy process and outcome.

TREATMENT PROGRAM

One essential requirement for such a process study is that all clients receive the same intervention techniques at the same stage of therapy. In order to investigate the contribution of the social interaction, it is necessary that the treatment program is standardized.

We chose the treatment of insomnia for this study, because we had previously developed a standardized broad-spectrum treatment for this kind of disorder (Schindler & Hohenberger-Sieber, 1985). This treatment program consists of 14 sessions and is divided into three parts: Behavior analysis, symptom related intervention and coping with stress.

DESIGN OF THE STUDY

Therapists. Therapy was conducted by 8 therapists, four female and four male, their age ranging from 25 to 39 years. They all were trained to carry out the treatment program and during the therapy they received weekly supervision sessions to ensure that the therapy was conducted comparably - as far as the technical aspects were concerned. Each therapist treated 4 cases, resulting in a total sample of 31 clients.

Clients. All clients suffered from chronic insomnia, most of them for several years. 75% of them were female and their age ranged from 25 to 45 years. They suffered either from sleep onset or from sleep maintenance insomnia and their mean sleep duration was 5.7 hours.

Assessment instruments. Before and after therapy the clients completed several questionnaires including a sleep questionnaire, scales measuring stress and coping, and a depression scale. This battery of questionnaires was also used for follow-up measures at 6, 12 and 18 months after the end of therapy. The "VEV" questionnaire (Zielke & Kopf-Mehnert, 1978) was chosen as the primary outcome criterion. This German instrument has 42 items and allows the client to rate the amount of change gained from the treatment. Normative data for this instrument are available. According to the total score one can ascertain if there has been significant change, no change or deterioration for the individual client. On the basis of this score the whole sample was divided into a high improvement group with 15 clients and a low improvement group with 16 clients.

All sessions were audiotaped and coded using our observation system CIP. The tapes were coded by three trained raters. Reliability was computed on the basis of several tapes and resulted in a kappa coefficient of about .80 for therapist as well as for client categories, indicating satisfactory inter-rater agreement.

EFFECTS OF THERAPIST BEHAVIORS

On the basis of these behavioral data we analyzed the contingent effect of the different therapist behaviors on the client reaction. This involved client responses following a particular therapist category. Comparing the base rate with the contingent probability one can obtain evidence of a significantly contingent effect (Revenstorf, Hahlweg, Schindler & Vogel, 1984).

For this analysis the data of all dyads were pooled together for the first and the second half of the treatment process. In the following the results for the first seven sessions shall be discussed.

Empathy. Figure 1 shows the contingent client reaction to empathy of the therapist. In can be seen that empathy is highly significantly contingent in proceeding self-disclosure as well as problem description. This means that the therapist can elicit client emotional disclosure by this behavior at a rate which is significantly higher than the rate that would be expected by chance. This is indicated in the figure by thick lines. Reactions which follow in rate that is significantly lower than chance are indicated by dotted lines. We can see that empathy is unlikely to be followed by short answers only, and it is also not helpful in eliciting client behavior that is relevant for change.

Figure 1: **Contingent client response to therapist's empathy pooled data (N = 31; Sessions 1 to 7) (p-values for the contingent probability of each transition)**

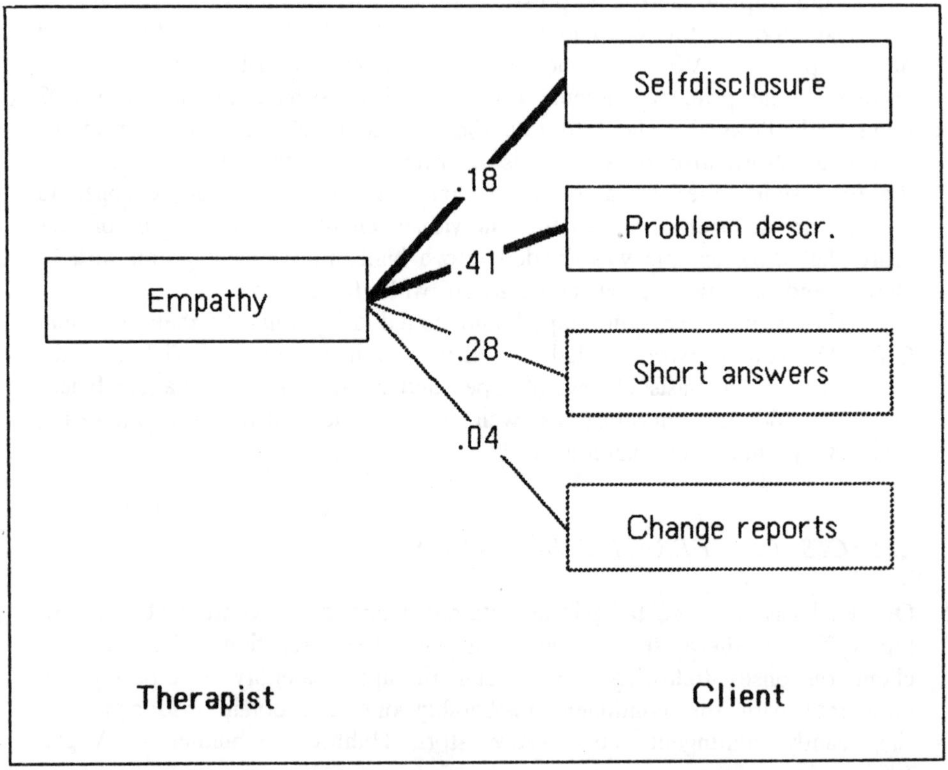

Support. The next primary therapist category is support. Here too we have a highly significant rate of contingent self-disclosure, but also of change reports and cooperative behavior (see figure 2). Support and reassurance is unlikely to be followed by simple answers as well as by problem description.

Exploration. If we look finally at explorative behavior of the therapist, then we can see that this kind of question has a self-disclosure rate lower than that expected by chance (see figure 3). The same is true for a contingent client reaction regarding change reports on cooperative behavior. Exploration will most likely be followed by problem description and short answers.

Figure 2: **Contingent client response to therapist's support pooled data (N = 31; Sessions 1 to 7) (p-values for the contingent probability of each transition)**

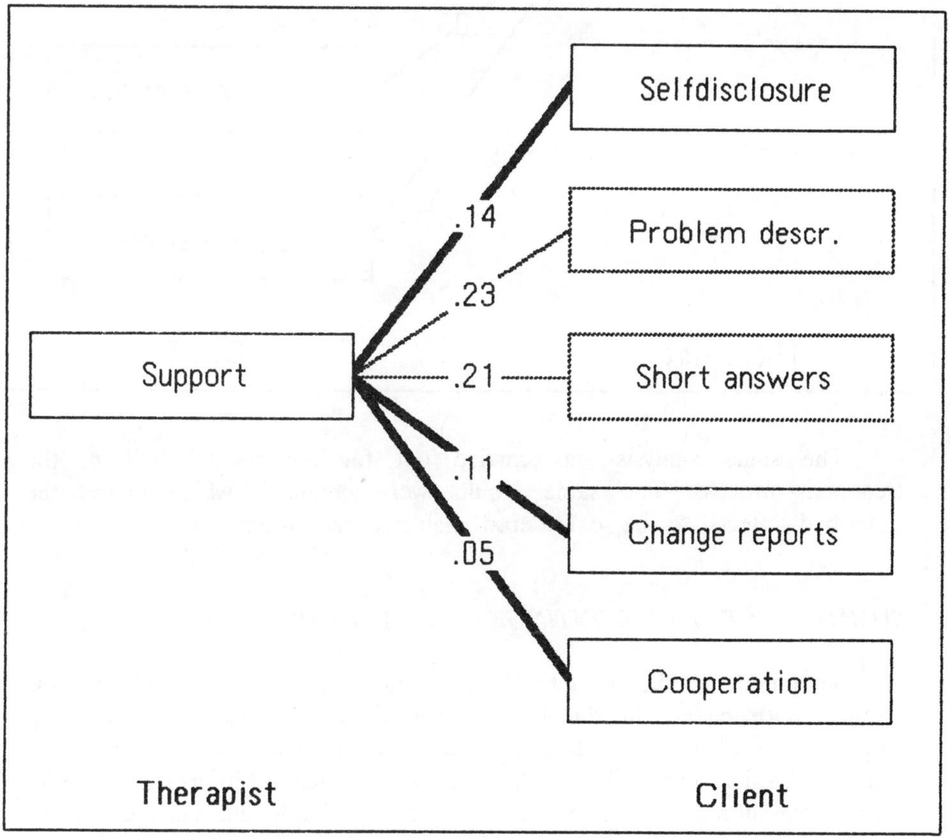

Figure 3: **Contingent client response on therapist's exploration pooled data (N = 31; Session 1 to 7) (p-values for the contingent probability of each transition)**

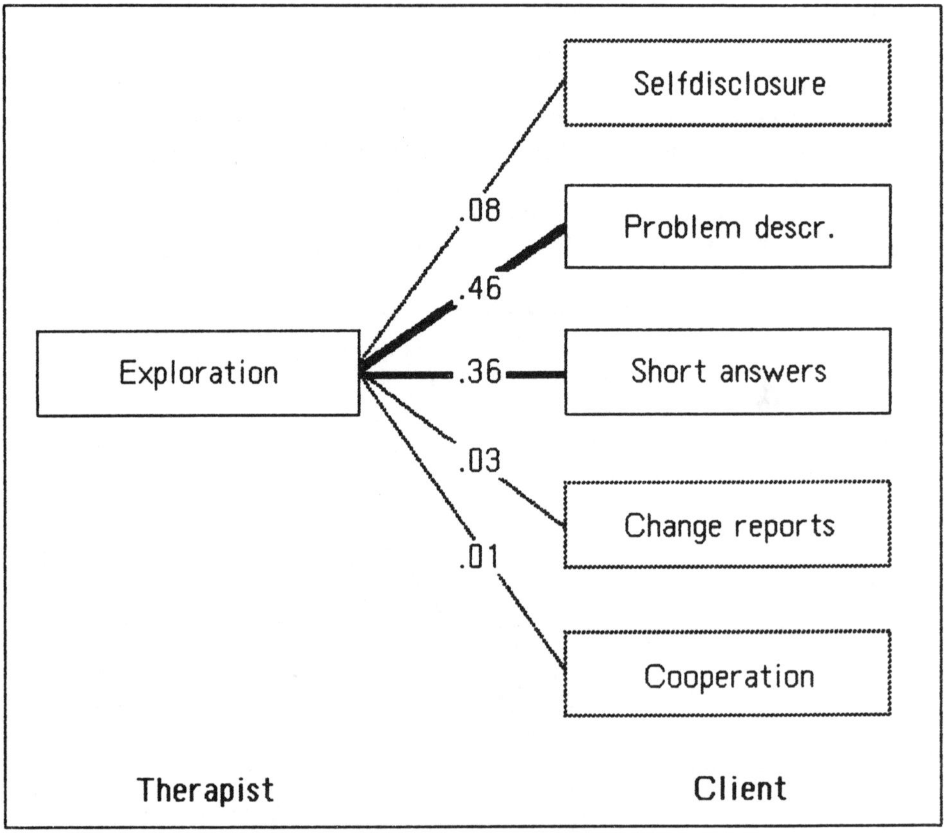

The same analysis was carried out for the second half of the treatment process. The same results were obtained, which allows the described effects to be considered stable over therapy.

SUMMARY OF THE CONTINGENT REACTIONS AT LAG 1

As mentioned at the outset, these results are true for both success groups. With clients in the low as well as in the high success group empathy will lead to self-disclosure but not to contributions relevant for change. Exploration will result mainly in factual information. With support/reassurance the therapist will most probably get change reports

Table 1: Comparison between high and low success group for lag 1—sequencies including therapist support

Sequence		High success group f [a]	High success group kappa [b]	Low success group f	Low success group kappa	U—test z—score
Support ⟶ self—disclosure	$\bar{X}$	43.5	.15	27.5	.08	2.53*
	SD	29.9	.05	21.7	.08	
Support ⟶ change reports	$\bar{X}$	44.1	.24	29.4	.17	2.73**
	SD	23.6	.07	24.0	.07	
Support ⟶ cooperation	$\bar{X}$	21.7	.18	11.9	.11	2.61**
	SD	9.2	.06	9.2	.07	
Self—disclosure ⟶ support	$\bar{X}$	49.9	.18	28.6	.13	2.29*
	SD	34.1	.07	21.7	.10	
Change reports ⟶ support	$\bar{X}$	53.9	.32	39.1	.25	2.21*
	SD	25.4	.08	30.3	.08	
Cooperation ⟶ support	$\bar{X}$	23.3	.20	15.4	.15	1.90*
	SD	9.1	.07	13.0	.08	

a) Mean frequency transition
b) Mean kappa—coefficient of the transition

and cooperation. These selected results illustrate that different therapist behaviors have a different reaction pattern on part of the client. And these effects are stable over the course of therapy.

DIFFERENCES BETWEEN HIGH AND LOW SUCCESS PATIENTS

Apart from the above findings, it is of interest whether there are differences in the contingent reactions between high and low success patients. For testing the differences between the two groups the kappa-statistic was used as proposed by Whitehurst, Fischel, DeBaryshe, Caulfield & Falco (1986). The kappa-coefficient is computed for a particular therapist-client transition per dyad. Kappa is the ratio of the obtained frequency of transitions to the maximum possible number of transitions, corrected by chance. Testing for group differences, the kappa-coefficient can ben considered as a usual individual parameter. We used the Mann-Whitney-U-test for comparing the high and low success group. The results for those transitions which include therapist support as antecedent or subsequent behavior are shown in table 1.

Clients in the low success group show significantly less contingent rates of self-disclosure, change reports and cooperation following supportive statements by the therapist. If we look at the therapist behavior, then we see that he also gives less support to the client's contribution of this kind. Therapist's support includes e.g. the categories "positive feedback" and "giving confidence". Thus the sequence "self-disclosure" - "support" means reinforcing the emotional reports of the client; secondly the sequence "change reports" - "support" can be understood as reassuring the client for new orientation or attempts of self-control; and thirdly "cooperation" - "support" means reinforcing client behavior like "goal formulation" or "proposals for change".

One could now say that the therapist's behavior is dependent on the contribution of the client; he can only give support for positive statements brought in by the client. However, the conditional probabilities describe the contingent rate of support. This means therapists immediately acknowledge positive contributions of the clients less often in the low success group in comparison to the more successful clients.

LONGER SEQUENCE IN THE INITIAL STAGE OF THERAPY

These differences can not only be found in the immediate contingencies but also in longer sequences. A longer sequence of interest for instance consists of several cooperative client statements followed by therapist empathy or support. Such an interaction pattern represents change relevant episodes as elaborating core emotional problems of the client or working out essential treatment goals. Figure 4 shows the differences in this sequence during the initial phase of treatment.

Figure 4: **Sequence of cooperation during behavior analysis for the high and the low success group**

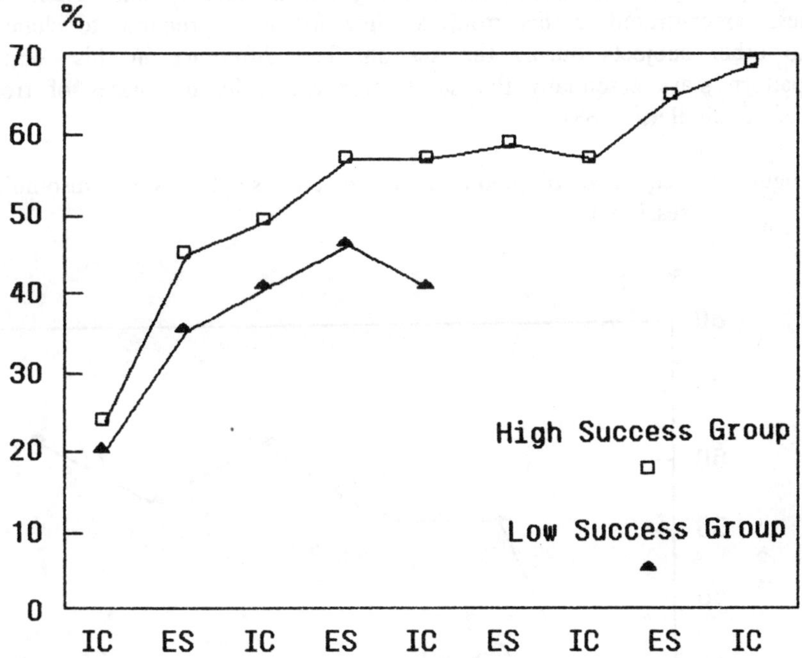

Client IC = Initiative / Cooperation
Therapist ES = Empathy / Support

One can see that during the two sessions of behavior analysis the two groups differ in the length of the sequences as well as in the probability of is occurrence. In the high success group clients react with initiative/cooperation in 23% of all their behavior. When the client showed this behavior the therapist reacted with "empathy/support" with a probability of p = .45, which means that this behavior occurs in 45% of all occasions when the client showed initiative. Given this sequential combination of client's initiative and therapist's support, the clients in the high success group react with cooperation again in 50% of all such incidents - and so on.

The clients in the low success group show "initiative/cooperation" with a base rate of 20%, which is about the same as in the other group. However, therapists react less often with contingent "empathy/support", and this lower rate is continued with the next client as well as therapist reaction. Thus the probability for participating in this kind of behavioral sequence is lower in this group for both the client and the therapist. The sequence is shorter as well, meaning that client and therapist spend less time on working out a certain topic. Their work is less concentrated in this group as they are more prepared to change over to other subjects during the session. The difference in this cooperation pattern stays essentially the same over the different phases of treatment (cf. Schindler, 1988).

Figure 5: **Sequence of cooperation in two single cases (insomnia; five sessions)**

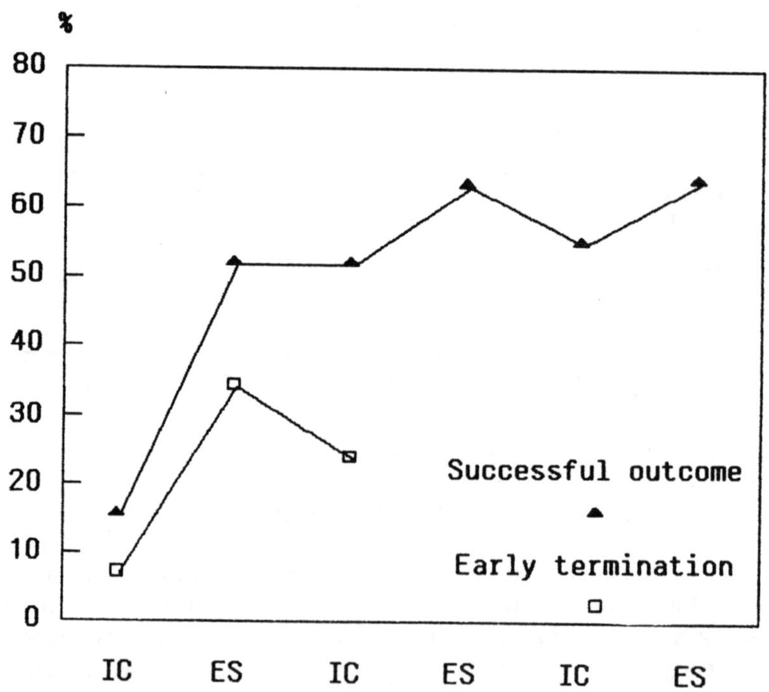

IC = Initiative / Cooperation of the client
ES = Empathy / Support of the therapist

REPLICATION BY SINGLE CASE STUDIES

These findings are confirmed by the results of two other studies we conducted. In the first study we compared the treatment of a successful patient with a drop out (Schindler & Hohenberger-Sieber, 1988). Both clients suffered from chronic insomnia and were treated by the same therapist. It can be seen in figure 5, that the same difference could be found.

Furthermore two treatments of depressive clients with different outcome were analyzed in a study by Kaimer, Reinecker & Schindler (1988). And again similar differences in the interaction could be found (see figure 6). These replications confirm that the kind of interaction style that evolves during the early phase in therapy obviously has prognostic value for the further progress and outcome.

Figure 6: **Sequence of cooperation in two single cases (depression; eight sessions)**

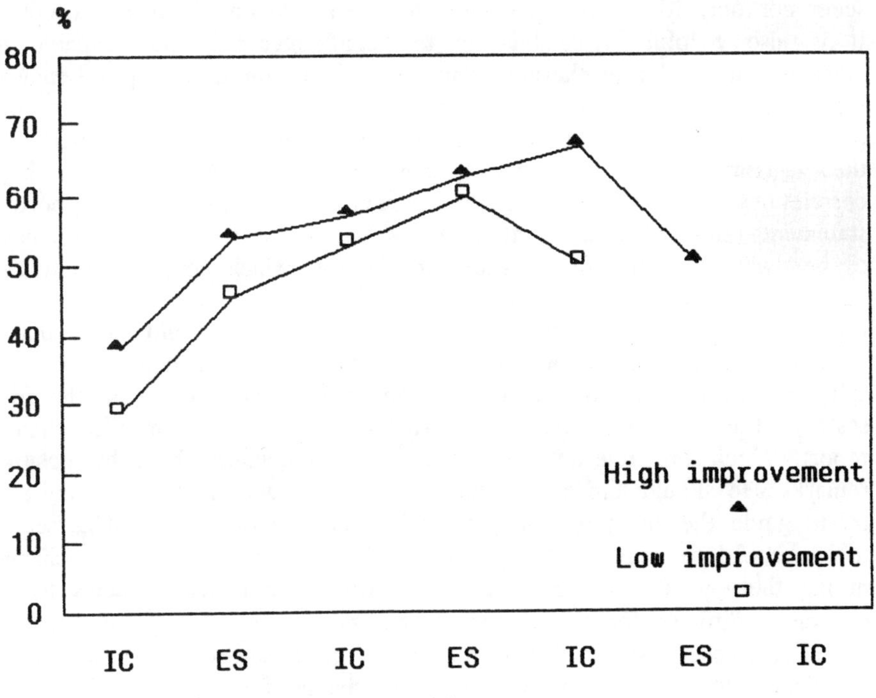

IC = Initiative / Cooperation of the client
ES = Empathy / Support of the therapist

CONCLUSION

These results allow us to draw several conclusions. Firstly, we were able to show that the therapeutic relationship has a significant influence on therapy process and outcome. When the technical components are standardized as far as possible, then distinct differences in interaction patterns can be found between the treatment processes of high versus low success clients.

Secondly, the initial phase of therapy seems to be crucial for the quality of the relationship during the further course of therapy. The style of interaction is evidently defined during the first therapeutic contacts and is very difficult to change as treatment continues.

Furthermore it could be shown that the different classes of the therapist behavior affect the client reaction in a distinct way. The most important dimension found in our studies has been "support/reassurance" by the therapist. This therapist dimension includes a broad range of behaviors as e.g. positive feedback, giving confidence and encouragement, positive reframing, and so on. Such signs of acknowledgement and support seem not only to be important for the client's feeling of being accepted. It is also helpful in establishing the confidence of being capable to manage change during therapy. Thus this dimension of therapist behavior seems to be of considerable importance for enhancing motivation and positive therapy expectations in the sense of Bandura's self-efficacy theory (Bandura, 1977). This becomes more evident with the high correlations ($r = .42$) between the frequency of the therapist's supportive statements and the client's rating of his benefit of the session. We have to be aware that the first sessions in therapy, which contain usually the behavior analysis, are not only important to gather information, but that during this phase the constitution of the therapeutic bond takes place.

As one recommendation for clinical practice we can conclude that in spite of possible disappointment with an uncooperative client in the first session, the therapist should be vigilant for aspects in the client's report, which are relevant for change, and recognize them by positive remarks. He should aim at structuring the interview in a directive way and try to guide the client to examples of his capacity for change. This seems to be crucial to convince the client that he is capable to manage change during therapy. To implement these behavior characteristics seems to be the more difficult for the therapist, the more reticent a client behaves. A reticent client offers fewer reports of past self-control attempts or contributes less often with proposals for change for instance. Thus it is more difficult for the therapist to find the opportunity to give support. Support however has the greatest capacity to elicit the mentioned change-relevant utterances on part of the client. Thus especially with a reticent client, it is the challenge for the therapist not only to gather information about symptomatic behavior during the very first sessions, but to guide the client to past self-control attempts or to areas in his life, which he is able to manage with success.

Of course we are still at the beginning in formulating strategies to use social influence in therapy. Observational studies are very time-consuming, but with this approach we think it is possible to further specify how to achieve a beneficial therapist-client relationship.

REFERENCES

Bandura, A. (1977). Self-efficacy: Toward a unifying theory of behavioral change. *Psychological Review, 84*, 151-215.

Chamberlain, P., Patterson, G., Reid, J., Kavanagh, K. & Forgatch, M. (1984). Observation of client resistance. *Behavior Therapy, 15*, 14-155.

Kaimer, P., Reinecker, H. & Schindler, L. (1988). Interaktionsmuster von Klient und Therapeut bei zwei unterschiedlich erfolgreich behandelten Fällen. *Zeitschrift fur Klinische Psychologie* (in press).

Maddux, J.E., Stoltenberg, C.D. & Rosenwein, R. (eds.) (1987). *Social processes in clinical and counseling psychology*. New York: Springer.

Revenstorf, D., Hahlweg, K., Schindler, L. & Vogel, B. (1984). Interaction analysis of marital conflict. In: Hahlweg, K. & Jacobson, N.S. (eds.), *Marital interaction: Analysis and modification*. New York: Guilford.

Russel, R.L. & Stiles, W.B. (1979). Categories for classifying language in psychotherapy. *Psychological Bulletin, 86*, 404-419.

Russell, R.L. & Trull, T.J. (1986). Sequential analysis of language variables in psychotherapy process research. *Journal of Consulting and Clinical Psychology, 54*, 16-21.

Schindler, L. (1988). Die soziale Interaktion von Therapeut und Klient in der Verhaltenstherapie: Ihr Einfluss auf Therapieverlauf und Erfolg (in preparation).

Schindler, L. & Hohenberger-Sieber, E. (1985). The need of a multifaceted behavioral approach to the treatment of insomnia. In: Koella, W.P., Rüther, E. & Schulz, H. (eds.) *Sleep '84*. New York: Fischer.

Schindler, L. & Hohenberger-Sieber, E. (1988). Interaction patterns of client and therapist in a successful and a drop-out case. Paper submitted for publication.

Schindler, L., Hohenberger-Sieber, E. & Hahlweg, K. (1988). Observing client-therapist interaction in behavior therapy: Development and validation of an observational system. Paper submitted for publication.

Strong, S.R. & Claiborn, C.D. (1982). *Change through interaction*. New York: Wiley.

Whitehurst, G.J., Fischel, J.E., DeBaryshe, B., Caulfield, M.B. & Falco, F.L. (1986). Analyzing sequential relations in observational data: A practical guide. *Journal of Psychopathology and Behavioral Assessment, 8*, 129-140.

Zielke, M. & Kopf-Mehnert, G. (1978). *Der Veränderungsfragebogen des Erlebens und Verhaltens (VEV)*. Manual. Weinheim: Beltz.

THE COMBINATION OF PARADOXICAL AND PROBLEM SOLVING ASSIGNMENTS IN THE TREATMENT OF FIGHTING COUPLES

A. Lange

University of Amsterdam, Department of Clinical Psychology, The Netherlands.

INTRODUCTION

The treatment of couples who are engaged in enduring arguments has become a topic of interest since the development of family and marital therapy. Innovating researchers, such as Jackson, Watzlawick, Weakland and Haley (Haley, 1963; Lederer & Jackson, 1968) have drawn attention to the phenomenon of the 'fighting couple', two people who are caught up in a series of vicious actions based on an irrational struggle for power and symmetrical escalations (Watzlawick et al., 1967).

Helping people to overcome this power struggle was in the beginning dominated by two theoretical frames. The 'Palo Alto' group (Watzlawick, Weakland, 1977) based their 'Brief Therapy' on communication theory. They proposed a system-theoretic therapy model which was mainly based on giving the patients insight into the communicational patterns and on giving directives which interrupted the vicious circles which were sustaining the symptomatic behavior. Although their general therapy model is widely used in family and couple therapy (Watzlawick et al., 1974; Papp, 1983; Selvini Palazzoli et al., 1978; Tomm, 1984 a and b) and although it includes paradoxical assignments in the form of prescribing the symptom, a thorough search of the literature does not reveal many studies in which paradoxical assignments were used in the treatment of distressed couples (Weeks & L'Abate, 1978 and 1982; Weeks, 1985; Seltzer, 1986; Shoham-Salomon & Rosenthal, 1987). To our knowledge it is described only by Herr & Weakland (1979) and Gilewsky, Kuppinger & Zarit (1985) who used it in the treatment of aging couples; by the behavioral therapists, Jacobson & Margolin (1979, p.152-153) and by Van Dyck & Hoogduin (1977), who mention the 'fractionated quarreling advice' (the instruction to quarrel for a fixed period every day).

Another frame of reference in the treatment of fighting couples was presented by behavioral marital therapists such as Stuart and Liberman (Stuart, 1969; Liberman, 1970). By combining learning theory and social psychological theories on exchange in interpersonal behavior (Homans, 1950; Thibaut & Kelley, 1959), they developed methods which were based on 'reciprocity'. The essence of their behavioral marital therapy is to induce the clients to break the negative spiral of punishment by making well-defined behavioral contracts (Lange & van der Hart, 1983) on a 'quid pro quo basis' and by training interpersonal social skills (Stuart, 1980; Jacobson, 1981; Margolin & Fernandez, 1985).

Behavioral marital therapy seems to work well with couples who, although their relationship is under stress, also have a considerable amount of problem solving ability. Most of the behavior-therapeutic outcome research with regard to couples in distress seems to deal with moderately distressed couples and not with couples who are caught in a severe, irrational struggle for power. Moreover, Gurman et al. (1986) argued, after re-examining some of the outcome studies, that the measures which were used in the reported studies, were not of clinical value. Applying new measures, like the Reliable Change Index, Jacobson et al. (1984) showed that the outcome of behavioral (problem solving) marital therapy is less promising than was previously assumed. Furthermore, analysis of clinical observations with fighting couples suggests that if the power struggle is strong and irrational, the congruent problem solving method is too rational to break the vicious circle (Lange, 1985a). Behavioral contracts are then not perceived as rewarding. The partners either do not keep to the assignments because they are afraid of losing the battle, or they disqualify the agreements as not being important because the positive acts of the partner are interpreted as not spontaneous and therefore unimportant. The circular process of "A is feeling hurt ➞ A reacts negatively ➞ B is hurt and reacts negatively ➞ A is hurt ➞ etc." is not broken.

The effectiveness of the 'non-behavioral', system-theoretic communication approach is less well-documented as there are only few controlled studies and even those seem to "bear little resemblance to the marital therapies they purportedly investigated" (Gurman et al., 1986, p.583). One of these studies is reported by Boelens et al. (1980) who compared behavioral versus system-theoretic marital therapy. On the basis of this and other studies Emmelkamp (1986) concludes that neither system-theoretic nor behavioral marital therapy is superior to the other. He furthermore quotes several studies in which it is argued that "behaviors exchanged by spouses is subjective and idiosyncratic and the planning of change must take into account the individuals' cognitive appraisals of the events in their relationship" (p.429).

Reviewing the literature it is striking how difficult it is to compare the different treatment paradigms in the way they are clinically used. The differences are often more in the labels assigned to them than in the therapies themselves. A behavioral problem solving marital therapy without feedback on communicational patterns is unthinkable. On the other hand, a system-theoretic therapy does fairly often call for communication training, directives and assignments and is generally not confined to just giving feedback. Both of these models are inconceivable without some kind of cognitive restructuring. Emphasis should not only lie on comparing these treatment models but in finding and testing ways of combining their most effective elements. In this paper a new combination of carefully chosen intervention strategies is examined by means of a detailed analysis of four cases out of a study of ten treatments of severely distressed couples. Essential is the unprecedented issuing of paradoxical assignments to one partner while giving problem solving assignment to the other.

THE CASES

Symmetrical escalation between Mr. and Mrs. Wilburn

Mr. and Mrs. Wilburn were in their 30s. They had been together for about seven years and did not want children. Their marital problems consisted in particular of escalating symmetrical quarrels emanating from a struggle for power. The pattern was as follows: Mrs. Wilburn would make sarcastic remarks to her husband, who would feel deeply hurt and humiliated. He could react, in the first instance, with resentful silence, after which he would enter into a confrontation, intended to hurt her in retribution. This process of escalation would go on for a while. They were affectionate towards one another, although Mr. Wilburn seemed more fond of his wife than she of him.

After the first two sessions, the picture was reasonably clear. Perhaps the most obvious course of action would have been to have examined possibilities for behavioral contracts. Mrs. Wilburn could be a little kinder and more considerate of her husband's feelings, in return for some positive behavior by him. The disadvantage of this approach was that even if certain things changed, the pattern would have been no different. The husband would still have been dependent on his wife's moods, the only difference being that she would have been trying to spare his feelings a little more. For this reason a strategy was chosen, which was based on the observation that Mr. Wilburn could have been less vulnerable, less dependent on his wife's being well-disposed towards him. It was introduced as follows:

> "*Mrs. Wilburn, we could try to help you to be less sarcastic and aggressive towards your husband, but ...* (long

pause) ... *I'm afraid that would be missing the point. I think that we should first find out why you, Mr. Wilburn, get so depressed when your wife is unkind to you, why you don't defend yourself immediately, why you take everything so personally instead of shrugging it off and saying, "that's Marg and her sarcasm again". I'd like to suggest that during the next two weeks, as soon as Marg makes a remark which hurts you, you go into another room to be on your own for ten minutes. When you are alone, you are to make yourself feel the hurt as keenly as possible. You are to think about the terrible thing she has said, how it's humiliated you and ask yourself whether this has anything to do with your family background.* (This had been discussed during the second session). *At the end of ten minutes, you are to write all this down. In order to make the most of the next two weeks, would you, Mrs. Wilburn, make sure that your husband has enough material to work on so that he is able to gain insight into what it is that is making him feel this way. Strange as it may seem, this means that over the next two weeks, you will have to make as many sarcastic remarks as you possibly can - you know the sort I mean."*

The instruction was accepted without objection, although with a degree of surprise. The result was perfect. Two weeks later, they came in laughing: Mr. Wilburn had tried to carry out the assignment to start with, but after two minutes had decided that he would not allow himself to be humiliated any longer, that he did not care what she said to him and he had then gone back into the sitting room. Mrs. Wilburn had tried several times, with increasing difficulty, to stick to the assignment. However, it no longer made any impression on her husband, so she had stopped. The therapist complimented Mrs. Wilburn on her efforts, but asked her to continue the assignment as, unfortunately, her husband had not used the opportunity to withdraw to another room very often. The assignment was, therefore, reissued, with similar result, i.e. Mr. Wilburn had not gone off to sit on his own at all and Mrs. Wilburn had hardly made any sarcastic remarks. The pattern appeared to be broken.

The assignment to Mrs. Wilburn was withdrawn and Mr. Wilburn was advised to watch himself in the future and, if necessary, to withdraw to be on his own. There were three more sessions spread over a long period in which the couple received guidance in sustaining and using the changes which had taken place. At the last session there was no question of a relapse.

Observations: By exposing Mr. Wilburn's weak attitude by means of learning assignment, the therapist was able to give Mrs. Wilburn a paradoxical assignment which made it unappealing for her to behave as she had previously. Furthermore, if she did behave in the old fashion, her husband was unaffected, because he interpreted it differently.

The Barclay's: a failure

Mr. and Mrs. Barclay were in their 40s and had two sons, aged 13 and 14. Mr. Barclay was a chemist and Mrs. Barclay did not have a job outside the home. They reported a long history of escalating fights. The husband, in particular, accused his wife in a loud voice of all manner of sins, upon which she took out a notebook, observed him critically and nervously made notes from time to time. She was gathering ammunition to use against him later. Despite this, she said that she loved him. His feelings were not quite so clear. He was grudging towards her and was not sure if it was worth all the effort. In the second session he again ranted and raved his wife for over fifteen minutes - how she treated him like a child, how she never agreed with him and was awkward about everything, how she sabotaged all his plans and, above all, how she had systematically humiliated him over the years. He said that he would no longer allow himself to be humiliated.

Although he certainly did not make a humiliated impression, the therapist decided to take this up as a theme. It would perhaps be possible to find out why he felt humiliated when his wife disagreed with him. To begin with, he was given an instruction similar to Mr. Wilburn's, i.e. every time his wife treated him like a child, he was to go and sit on his own for fifteen minutes and contemplate what had taken place (the first step in problem solving). Mrs. Barclay was asked to provide him with as much opportunity to do so as possible by behaving in a humiliating and contrary fashion. They did not like the idea, but they were, nevertheless, prepared to try the assignment. Two weeks later it emerged that Mrs. Barclay had tried to carry out the assignment of being nasty, even though she had found it extremely difficult, but that her husband had not even tried to carry out his assignment al all. He was no longer interested in therapy and had decided he wanted a divorce as, according to him, there was no hope that his wife would ever change. Mrs. Barclay was very upset and tried in a touching but awkward way to refute his arguments. A trial separation (Lange & van der Hart, 1983) was arranged. During this time, problems with their children led them to a sort of 'working relation' and they agreed to stay together on these terms. The fighting diminished somewhat, but the disruptive pattern was not really broken.

Observations: Although the final results of the treatment were not negative, the combination of a paradoxical and a congruent assignment did not have the intended effect. The following factors may have played a role in this. During the phase in which the assignment was issued, the level of affection between the clients was not equal. Mr. Barclay was not enthusiastic about being involved in the treatment. He was in the process of "getting rid of his wife" and was not amenable to the idea that he could perhaps change in some way. There was no treatment contract in that respect. Furthermore, the therapist made an incorrect choice: the problem solving part of the assignment can only be given to a partner who is interested and motivated to "work". This was not the case with Mr. Barclay. If the strategy should have been used at all he should have been given the paradoxical part of it.

Lack of attention: the Whites

Mrs. White complained that her husband (both were in their early thirties) did not pay enough attention to her. After some probing by the therapist the pattern became clear: Mr. White's feelings for his wife had not disappeared but her constant demand for attention and affection made it rather difficult for him to show the desired behavior. He felt like a fool, being expected to show spontaneous behavior on command.

The therapist intervened in the following way. First he explained the vicious circle they were in: "the wife shows that she expects affectionate behavior from her husband (verbally as well as non-verbally) ---> his responses are blocked and he withdraws ---> she feels rejected and shows this ---> he withdraws ---> etc." In theory this pattern might be broken by reciprocal behavioral exchanges. The husband could try to conform more to his wife's wishes which could be rewarded by her. In fact, however, this would not really break the pattern, for the wife would still not be satisfied as his behavior would not be interpreted as "affectionate" but as "commanded". It would be more promising if the wife were less dependent on her husband. That would be better for her and make it easier for the husband. The less she needed her husband the more she would get from him.

The wife agreed to this reasoning. The first step contained the following elements: the wife would monitor each moment that she felt a lack of attention in her husband's behavior, and write down the antecedents (Watson & Tharp, 1981). Furthermore she would take time-out and reflect on the question of "how important this lack of attention was and whether she could live without it and how". This was the start of the congruent, problem solving part. The husband received the paradoxical instruction: he was warned that he might feel the urge to be extra nice to his wife, but that would not help her for it would keep her dependent. She would not learn to be independent of his behavior. He was therefore requested not to change his usual behavior.

In five sessions the vicious circle was dramatically broken. The wife did not "harass" her husband anymore and she started re-orienting herself. The husband felt under less strain and therefore "could not" keep the assignment of not changing his behavior. He was more attentive than ever. The fights about "giving and getting attention" were over. A follow-up, six months later showed that there had been no relapse.

The endless discussions of the Greens

Mr. and Mrs. Green were in their thirties and showed all the elements of a continuing power struggle. A special feature was the length of their fights which could go on for hours. In the third session one of their arguments was re-enacted and analyzed. The therapist then focused on their inability to stop a discussion, especially when alcohol had been drunk. His suggestion to monitor and consequently reduce drinking was followed by the couple. They also agreed with him that it would be good for both of them to train certain skills for ending a discussion. He then gave them the following instruction: Arguments were not allowed for longer than half an hour. They would be alternately responsible for keeping this assignment. Standard phrases, like "you know that we agreed not to talk for longer than half an hour" were exercised during role playings. One the days the husband was responsible, the wife was instructed to give her husband "learning material". If she were to give in easily he would not learn to stop a difficult discussion. She had to go on and try to prolong the conflicts. The husband could then practice stopping her. On the other days the instructions were reversed.

The problem solving instructions - including the reduction in alcohol consumption - were followed, but prolonging the discussion on the command of the therapist in order to help the problem solving ability of the partner, proved to be quite difficult. The eternal daily conflicts were over and did not come back. The therapy took five more sessions, spread over four months, during which the clients were taught general social skills for solving interpersonal problems in order to maintain the acquired positive changes.

Observations: The assignments to Mr. and Mrs. Green differed from others in one respect. They were fully symmetrical. Each partner alternately received the problem solving assignment and the other the paradoxical instruction, rather than one partner receiving only the former and the other only the latter. The principal idea, however, is the same. On the days Mrs. Green had to practice gaining new skills, the paradoxical instruction to her husband would detract from the attractiveness of fighting her. The next day it would be the other way round.

DISCUSSION

1. The strategy which is introduced here is specially designed for couples who fight verbally, not for violent couples. This conforms to the rule that paradoxical assignments may be used only when obeying them would not

harm the clients. Suggestions for treating partners who are involved in physical abuse are reviewed by Rosenbaum & O'Leary (1986).

2. A meta-analysis on controlled outcome studies by Shoham-Salomon & Rosenthal (1987) and an experimental study by Shoham-Salomon & Jancourt (1985) suggest that, in general, paradoxical methods seem to be more effective and appropriate with extreme cases. This makes the question of why there is no tradition of using paradoxical assignments with severely distressed couples, even more compelling. The answer might be that none of the well-known rationales for 'selling' paradoxical directives to patients is appropriate for fighting couples. Contrary to the opinion of early authors, such as Haley (1963), several studies point out that paradoxical assignments should not be issued as though they were magic, but should be accompanied by some sort of explanation which makes it reasonable for the clients to try to carry them out (O'Connell, 1983; Riebel, 1984; Lange, 1985a). In a review, Lange (1985b) distinguishes three categories of these motivating paradigms which were then found in the literature on paradoxical assignments:

a. *Honest explanation*: the therapist explains why trying on purpose to behave in the symptomatic way will change the interaction. This paradigm, which is based on Frankl's (1960) concept of paradoxical intention, is more appropriate for individuals, such as social phobics, who suffer from an intrapsychic anticipation anxiety (Ascher & Turner, 1980) than for couples in distress.

b. *Positive reframing*: Several authors have argued that paradoxical interventions are most effective if they are used in a way that involves positive reframing of the symptomatic behavior (Fisher et al., 1981; Riebel, 1984 and Shoham-Salomon & Rosenthal, 1987). Their studies, however, do not include interpersonal problems and their findings can certainly not be generalized to fighting couples. Positive connotation is also used in systemic family therapy, when the function of individual psychopathology for the well being of the family is emphasized and the entire family is instructed not to change (Tomm, 1984a and 1984b). There is no evidence that this sort of positive reframing, which might be usable in homeostatic families who deny the existence of conflicts, is appropriate for fighting couples.

c. *Awareness*: the therapist explains that by exaggerating or monitoring the symptoms, the patients will acquire more insight into the dynamics of their behavior and that this will enable them to change their behavior later. This, is the most widely used paradigm. However, as explained by Lange (1985a), it is not the most powerful one, if used with interpersonal problems, because the same assignment is given to both partners. This makes them feel less responsible than if they were each given a separate assignment and it often does not bring the desired breakthrough in the vicious circle.

The *helping paradigm*, as it is introduced here for the treatment of fighting couples, was first mentioned by Teisman (1979) in a case study of the treatment of jealousy. It was also described by Coyne & Biglam (1984) in their behavioral analysis of a paradoxical treatment of a family with a "nasty daughter" and, independently, by Lange (1983 and 1987). It seems to provide a stronger rationale and is more appropriate in breaking the vicious circles than the paradigms distinguished above. Its strength lies in the dramatic cognitive reframing (Sanderman & Rüphan, 1987) which occurs when one partner is requested to continue fighting in order to help the other to gain more of the upper hand in the relationship. Fighting is then no longer rewarding.

3. In three of the four cases which were examined here, the disruptive pattern was effectively broken in only a few sessions spread over several months. Regarding the Barclays we discussed why the intervention probably failed. Inspecting the four cases together we may cautiously draw the following conclusions:

- The paradigm described can be a strong intervention for couples who are engaged in a power struggle but who are not characterized by a lack of minimal affection on the part of either of them.
- The strategy calls for a precise analysis of the interplay between individual traits of the partners and interactional processes. The congruent problem solving part of the intervention should be given to the partner who can and is willing to benefit from a social skills program, e.g. the vulnerable Mr. Wilburn, the sub-assertive Mrs. Fulbright and the dependent Mrs. White.
- The interventions should not be considered as isolated from the rest of the therapy. In all the cases the assignments were preceded by a thorough investigation of the exact nature of the fights, by re-enacting some of the fights for example. This is necessary in order to find the best starting-points for applying the strategy. Feedback and explanation were considered important by the clients. A good working relationship between therapist and client had already been established. Sometimes the intervention will have to be combined with other interventions, as in the case of the Green couple who agreed to a significant reduction in their alcohol consumption.
- In most cases the therapy is not finished after the first breakthrough. The therapist should not be too jubilant. As with other paradoxical assignments which the clients did not carry out, a concerned attitude is more appropriate, as well as a repetition of the assignment, accompanied by an earnest request to try even harder to carry it out (Lange, 1985b). Only when the fighting has been absent for quite some time should the paradoxical assignment be withdrawn and a symmetrical problem solving strategy should be pursued in order to help the clients to maintain the newly-acquired pattern.

4. The conclusions we have drawn above are based on systematic clinical observations. The next phase of investigation calls for quantitative research in which fighting couples are singled out for different forms of treatment. First, fighting couples should be screened on the dimensions mentioned above. Only those couples who conform to the criteria for the strategy are taken into the study. Secondly, a group of therapists will have to be trained, not only in using this method, but also in other aspects of marital therapy, as we have argued that the techniques should not be used in isolation. After random allocation of clients to one of the experimental conditions of different strategy and after random allocation to therapists, it might be possible to compare the results of the "combination" strategy with "pure" paradoxical strategies and/or with "pure" non-paradoxical, congruent, strategies in pre-post-test designs, on measures like the Interactional Problem Solving Scale (Lange, 1984) or the Maudsley Marital Questionnaire, (Arrindell, 1987), applying criteria like the "reliable change index" (Jacobson et al., 1984). We hope to report on this in the near future.

REFERENCES

Arrindell, W.A. (1987). *Marital conflict and agoraphobia: Fact or phantasy*. Delft: Eburon.

Ascher, L.M. & Turner, R.M. (1980). A comparison of two methods for the administration of paradoxical intention. *Behaviour Research & Therapy, 18*, 121-126.

Boelens, W., Emmelkamp, P., MacGillavry, D. & Markvoort, M. (1980). A clinical evaluation of marital treatment: reciprocity counseling vs. system-theoretic counseling. *Behavioural Analysis & Modification, 4* (2), 85-96.

Coyne, J.C. & Biglan, A. (1984). Paradoxical techniques in strategic family therapy: a behavioral analysis. *Journal of Behavior Therapy and Experimental Psychiatry, 15* (3), 221-227.

Emmelkamp, P.M.G. (1982). *Phobic and Obsessive-Compulsive Disorders; Theory, Research and Practice*. New York: Plenum.

Emmelkamp, P.M.G. (1982). Behavior therapy with adults. In: Garfield, S.L. & Bergin, A.E. (Eds.), *Handbook of Psychotherapy and Behavior Change*. New York: Wiley.

Fisher, L., Anderson, A. & Jones, J.E. (1981). Types of paradoxical interventions and indications/contra-indications for use in clinical practice. *Family Process, 20*, 25-35.

Frankl, V.E. (1960). Paradoxical intention. *American Journal of Psychiatry, 14*, 520-535.

Gilewsky, M.J., Kuppinger, J. & Zarit, S.H. (1985). The aging marital

system: A case study in life changes and paradoxical intervention. *Clinical Gerontologist, 3* (3), 3-15.
Gurman, A.S., Kniskern, D.P. & Pinsof, W.M. (1986). Research on the process and outcome of marital and family therapy. In: Garfield, S.L. & Bergin, A.E. (Eds.), *Handbook of Psychotherapy and Behavior Change*. New York: Wiley.
Haley, J. (1963). *Strategies of Psychotherapy*. New York: Grune & Stratton.
Herr, J.J. & Weakland, J. (1979). *Counseling Elders and Their Families: Practical Techniques for Applied Gerontology*. New York: Springer.
Homans, G.C. (1950). *The Human Group*. New York: Harcourt, Brace.
Jacobson, N.S. (1981). Behavioral Marital Therapy. In: Gurman, A.S. & Kniskern, D.P. (Eds.), *Handbook of Family Therapy*. New York: Brunner/Mazel.
Jacobson, N.S. & Margolin, G. (1979). *Marital Therapy*. New York: Brunner/Mazel.
Jacobson, N.S., Follette, W.C., Revenstorf, D., Baucom, D.H., Hahlweg, K. & Margolin, G. (1984). Variability in outcome and clinical significance of behavioral marital therapy: a reanalysis of outcome data. *Journal of Consulting and Clinical Psychology, 52* (4), 497-504.
Lange, A. & Hart, O. van der (1983). *Directive Family Therapy*. New York: Brunner/Mazel.
Lange, A. (1983). De combinatie van een paradoxale en congruente strategie. *Kwartaalschrift Directive Therapie en Hypnose, 3* (2), 124-143.
Lange, A. (1984). *De Interactionele Probleem Oplossings-Vragenlijst (IPOV)*. Deventer: Van Loghum Slaterus.
Lange, A. (1985a). *Gedragsverandering in gezinnen*. Fifth revised edition. Groningen: Wolters Noordhoff.
Lange, A. (1985b). Paradoxale opdrachten. *Kwartaalschrift Directieve Therapie en Hypnose, 5* (2), 145-174.
Lange, A. (1987). A new way of motivating clients to carry out paradoxical assignments: the combination of the paradoxical and the congruent. In: Zeig, J.K. & Lankton, S. (Eds.), *Ericksonian Psychotherapy: State of the Art*. New York: Brunner/Mazel.
Lederer, W.J. & Jackson, D.D. (1968). *The Mirages of Marriage*. New York: Norton.
Liberman, R.P. (1970). Behavioral approaches to family and couple therapy. *American Journal of Orthopsychiatry, 40* (1), 106-118.
Margolin, G. & Fernandez, V. (1985). Marital dysfunction. In: M. Hersen & A.S. Bellack (Eds.), *Handbook of Clinical Behavior Therapy*. New York: Plenum Press.
O'Connell, D.S. (1983). Symptom prescription in psychotherapy. *Psychotherapy: Theory, Research and Practice, 20* (1), 12-20.
Papp, P. (1983). *The Process of Change*. New York: Guilford Press.

Rachman, S.J. & Hodgson, R.J. (1980). *Obsessions and compulsions*. Englewood Cliffs, N.J.: Prentice Hall.

Riebel, L. (1984). Paradoxical intention strategies: a review of rationales. *Psychotherapy, 21* (2), 260-272.

Rosenbaum, A. & O'Leary, K.D. (1986). The treatment of marital violence. In: Jacobson, N.S. & Gurman, A.S. (Eds.), *Clinical Handbook of Marital Therapy*. New York: Guilford Press.

Sanderman, R. & Rüphan, M. (1987). Een cognitieve benadering van partnerrelatietherapie. *Gedragstherapie, 20* (1), 77-88

Seltzer, L.F. (1986). *Paradoxical Strategies in Psychotherapy. A Comprehensive Overview and Guidebook.* New York: Wiley.

Selvini Palazzoli, M., Boscolo, L., Cecchin, G.F. & Prata, G. (1978). *Paradox and Counterparadox*. New York: Jason Aronson.

Shoham-Salomon, V. & Jancourt, A. (1985). Differential effectiveness of paradoxical interventions for more versus less stress-prone individuals. *Journal of Counseling Psychology, 32* (3), 449-453.

Shoham-Salomon, V. & Rosenthal, R. (1987). Paradoxical interventions: a meta-analysis. *Journal of Consulting and Clinical Psychology, 55* (1), 22-28.

Stuart, R.B. (1969). Operant-interpersonal treatment for marital discord. *Journal of Consulting and Clinical Psychology, 33*, 675-682.

Stuart, R.B. (1980). *Helping Couples Change: A Social Learning Approach to Marital Therapy.* New York: Guilford Press.

Thibaut, J.W. & Kelley, H.H. (1959). *The Social Psychology of Groups*. New York: Wiley.

Tomm, K. (1984a). One perspective on the Milan systemic approach: Part I. Overview of development, theory and practice. *Journal of Marital and Family Therapy, 10* (2), 113-125.

Tomm, K. (1984b). One perspective on the Milan systemic approach: Part II. Description of session format, intervening style and interventions. *Journal of Marital and Family Therapy, 10* (3), 253-271.

Van Dyck, R. & Hoogduin, K. (1977). Ruziemakende paren. In: Velden, K. van der (ed.), *Directieve therapie 1.* Deventer: Van Loghum Slaterus.

Van Dyck, R. & Velden, K. van der (1977). Valkuilen voor directieve therapeuten. In: Velden, K. van der (ed.), *Directieve therapie I.* Deventer: Van Loghum Slaterus.

Van Dyck, R., Velden, K. van der & O. van der Hart (1980). Een indeling van directieve interventies. In: Velden, K. van der (ed.), *Directieve therapie 2.* Deventer: Van Loghum Slaterus.

Watson, D.L. & Tharp, R.C. (1981). *Self Directed Behavior; Self-Modification for Personal Adjustment*, Monterey, Cal.: Brooks/Cole.

Watzlawick, P. & Weakland, J.H. (1977). (eds.), *The Interactional View; Studies at the Mental Research Institute Palo Alto 1965-74.* New York: Norton.

Watzlawick, P., Beavin, J. & Jackson, D.D. (1967). *Pragmatics of Human Communication*. New York: Norton.

Watzlawick, P., Weakland, J.H. & Fish, R. (1974). *Change: Principles of Problem Formation and Problem Resolution*. New York: Norton.

Weakland, J., Fish, R., Watzlawick, P. & Bodin, A. (1974), Brief therapy: Focused resolution. *Family Process, 13*, 141-168.

Weeks, G.R. (ed.) (1985). *Promoting Change Through Paradoxical Therapy*. Homewood, Ill.: Dow-Jones-Irwin.

Weeks, G.R. & L'Abate, L. (1982). *Paradoxical Psychotherapy, Theory and Practice with Individuals, Couples and Families*. New York: Brunner/Mazel.

Weeks, G.R. & L'Abate, L. (1978). A bibliography of paradoxical methods in psychotherapy of family systems. *Family Process, 17*, 95-98.

PART III:

DEPRESSIVE DISORDERS

COGNITIVE-BEHAVIOUR THERAPY FOR DEPRESSION: THE STATE OF THE ART

M.J.V. Fennell

Oxford University, Department of Psychiatry,
The Warneford Hospital, Oxford, U.K.

INTRODUCTION

Beck's cognitive model of emotional disorder (Beck, 1976) proposes that depression is rooted in dysfunctional assumptions, formed in response to early experience. These are activated by appropriate precipitating events (in the case of depression, loss). Once activated, they give rise to an upsurge of negative automatic thoughts - "negative" in that they are associated with distressing emotions, "automatic" in that they are not the product of any deliberate reasoning process. These in turn lead on to the other symptoms of clinical depression. A vicious circle is established. The more depressed a person becomes, the more depressing thoughts they think. And the more depressing thoughts they think, the more depressed they become.

The first goal of cognitive-behaviour therapy (CBT) (Beck, Rush, Shaw and Emery, 1979) is to break the vicious circle, and thus to overcome the depression, by reducing the frequency and credibility of negative automatic thoughts. The second goal is to decrease the chances of relapse by undermining the dysfunctional assumptions upon which the thoughts are based. These goals are achieved through a combination of behavioural and cognitive strategies. Over the course of treatment, patients learn to manage their depression independently, acquiring the necessary skills within the context of an active, collaborative relationship with the therapist.

In the ten years since Rush and his colleagues reported the first controlled outcome trial of CBT for depression (Rush, Beck, Kovacs and

Hollon, 1977), the approach has been adopted with increasing enthusiasm by clinicians. Indeed, it has revolutionized the treatment of depression. Equally, the principles of the cognitive model have stimulated an expanding body of empirical research.

This is an area in which the dialogue between scientist and practitioner has proved particularly fruitful. The model itself is rooted firmly in clinical observation. Conversely, the approach is notable for its emphasis on the necessity for controlled evaluation, and for the extent to which the results of empirical investigations have informed clinical practice. A glance at recent publications reveals an impressive range in terms both of methodology and content. Research includes fine-grained experimental manipulations (e.g. Dobson and Shaw, 1987), large-scale comparative outcome trials (e.g. Murphy, Simons, Wetzel and Lustman, 1984; Simons, Murphy, Levine and Wetzel, 1986), studies examining the association between thinking, affect and other variables (e.g. Blackburn, Jones and Lewin, 1986), and, at the clinical end of the scale, more or less impressionistic attempts to systematize observations of the process of therapy (e.g. Murphy, 1985; Persons and Burns, 1986; Safran, Vallis, Segal and Shaw, 1986).

RECENT RESEARCH

It is impossible in the space available to review in detail the full range of current research. I think however that recent findings may be summarized under 3 main headings: (1) evidence for an association between thinking and depression; (2) evidence for cognitive vulnerability to depression; and (3) evidence for the immediate and longterm effectiveness of CBT.

The association between thinking and depression

Plentiful evidence, both from experimental manipulations and from correlational questionnaire data, supports an association between depression and negative thinking. In depressed patients, disturbances have been found in a number of areas of cognitive functioning. These include frequency of negative automatic thoughts (e.g. Hollon, Kendall and Lumry, 1986), belief in dysfunctional assumptions (e.g. Dobson and Shaw, 1986), attentional processes (e.g. Ingram, Lumry, Cruet and Sieber, 1987), and the encoding and retrieval of self-referent information (see Blaney, 1986).

Equally, it would appear that modifying thinking can modify mood. Interventions which successfully reduce the frequency or intensity of negative thoughts have been shown to produce immediate improvements in depressed mood and (less consistently) in other aspects of clinical depression. These include distraction (e.g. Fennell and Teasdale, 1987b), "distancing" from depressing thoughts (Blackburn and Bonham, 1980), challenging depressing thoughts (e.g. Teasdale and Fennell, 1982) and focussing on positive aspects of the self (e.g. Roetzer, 1978).

Taken together, these findings support the vicious circle between thinking and affect which the cognitive model suggests can maintain clinical depression. Nonetheless, recent failures to replicate early findings (see Bower, 1987) suggest that we still have much to learn about the appropriate setting conditions for this reciprocal interaction, and about the cognitive-affective processes which underlie it.

Cognitive vulnerability to depression

A number of factors have been tentatively identified which might reflect an enduring depressogenic cognitive style. These include: neuroticism (e.g. Teasdale and Dent, 1987); deficits in recall of self-referent information in normal and induced mood (ibid.); elevated scores on the Dysfunctional Attitude Scale, a measure of depressive assumptions (e.g. Dobson and Shaw, 1986; Simons et al., 1986); high levels of depressive distortion (e.g. Miller and Norman, 1986); and longstanding low self-esteem (e.g. Brown and Harris, 1986). However, there is as yet no solidly replicated, consistent evidence for lasting cognitive features which reliably predict onset or relapse into depression. Generally speaking, scores on measures of depressive thinking return to normal when the person is no longer depressed (e.g. Blackburn et al., 1986; Hollon et al., 1986). Where this is not the case (e.g. Rush, Weissenburger and Eaves, 1986), it is often unclear whether this simply reflects residual symptomatology.

The failure to establish convincing evidence for cognitive vulnerability to depression may indicate that no such thing exists. Or it may simply reflect the difficulty of measuring processes which, according to the model, are activated only in the presence of appropriate precipitating stimuli. Recent attempts to tease out the relationships between dysfunctional assumptions, categories of life stress, and depression (e.g. Hammen, Marks, Mayol and DeMayo, 1985; Olinger, Kuiper and Shaw, 1987) provide a promising opening here.

The effectiveness of CBT for depression

Several major controlled outcome trials using moderately-to-severely depressed, nonbipolar, nonpsychotic patients meeting formal diagnostic criteria for Major Depressive Disorder have now been reported. These show that on average CBT leads to post-treatment improvements at least comparable to those produced by antidepressant drugs (Beck, Hollon, Young, Bedrosian and Budenz, 1985; Blackburn, Bishop, Glen, Whalley and Christie,

1981; Hollon, Evans and DeRubeis, 1983; Murphy et al., 1984; Rush et al., 1977; Teasdale, Fennell, Hibbert and Amies, 1984). Perhaps more importantly, CBT may in the longer term reduce relapse rates more effectively than such drugs (Blackburn, Eunson and Bishop, 1986; Hollon et al., 1983; Kovacs, Rush, Beck and Hollon, 1981; Simons et al., 1984; Zimmer, Axmann, Koch, Giedke, Pflug and Heimann, 1985).

Whether CBT is more effective than other equally structured, problem-focussed, short-term psychological treatments remains to be seen. The results of the NIMH collaborative treatment trial (Elkin, Parloff, Hadley and Antry, 1985), when they become available, may tell us more. Equally, in the absence of consistent treatment-specific effects, we cannot yet say *how* CBT works. In particular, it is not clear whether its efficacy derives from modifying depressive thoughts and beliefs *per se*, or whether "non-specifics" such as a credible rationale, high treatment structure, a collaborative therapeutic relationship, and the like, are responsible for its success. Effective treatments for depression, whatever their immediate focus, apparently influence the full range of depressive symptomatology (Blackburn and Bishop, 1983; Simons, Garfield and Murphy, 1984).

DIFFERENTIAL RESPONSIVENESS TO CBT FOR DEPRESSION

The evidence summarized above suggests that *on average* CBT is an effective treatment for depression. It is clear, however, that it is more successful with some patients than with others. In a comparative outcome trial carried out in general practice (Teasdale et al., 1984), we found that about 50% of CBT patients improved substantially within 3-4 sessions. These gains were maintained at post-treatment, and indeed up to one-year follow-up. A further 35% were also well at post-treatment but improved more slowly and did not maintain their gains so consistently. The other 15% remained obdurately depressed throughout (Fennell and Teasdale, 1987a).

What accounts for these marked differences in treatment responsiveness? Why is it that some people take to cognitive therapy like ducks to water and use it creatively and vigorously to deal with their depression, whereas in others the production of even minimal change is like pulling teeth? Is it that some people's cognitive processes are particularly inaccessible or resistant to change? Or is it that, in some cases, factors other than cognitive processes have a major role in maintaining the depression? In particular, what part do biological and interpersonal variables play?

Cognitive factors

I should like first to consider factors that might encourage chronicity and undercut patients' ability to make full use of psychological treatment. Two studies have shown that a well-developed preexisting repertoire of cognitive-behavioural coping skills and endorsement of a self-control rationale (high learned resourcefulness) predict a good response to cognitive-behavioural interventions (Rehm, Kaslow and Rabin, 1987; Simons, Lustman, Wetzel and Murphy, 1985). Readiness to accept and act on the CBT rationale has also been found to predict a positive outcome (Fennell and Teasdale, 1987a). In the longer term, relatively high scores on the Dysfunctional Attitude Scale, in association with continued minimal depressive symptomatology, have been shown to predict relapse following CBT (Simons et al., 1984).

Beyond prediction of treatment response, little systematic attempt has yet been made to determine how dysfunctional beliefs or patterns of interpretation become entrenched, override the normal process of recovery, and lead to chronic, treatment-resistant, and even characterological depression. Tentative conceptualizations (e.g. Bruch, Chessler and Meyer, 1985: Rowe, 1983; Young, in preparation) agree in assigning a core role to fundamental, absolute, negative self-schemas, and to their cognitive and behavioural consequences. However, they remain largely speculative. Similarly, only isolated studies have so far attempted to evaluate cognitive-behavioural treatment of chronic depression (e.g. De Jong, Triebe and Heinrich, 1986; Fennell and Teasdale, 1982; Shaw, cited in Beck et al., 1979, p.392). The need for more precise and reliable identification of cognitive factors contributing to chronicity and to treatment-resistance is clear. Equally, as clinicians, we must examine how the CBT delivery system may be modified and elaborated to take account of these.

Biological factors

Rush and Shaw (1982) suggested that CBT is not the treatment of choice for bipolar, psychotic, and endogenous or melancholic depressions. They also acknowledge that controlled outcome studies were not available to substantiate this claim.

Limited experimental evidence supports a distinction between endogenous and nonendogenous depressions in response to cognitive interventions. Davies (1982, cited in Williams, 1984) and Fennell and Teasdale (1987b) used distraction procedures to reduce the frequency of depressing thoughts and the intensity of depressed mood, and found them to be less effective with endogenous than with nonendogenous patients. These results might indicate a different role for negative thinking in the two groups. On the other hand, controlled outcome trials show endogenous and nonendogenous patients responding equally well to CBT (Blackburn et al., 1981; Kovacs et al., 1981), and no consistent differences have emerged between them on questionnaire measures of depressive thinking (e.g. Hollon et al., 1986; Zimmerman and Coryell, 1986).

This could be because the criteria usually employed to define endogeneity (which generally assess only presenting symptomatology) fail to identify crucial differences, and that more elaborate or sensitive measures are required. Recent work on the discriminative power of the Newcastle Diagnosis Scale (which takes account not only of symptoms but also of other factors such as previous functioning and current stressors), and on biological markers such as the dexamethasone suppression test, seem particularly promising here (e.g. Carney, Reynolds and Sheffield, 1986; Rush, 1983; Zimmerman, Coryell and Pfohl, 1986).

Interpersonal factors

Zeiss and Jones (1983) have identified the entrenchment of depressed clients in powerful, noxious environmental systems as a possible cause of treatment failure. This includes not only marital or equivalent relationships but also broader social networks. It may refer to a lack of such relationships (e.g. Brown and Harris, 1978; Surtees, 1980), or to actively harmful existing relationships (e.g. Hooley, 1987; Hooley, Orley and Teasdale, 1986).

The importance of social support in reducing the likelihood of depression and in promoting recovery has been extensively documented (e.g. Brown, Adrews, Harris, Adler and Bridge, 1986; Cohen and Wills, 1985; Parry and Shapiro, 1986). Equally, Rush and Shaw (1983) state unequivocally that where hostile or unhelpful relationships are contributing to the maintenance of depression, "it is imperative that the couple or family system members be engaged in the process of cognitive change" (p.227).

Yet in practice cognitive therapists often pay little more than lip service to the social environment as a possible maintaining factor. There is thus a need, both theoretical and practical, to examine how knowledge of social support networks may be integrated with a cognitive perspective, and how cognitive factors which prevent the depressed person from taking advantage of potential support may be assessed and changed. Similarly, we should explore more fully the contribution of marital distress to persistent depression and to treatment resistance, and work to develop integrated treatment approaches which will address the problem directly.

CONCLUSIONS

I have aimed to summarize recent research relating to the cognitive model of depression and to CBT. I have suggested that the puzzle of differential treatment responsiveness may be solved if we examine more closely those cognitive factors which contribute to chronic depression and to treatment resistance, and if in addition we integrate cognitive principles and methods with information and ideas from other fields of research.

The cognitive model of depression has always assumed an interaction between cognition and other intrapersonal and environmental variables. In practice, however, attention has often been confined to the cognitive components of that interaction. This is admitted both by the model's supporters (e.g. Segal and Shaw, 1986) and by its critics (e.g. Coyne and Gotlib, 1986). It would be useful in our current state of knowledge to make the interactional nature of the model more explicit. The work of George Brown and his colleagues, which has been referred to above, provides a valuable example. Brown and others have carried out a series of large-scale prospective community studies, examining the development of depression in women following significant negative life events. They have attempted to integrate and explore historical factors (e.g. early loss or neglect), current environmental and interpersonal factors (e.g. anticipated and actual support), and cognitive factors (e.g. self-esteem, overgeneralization from specific negative events). As yet a treatment dimension is lacking.

In conclusion, I should like to suggest that we will increase our theoretical grasp of depression most fully if we extend the cognitive model to encompass biological, environmental and interpersonal factors, and work to map the relationships between them. Similarly, we will maximize our effectiveness as clinicians if we use what we learn to assess the relative importance of each factor in the individual, and to treat him or her accordingly.

REFERENCES

Beck, A.T. (1976). *Cognitive therapy and the emotional disorders*. New York: International Universities Press.

Beck, A.T., Hollon, S.D., Young, J.E., Bedrosian, R.C. & Budenz, D. (1985). Treatment of depression with cognitive therapy and amitriptyline. *Archives of General Psychiatry, 42*, 142-148.

Beck, A.T., Rush, A.J., Shaw, B.F. & Emery, G. (1979). *Cognitive therapy of depression*. New York: Guilford.

Blackburn, I.M. & Bishop, S. (1983). Changes in cognition with pharmacotherapy and cognitive therapy. *British Journal of Psychiatry, 143*, 609-617.

Blackburn, I.M. & Bonham, K.G. (1980). Experimental effects of a cognitive therapy technique in depressed patients. *British Journal of Social & Clinical Psychology, 19*, 353-363.

Blackburn, I.M., Bishop, S., Glen, A.I.M., Whalley, L.J. & Christie, J. (1981). The efficacy of cognitive therapy in depression: A treatment trial using cognitive therapy and pharmacotherapy, each alone and in combination. *British Journal of Psychiatry, 139*, 181-189.

Blackburn, I.M., Eunson, K.M. & Bishop, S. (1986). A two-year naturalistic follow-up of depressed patients treated with cognitive therapy, pharmacotherapy and a combination of both. *Journal of Affective Disorders, 10*, 67-75.

Blackburn, I.M., Jones, S. & Lewin, R.J.P. (1986). Cognitive style in depression. *British Journal of Clinical Psychology, 25*, 241-251.

Blaney, P.H. (1986). Affect and memory: A review. *Psychological Bulletin, 99*, 229-246.

Bower, G.H. (1987). Commentary on mood and memory. *Behaviour Research & Therapy, 25*, 443-455.

Brown, G.W. & Harris, T.O. (1978). *Social origins of depression: A study of psychiatric disorder in women*. London: Tavistock.

Brown, G.W. & Harris, T.O. (1986). Stressor, vulnerability and depression: A question of replication. *Psychological Medicine, 16*, 739-744.

Brown, G.W., Andrews, R., Harris, T., Adler, Z. & Bridge, L. (1986). Social support, self-esteem and depression. *Psychological Medicine, 16*, 813-831.

Bruch, M.H., Chessler, E.S. & Meyer, V. (1985). *Towards a self-schema model of complex behavioural disorders: Clinical observations and research findings in individualized behaviour therapy*. Paper presented at the 15th Annual Meeting of the European Association of Behaviour Therapy, Munich, Federal Republic of Germany.

Carney, M.W.P., Reynolds, E.H. & Sheffield, B.F. (1986). Prediction of outcome in depressive illness by the Newcastle Diagnosis Scale: Its relationship with the unipolar/bipolar and DSM III systems. *British Journal of Psychiatry*, 150, 43-48.

Cohen, S. & Wills, T.A. (1985). Stress, social support, and the buffering hypothesis. *Psychological Bulletin, 98*, 10-357.

Coyne, J.C. & Gotlib, I. (1986). Studying the role of cognition in depression: Well-trodden paths and cul-de-sacs. *Cognitive Therapy & Research, 10*, 695-705.

DeJong, R., Treiber, R. & Heinrich, G. (1986). Effectiveness of two psychological treatments for inpatients with severe and chronic depressions. *Cognitive Therapy & Research, 10*, 645-663.

Dobson, K.S. & Shaw, B.F. (1986). Cognitive assessment with major depressive disorders. *Cognitive Therapy & Research, 10*, 13-29.

Dobson, K.S. & Shaw, B.F. (1987). Specificity and stability of self-referent encoding in clinical depression. *Journal of Abnormal Psychology, 96*, 34-40.

Elkin, I., Parloff, M.B., Hadley, S.W. & Antry, J.H. (1985). NIMH Treatment of Depression Collaborative Research Program. *Archives of General Psychiatry, 42*, 305-316.

Fennell, M.J.V. & Teasdale, J.D. (1982). Cognitive therapy with chronic, drug-refractory depressed outpatients: A note of caution. *Cognitive Therapy & Research*, 6, 455-460.

Fennell, M.J.V. & Teasdale, J.D. (1987a). Cognitive therapy for depression: Individual differences and the process of change. *Cognitive Therapy & Research, 11*, 253-271.

Fennell, M.J.V. & Teasdale, J.D. (1987b). Distraction in neurotic and endogenous depression: An investigation of negative thinking in Major Depressive Disorder. *Psychological Medicine, 17*, 441-452.

Hammen, C., Marks, T., Mayol, A. & DeMayo, R. (1985). Depressive self-schemas, life stress and vulnerability to depression. *Journal of Abnormal Psychology, 94*, 308-319.

Hollon, S.D., Evans, M.D. & DeRubeis, R.J. (1983). *Final report of the cognitive-pharmacotherapy trial.* Paper presented at the World Congress of Behaviour Therapy, Washington, D.C.

Hollon, S.D., Kendall, P.C. & Lumry, A. (1986). Specificity of depressotypic cognitions in clinical depression. *Journal of Abnormal Psychology, 95*, 52-59.

Hooley, J.M. (1986). Expressed emotion and depression: Interactions between patients and high- vs. low-expressed emotion spouses. *Journal of Abnormal Psychology, 95*, 237-246.

Hooley, J.M, Orley, J. & Teasdale, J.D. (1987). Levels of expressed emotion and relapse in depressed patients. *British Journal of Psychiatry, 148*, 642-647.

Ingham, J.G., Kreitman, N.B., Miller, P.McC., Sahidharan, S.P. & Surtees, P.G. (1986). Self-esteem, vulnerability and psychiatric disorder in the community. *British Journal of Psychiatry, 148*, 375-385.

Ingram, R.E., Lumry, A.E., Cruet, D. & Sieber, W. (1987). Attentional processes in depressive disorders. *Cognitive Therapy & Research, 11*, 357-360.

Kovacs, J., Rush, A.J., Beck, A.T. & Hollon, S.D. (1981). Depressed outpatients treated with cognitive therapy or pharmacotherapy: A one-year follow-up. *Archives of General Psychiatry, 38*, 33-39.

Miller, I.W. & Norman, W.H. (1986). Persistence of depressive cognitions within a subgroup of depressed inpatients. *Cognitive Therapy & Research, 10*, 211-224.

Murphy, G.E. (1985). A conceptual framework for the choice of interventions in cognitive therapy. *Cognitive Therapy & Research, 9*, 127-134.

Murphy, G.E., Simons, A.D., Wetzel, R.D. & Lustman, P.J. (1984). Cognitive therapy and pharmacotherapy: Singly and together in the treatment of depression. *Archives of General Psychiatry, 41*, 33-41.

Olinger, L.J., Kuiper, N.A. & Shaw, B.F. (1987). Dysfunctional assumptions and stressful life events: An interactive model of depression. *Cognitive Therapy & Research, 11*, 25-40.

Parry, G. & Shapiro, D.A. (1986). Social support and life events in working class women. *Archives of General Psychiatry, 43*, 315-323.

Persons, J.B. & Burns, D.D. (1986). The process of cognitive therapy: The first thought changes less than the last one. *Behaviour Research & Therapy, 42*, 619-624.

Rehm, L.P., Kaslow, N.J. & Rabin, A.S. (1987). Cognitive and behavioural targets in a self-control program for depression. *Journal of Consulting & Clinical Psychology, 55*, 60-67.

Roetzer, F.T. (1978). Building up positive self-evaluations in hospitalized depressives: A controlled trial of a cognitive-behavioural treatment intervention. in: *Clinical psychology: Advances in diagnosis and therapy*. Congress Proceedings II, Hamburg.

Rowe, D. (1983). *Depression: The way out of your prison.* London: Routledge and Kegan Paul.

Rush, A.J. (1983). A phase II study of cognitive therapy of depression. In: J.B. Williams and R.D. Spitzer (Eds.), *Psychotherapy research: Where are we and where should we go?* (pp.216-234). New York: Guilford.

Rush, A.J. & Shaw, B.F. (1983). Failures in treating depression by cognitive-behavioural therapy. In: E.B. Foa & P.M.G. Emmelkamp (Eds.) *Failures in behaviour therapy*. (pp.217-228). New York: Wiley.

Rush, A.J., Beck, A.T., Kovacs, M. & Hollon, S.D. (1977). Comparative efficacy of cognitive therapy and pharmacotherapy in the treatment of depressed outpatients. *Cognitive Therapy & Research, 1*, 17-37.

Rush, A.J., Weissenburger, J. & Eave, G. (1986). Do thinking patterns predict depressive symptoms? *Cognitive Therapy & Research, 10*, 225-236.

Safran, J.D., Vallis, T.M., Segal, Z.V. & Shaw, B.F. (1986). Assessment of core cognitive processes in cognitive therapy. *Cognitive Therapy & Research, 10*, 509-526.

Segal, Z.V. & Shaw, B.F. (1986). Cognition in depression: A reappraisal of Coyne and Gotlib's critique. *Cognitive Therapy & Research, 10*, 671-

693.
Simons, A.D., Garfield, S. & Murphy, G.E. (1984). The process of change in cognitive therapy and pharmacotherapy for depression: Changes in mood and cognition. *Archives of General Psychiatry, 41*, 45-51.

Simons, A.D., Lustman, P.J., Wetzel, R.D. & Murphy, G.E. (1985). Predicting response to cognitive therapy for depression: The role of learned resourcefulness. *Cognitive Therapy & Research, 9*, 79-89.

Simons, A.D., Murphy, G.E., Levine, J.L. & Wetzel, R.D. (1986). Cognitive therapy and pharmacotherapy for depression: Sustained improvement over one year. *Archives of General Psychiatry, 43*, 43-48.

Surtees, P.G. (1980). Social support, residual adversity and depressive outcome. *Social Psychiatry, 15*, 71-80.

Teasdale, J.D. & Dent, J. (1987). Cognitive vulnerability to depression: A test of two hypotheses. *British Journal of Clinical Psychology, 26*, 113-126.

Teasdale, J.D. & Fennell, M.J.V. (1982). Immediate effects of depression of cognitive therapy interventions. *Cognitive Therapy & Research, 6*, 343-351.

Teasdale, J.D., Fennell, M.J.V., Hibbert, G.A. & Amies, P.L. (1984). Cognitive therapy for major depressive disorder in primary care. *British Journal of Psychiatry, 144*, 400-406.

Williams, J.M.G. (1984). Cognitive-behaviour therapy for depression: Problems and perspectives. *British Journal of Psychiatry, 145*, 254-262.

Young, J.E. (In preparation). Schema-focussed cognitive therapy for personality disorders. In: A.T. Beck & A. Freeman (Eds.), *Cognitive therapy for personality disorders*. New York: Guilford.

Zeiss, A.M. & Jones, S.L. (1983). Behavioural treatment of depression: Examining treatment failures. In: E.B. Foa & P.M.G. Emmelkamp (Eds.), *Failures in behaviour therapy*. (pp.197-216). New York: Wiley.

Zimmer, F.T., Axmann, D., Koch, H., Giedke, H., Pflug, B. & Heimann, H. (1985). *One-year follow-up of cognitive-behaviour therapy for depressed outpatients: A comparison of cognitive-behaviour therapy alone, in combination with pharmacotherapy and pharmacotherapy alone*. Paper presented at the 15th Annual Meeting on the European Association for Behaviour Therapy, Munich, Federal Republic of Germany.

Zimmerman, M. & Coryell, W. (1986). Dysfunctional assumptions in endogenous and nonendogenous depressed inpatients. *Cognitive Therapy & Research, 10*, 339-346.

Zimmerman, M., Coryell, W. & Pfohl, B. (1986). The validity of the dexamethasone suppression test as a marker for endogenous depression. *Archives of General Psychiatry, 43*, 347-355.

PSYCHOLOGICAL AND BIOLOGICAL CHANGES WITH COGNITIVE THERAPY

I.M. Blackburn

MRC Unit, Royal Edinburgh Hospital, Edinburgh, U.K.

The title of this paper implies the question: "Can a psychological treatment induce biological changes?" which itself reflects the deeply anchored dualistic, mind-body, thinking which still pervades our thinking. The converse question, "Can a biological treatment induce psychological changes ?", paradoxically, appears to cause less problems, as it is taken for granted and moreover, the evidence is there to back it, that the answer is yes. What I would like to put across in this short presentation is some evidence, direct and indirect, that a psychological method of treatment does change not only psychological, but also biological symptoms.

I will review what transpires from the literature and describe some of our work in Edinburgh relating to this question. The answers may lead to greater understanding of the mechanism of action of cognitive therapy (CT) and of the processes of depressive illnesses. The areas of evidence which I shall consider are:

1. The efficacy of cognitive therapy for endogenous depression.
2. The relative changes in psychological and biological symptoms with CT and pharmacotherapy.
3. Changes in a biological variable, cortisol, and in thinking style with cognitive therapy alone or in combination with pharmacotherapy.

ENDOGENOUS DEPRESSION AND CT

Several treatment trials of cognitive therapy versus pharmacotherapy have found that cognitive therapy was as effective with endogenous depressed patients as with non-endogenous depressed patients. Endogenous symptoms-that is, sleep and libido disturbance, weight loss, loss of appetite, psychomotor disturbance, diurnal mood variation, lack of reactivity, pervasive anhedonia and guilt, are, of course, considered to be biological symptoms which are due to a functional lesion in the hypothalamic-pituitary-adrenal (HPA) system.

Kovacs et al. (1981), using Klein's system (Klein, 1974) of classifying endogenomorphic symptoms, reanalyzed the data of Rush et al. (1977). They found that both their treatment groups, CT and imipramine, had equal frequencies of high vs. low endogenomorphic patients. Moreover, when they examined the relationship between pretreatment level of endogenous symptomatology and end of treatment outcome, they found that patients with high endogenicity had the lowest scores on the Beck Depression Inventory (BDI, Beck et al., 1961) at the end of treatment and had a better response on both treatments relative to patients with low endogenicity scores.

In our study, Blackburn et al. (1981), dividing patients who completed treatment into definite endogenous and non-endogenous groups according to Research Diagnostic Criteria (RDC, Spitzer et al., 1978), we found that: comparing the frequencies of endogenous responders and non-responders with non-endogenous responders and non-responders to cognitive therapy or pharmacotherapy alone and to both treatments compared (Fisher's exact probability test), there were no significant differences. That is, the presence of endogenicity made no difference to response within each of the three treatment modalities. Moreover, within the endogenous group and within the non-endogenous group, the frequencies of responders and non-responders did not differ (X^2 = .70, df = 2 and X^2 = .89, df = 2 respectively), indicating that endogenous patients responded similarly to the three treatments, as did the non-endogenous patients.

Finally, in the outcome study by Teasdale et al. (1984), where general practice patients received "usual" treatment from their doctors or had CT in addition, 32/34 of the total patient group satisfied RDC criteria for definite or probable endogenous depression. At the end of the treatment period, the group receiving CT had a better outcome than the treatment as usual group. Since a proportion of both samples of patients were on antidepressant medication, we can conclude that the addition of CT to treatment as usual was beneficial to a predominantly endogenous group.

CHANGES IN PSYCHOLOGICAL AND BIOLOGICAL SYMPTOMS WITH CT AND DRUGS

The other class of evidence relates to changes in specific symptoms of depression with CT relative to pharmacotherapy. Rush et al. (1981) have investigated this relationship in the weekly data from their treatment trial study. They used cross-lagged correlations for treatment weeks 1-2, 2-3 and 3-4 to analyze the pattern of change in psychological and biological variables in their two treatment groups (CT and imipramine). They found that, as expected, with CT, cognitive symptoms changed before vegetative symptoms and before motivational symptoms; mood changed before cognitive, vegetative and motivational symptoms; motivational symptoms were the last to change. No such consistent pattern of change was obtained with drug treatment.

In a subsequent study (Rush et al., 1982), they found that regardless of initial level of depression, CT had more impact than imipramine on degree of hopelessness (The Hopelessness Scale, Beck et al., 1974) and on general and social aspects of self-concept, but emotional well-being was equally improved by CT and drugs (Miskimins Self-Goal-Other II, MSGO, bipolar scales rated on a 9-point continuum, Miskimins, 1972).

CHANGE IN BIOLOGICAL VARIABLES AND IN THINKING STYLE

I would like now to consider the third aspect of this paper, that is, change in biological variables and in thinking style with cognitive therapy.

MR (Figure 1a) was an in-patient with psychotic symptoms (paranoid delusions relating to people following her and talking about her because they suspected her of having an affair with the minister). Her RDC diagnosis was primary major depressive disorder, endogenous and psychotic sub-type. She was treated with CT alone and took part in a follow-up study of neuroendocrine changes during in-patient treatment. The hormones measured were prolactin, growth hormone and cortisol in plasma taken through the day at fortnightly intervals through in-patient stay. The three points of measurement at each date represent the average of the morning samples (07.00, 07.30 and 08.00 h), the average of the afternoon samples (15.00, 15.30 and 16.00 h) and the average of the evening samples (23.00, 23.30 and 24.00 h). This technique of frequent sampling is designed to take account of the diurnal and pulsatile pattern of hormone concentrations. The decrease, over the course of admission, in cortisol and growth hormone concentrations, with no significant change in prolactin, is typical of recovery from depression as reflected by the

Figure 1: **Changes in prolactin (PRL), growth hormone (GH) and cortisol during treatment for depression.**

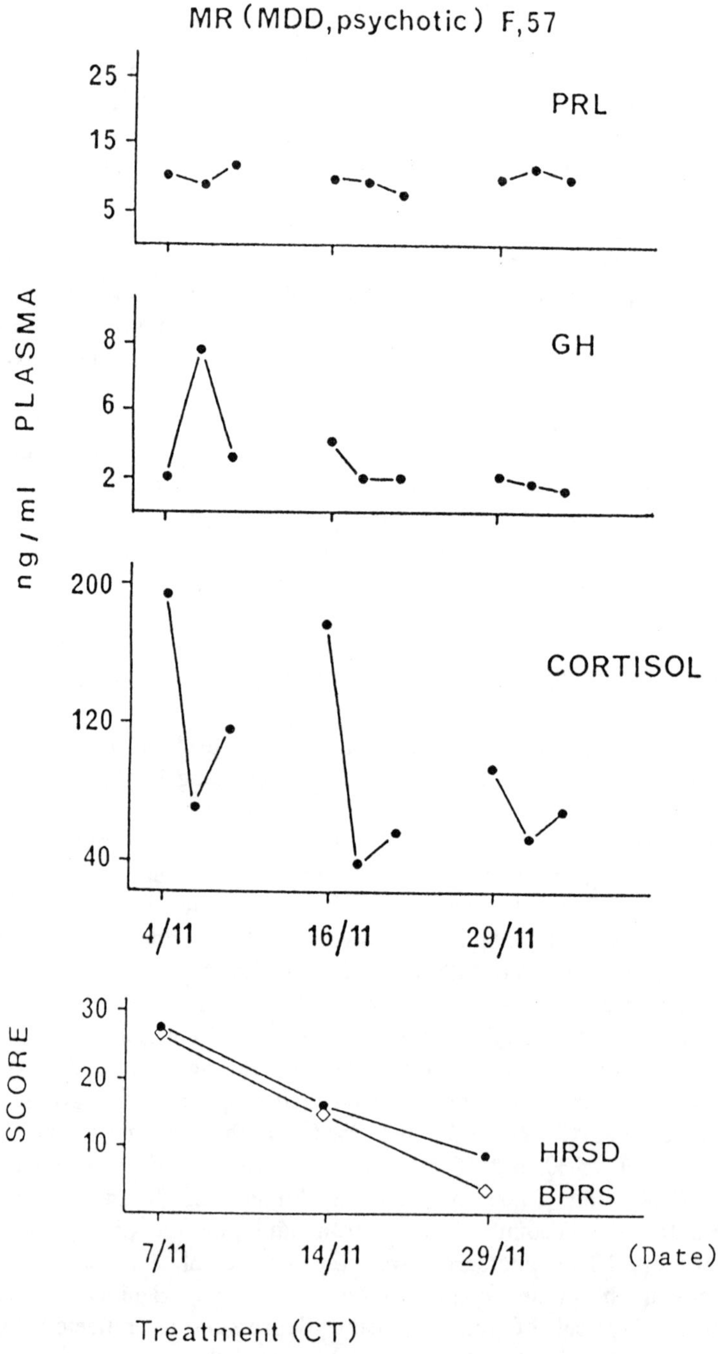

Fig.1b : **Changes in prolactin (PRL), growth hormone (GH) and cortisol during treatment for depression.**

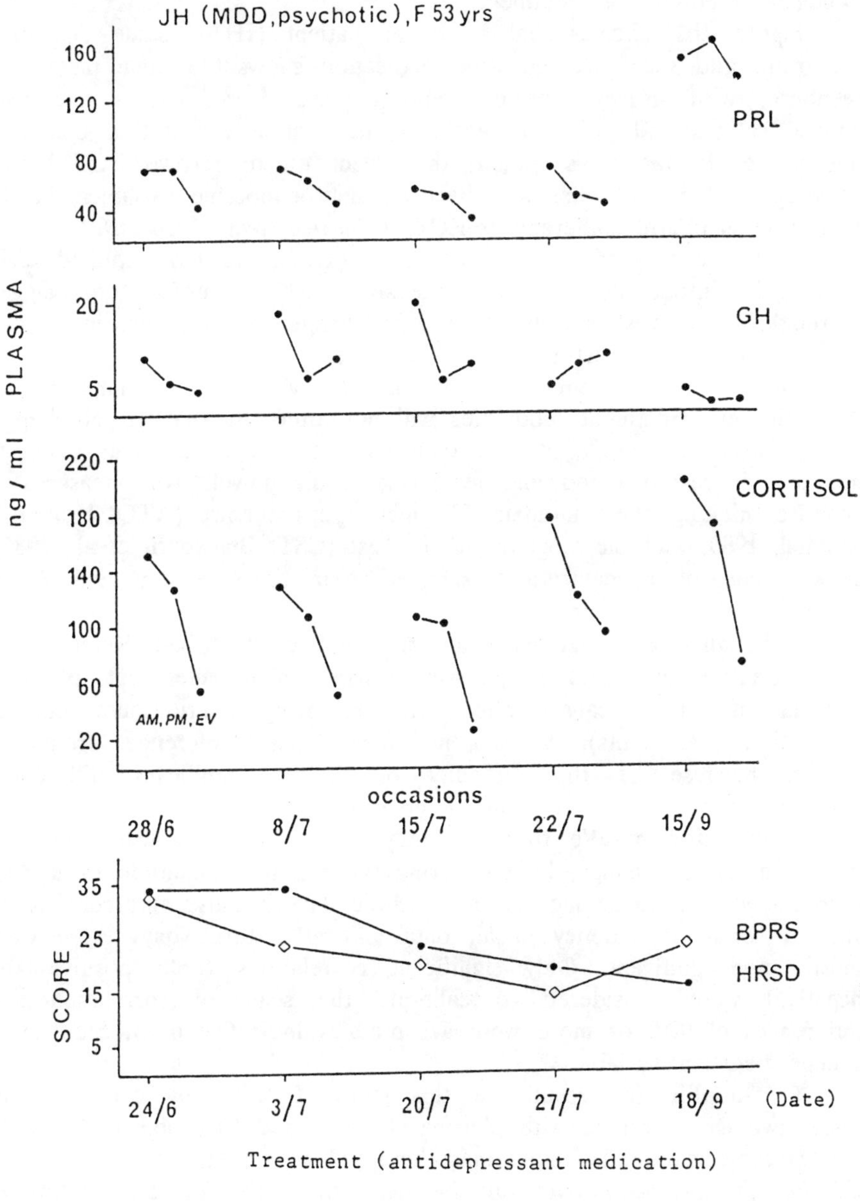

HRSD = Hamilton Rating Scale for Depression (17 items)
BPRS = Brief Psychiatric Rating Scale

clinical scales, BPRS (Brief Psychiatric Rating Scale, Overall & Gorham, 1962) and HRSD (Hamilton Rating Scale for depression, 17 item version, Hamilton, 1960) and similar to the pattern observed in patients receiving biological methods of treatment.

Figure 1b indicates that a similar patient (JH) - same diagnostic sub-group and sex - treated with medication shows the same pattern of response, with growth hormone and cortisol decreasing in line with clinical ratings and going up again as the patient's condition began to deteriorate. In fact, this patient then went on to receive ECT before discharge. Thus, CT has an effect on neuroendocrine variables, in the same way as pharmacotherapy or ECT, *if the treatment is successful.*

In a recent study, Blackburn et al (1987), we have studied eight depressed in-patients in an intensive design, using cross-lagged correlations to investigate the pattern of change with recovery in mood, cognitive style and cortisol. Our hypotheses were that:

1. Changes in different functions will not occur at the same time.
2. Different treatment modalities will not affect the pattern of change.

Several measures were used on a daily basis: two visual analogue scales to measure depressed mood and feeling generally unwell; two measures of negative thinking, the Automatic Thoughts Questionnaire (ATQ, Hollon & Kendall, 1980) and the Cognitive Style Test (CST, Blackburn et al., 1986); salivary cortisol concentrations sampled four times a day and 24 h. urinary cortisol concentration.

Although cross-lagged panel analysis has been described (Kenny, 1975) as a quasi-experimental single-case design which rules out plausible explanations of a causal effect (by removing spuriousness out of correlation coefficients), we did not make causal inferences from our results, because of the difficulty of finding significant differences between cross-lagged correlations. Even sample numbers of up to 300 are usually not sufficient. We, therefore, only attempted to establish *order of precedence* of change, by comparing the relative magnitude of lagged correlations. We chose lags of up to three days because auto-correlations showed serial dependency in all data and after three days these were mostly non-significant. Only significant correlations (both positive and negative) were considered to calibrate the scale of correlation and differences of 0.10 or more were accepted as indicative of precedence of change between variables.

To simplify the results of this study, I will only consider four cases: two cases treated with pharmacotherapy and Ct (subjects 1 and 6) and two subjects treated with pharmacotherapy alone (subjects 4 and 5). *If CT has a specific impact on the dependent variables, the pattern of response for the two subjects receiving CT should differ from that of the two subjects who were treated with medication alone.* All patients got

Table 1: Cross-lagged (1,2,3) and synchronous (o) correlation

S	Lags (days) 1	2	3	0	Lags (days) 1	2	3
	Unwellness ⟶ SC ev				SC ev ⟶ Unwellness		
M	-.17	_-.23**_	_-.25**_	-.06	-.11	-.14	-.13
S1	-.19	-.29	_-.38*_	-.13	-.09	-.16	-.19
S4	-.30	_-.43*_	-.12	-.32	-.16	-.18	-.16
	ATQ ⟶ SC ev				SC ev ⟶ ATQ		
M	_-.39**_	-.24	-.27	-.26	-.18	-.06	-.03
S1	-.32	-.40	_-.51**_	-.37	-.47	-.20	-.19
S4	-.31	-.37	_-.42*_	-.33	-.30	-.28	-.17
S5	-.37	-.23	_-.41*_	-.25	-.36	-.22	-.06
	Depression ⟶ ATQ				ATQ ⟶ Depression		
M	_.69**_	.63	.62	.72	.62	.64	.56+
S1	_.65**_	.41	.48	.59	.19	.43	.58
S4	_.81**_	.74	.63	.83	.83	.77	.84+
S5	_.79**_	.77	.75	.79	.74	.79	.71+
S6	_.73**_	.69	.63	.68	.65	.77	-.06+
	Unwell ⟶ ATQ				ATQ ⟶ Unwell		
M	.49	.55	_.55**_	.68	.45	.45	.41
S1	.62	.77	_.81**_	.62	.46	.48	.33
S4	.38	.48	.45	.61	.56	_.64**_	.50
S5	.69	.72	_.73**_	.73	.65	.63	.47
S6	.40	_.47*_	.33	.27	.03	.11	.16
	Depression ⟶ CST				CST ⟶ Depression		
M	.17	.06	.04	.33	.42**	.23	.32
S4	.74	.57	.38	.76	.62	.65	.76**
S6	-.13	-.05	-.10	.24	.90**	.15	.63
	Unwell ⟶ CST				CST ⟶ Unwell		
M	.13	.19	.03	.19	_.21**_	.21	.15
S1	.49	_.67**_	.42	.52	.23	.16	.15
S4	.30	.12	.21	.54	.61	_.62**_	.27

M = Mean Correlation; SE ev = Salivary Cortisol evening;
ATQ = Automatic Thought Questionnaire; CST = Cognitive Style Test;
---> indicates direction of precedence. Italics indicate precedence of change; + indicates ambiguous pattern of change.
$* p < .05$; $** p < .01$

better (there were significant differences between base-line and discharge scores in depression, feeling of unwellness and ATQ) and there was a significant difference in urinary free cortisol concentrations and the ratio of urinary free cortisol to creatinine. The best relationship between mood, cognition and cortisol level were with evening salivary cortisol (SC ev) (Table 1).

For the group as a whole (eight subjects), feeling unwell and scores on the Automatic Thought Questionnaire (negative thinking) predicted cortisol concentration. This relationship was true whether the patient received CT in combination or not. The association was not very strong, however, and the negative association indicates that the higher the cortisol level, the better is mood and the less negative the thinking. Thus, although cortisol levels decrease from admission to discharge, on a day-to-day basis cortisol acts as an adaptive mechanism, what Frankenhauser (1979) and Lundberg (1979) described as "pulling themselves together" to maintain coping behaviour.

There were strong positive relationships between depressed mood and negative thinking as measured by the ATQ, but the pattern of precedence was equivocal except for subject 1, who although he had CT, showed changes in depressed mood before changes in negative thinking.

For the group as a whole, changes in feeling unwell preceded change in negative thinking, as measured by the ATQ, and this was true for both CT subjects (S1 and S6) and one drug patient (S5). Subject 4, treated with drugs, showed the reverse pattern with negative thinking changing before feelings of unwellness.

The association between depressed mood and CST followed a different pattern - negative cognitive style preceding change in mood for the group and for subjects 4 and 6, although they received different treatments. The same was true for the group as far as feeling unwell and negative interpretations were concerned. However, as shown in Table 1, paradoxically, for S1 who had CT, feeling unwell changed first, whereas for S4, who received only drugs, cognition changed first.

Thus, the addition of cognitive therapy to pharmacological treatment does not appear to change the pattern of precedence of change in psychological and biological variables during the process of recovery in any predictable direction. The general pattern appears to be negative interpretations ➞ depression and feeling unwell ➞ negative automatic thoughts ➞ late cortisol production.

The two cognitive scales apparently measure different aspects of cognition: negative interpretations (CST) and negative stream of thought (ATQ). There are individual differences in pattern of response, which, if studied further, may lead to the better understanding and treatment of individual cases. The individual differences made sense to the clinicians, that is, we could understand why in patient 1 mood changed before thinking while in patient 4 cognition changed before mood. This could reflect the phenomenon of being "wise after the event", but difficult as it is to carry out studies of this type, it may be that we need to pursue them with a better methodology.

CONCLUSION

The diverse studies that I have described briefly show at least one clear finding, namely that CT has an effect on biological variables whether they be syndromes, symptoms or neuroendocrine variables.

If Rush's et al. findings are replicated, they would indicate that, in group data, CT affects cognitive symptoms before vegetative symptoms, but that mood changes first. The cross-lagged analysis (Blackburn et al., 1987) suggests individual differences in response irrespective of treatment, which it may be important to study further.

The psychobiological model of depression (Akiskal, 1985; Beck, 1987) which states that "cognitive and biological phenomena represent different sides of the same coin" remains the most viable model in view of the results presented. Thus, it is not al all surprising that CT should affect biological variables. If the patient gets better, his biology must change, whatever the treatment.

REFERENCES

Akiskal, H. (1985). Interaction of biologic and psychologic factors in the origin of depressive disorders. *Acta Psychiatrica Scandinavia, 71*, 131-139.

Beck, A.T. (1987). Cognitive models of depression. *Journal of Cognitive Psychotherapy, 1*, 5-37.

Beck, A.T., Ward, C.H., Mendelson, M., Moch, J., Erbaugh, J. (1961). An inventory for measuring depression. *Archives of General Psychiatry, 4*, 561-571.

Beck, A.T., Weissman, A., Lester, D., Trexler, L. (1974). The measure of pessimism. The hopelessness scale. *Journal of Consulting and Clinical Psychology, 42*, 861-865.

Blackburn, I.M., Bishop, S., Glen, A.I.M., Whalley, L.J., Christie, J.E. (1981). The efficacy of cognitive therapy in depression: A treatment trial using cognitive therapy and pharmacotherapy, each alone and in combination. *British Journal of Psychiatry, 139*, 181-189.

Blackburn, I.M., Jones, S., Lewin, R.J.P. (1986). Cognitive style in

depression. *British Journal of Clinical Psychology, 25*, 241-251.
Blackburn, I.M., Whalley, L.J., Christie, J.E., Shering, A., Foggo, M., Bennie, J., Farrer, D., Watts, G., Wilson, H., Fink, G. (1987). Mood, cognition and cortisol: their temporal relationships during recovery from depressive illness. *Journal of Affective Disorders, 13*, 31-43.
Frankenhauser, M. (1979). Psychoneuroendocrine approaches to the study of emotion as related to stress and coping. In: H.E. Howe & R.A. Diensbier (eds.), *Nebraska Symposium on Motivation*. University of Nebraska Press, Lincoln, NE.
Hamilton, M. (1960). A rating scale for depression. *Journal of Neurology, Neurosurgery and Psychiatry, 23*, 56-61.
Hollon, S.D. & Kendall, P.C. (1980). Cognitive self-statements in depression. Development of an Automatic Thoughts Questionnaire. *Cognitive Therapy and Research, 4*, 383-395.
Kenny, D.A. (1975). Cross-lagged panel correlation: A test for spuriousness. *Psychological Bulletin, 82*, 887-903.
Klein, D.F. (1974). Endogenomorphic Depression. *Archives of General Psychiatry, 31*, 447-454.
Kovacs, M., Rush, A.J., Beck, A.T. & Hollon, S.D. (1981). Depressed outpatients treated with cognitive therapy and pharmacotherapy. *Archives of General Psychiatry, 38*, 33-39.
Lundberg, U. (1979). Psychophysiological aspects of performance and adjustment to stress. In: H.W. Krokne & L. Laus (Eds.), *Achievement stress and Anxiety*. Hemisphere Publishing Corporation, Washington D.C.
Miskimins, R.W. (1972). *Manual: MSCO II.* Fort Collins Colo Rocky Mountains Behavioural Science Institute.
Overall, J.E. & Gorham, D.R. (1962). The Brief Psychiatric Rating Scale. *Psychological Reports, 10*, 799-812.
Rush, A.J., Kovacs, M., Beck, A.T., Weissenburger, J. & Hollon, S.D. (1981). Different effects of cognitive therapy and pharmacotherapy on depressive symptoms. *Journal of Affective Disorders, 3*, 221-229.
Rush, A.J., Beck, A.T., Kovacs, M., Weissenburger, J. & Hollon, S.D. (1982). Comparison of the effects of cognitive therapy and pharmacotherapy on hopelessness and self-concept. *American Journal of Psychiatry, 139*, 862-866.
Spitzer, R.L., Endicott, J. & Robins, E. (1978). *Research diagnostic criteria (RDC) for a selected group of functional disorders.* 3rd edition New York State Psychiatric Institute, Biometrics Research, New York.
Teasdale, J.D., Fennell, M.J.V., Hibbert, G.A. & Amies, P.L. (1984). Cognitive therapy for major depressive disorder in primary care. *British Journal of Psychiatry, 144*, 400-406.

COGNITIVE BEHAVIOUR THERAPY IN THE SOCIAL CONTEXT

G. Parry

University of Southampton, Royal South Hants Hospital, Department of Psychiatry, U.K.

A cognitive approach to depression teaches clients to identify and change automatic negative thoughts. The emphasis on dysfunctional cognition, particularly in a paradigm derived from laboratory experimentation, has led to some concern that insufficient attention has been paid to the social interactions of depressed people in their natural environment which may influence their perceptions (Coyne & Gotlib. 1983). Cognitive behaviour therapy (CBT) has developed independently of the client's social ecology, although cognitive behaviour therapists have become aware that social network factors can either enhance or undermine treatment effects.

From epidemiological research we know that factors in the social environment, such as severely stressful life events and social support, have a role in triggering depressive episodes. It is possible (although as yet untested) that clients who lack social support at the end of therapy will remain vulnerable to further episodes, and less able to maintain their clinical improvement. If problems in social support can be addressed, the value of CBT may be enhanced, as an effective therapy which has a curative as well as preventive function.

Of course, problems in social relationships are commonly addressed within CBT, but this may be done in an unfocussed and unsystematic way. An understanding of the main theoretical issues in the perception and mobilization of social support is essential to plan CBT intervention techniques which take account of the social dimension[1].

First I define social support and briefly review the evidence that it is a risk factor in depression. Epidemiological research tends to view social factors as external to the individual, but a clinical application depends on understanding the role played by psychological processes in the perception and mobilization of support. A formulation made that there is a link between negative self-referent cognitions and failures to use support. From this theoretical base, I outline a treatment approach which is designed to follow a typical CBT. Assessment tools for planning and monitoring the intervention are described, and details given of specific techniques for eliciting and challenging dysfunctional cognitions about social support interactions. Behavioural skills training in support mobilization is outlined. Finally, I state some general principles for this type of therapeutic work.

WHAT IS SOCIAL SUPPORT ?

Sidney Cobb has formulated a widely adopted definition of social support:

> "*Information leading individuals to believe (they) are (1) cared for and loved, (2) esteemed and valued; and that they (3) belong to a network of communication and mutual obligation*" (Cobb, 1976).

This is essentially a cognitive definition and as such is particularly useful to cognitive behaviour therapists. It is worth examining other authors' definitions too:

> "*Interpersonal transactions that involve the expression of positive affect, the affirmation or endorsement of the person's beliefs or values and/or the provision of aid or assistance*" (Kahn and Antonucci, 1980).
>
> "*The degree to which a person's basic social needs are gratified through interaction with others*" (Kaplan, Cassel and Gore, 1977).
>
> "*Behavior which assures people that their feelings are understood by others and considered normal in the situation*" (Walker, MacBride and Vachon, 1977).

We see from these that the term 'social support' refers to a range of different psychosocial processes and is not a unitary entity. Various authors have developed taxonomies of different types of support (House, 1981; Caplan, 1974; Cobb, 1976). These can be summarized as follows (adapted from Wortman, 1984):

* the expression of positive affect (including information that one is loved, cared for and esteemed);
* the expression of agreement with (or acknowledging the appropriateness of) a person's belief, interpretations or feelings; encouraging their open expression;
* offering advice or information, or access to new, diverse information;
* provision of material aid;
* provision of information that the person is part of a network of mutual obligation or reciprocal help.

Social support becomes available in the context of a social network, but is not synonymous with it - hence the term 'social support network' is rather confusing and is best avoided. Not all network relationships are supportive, but the type of network one inhabits may affect the way support is mobilized. One crucial concept here is that the people in an

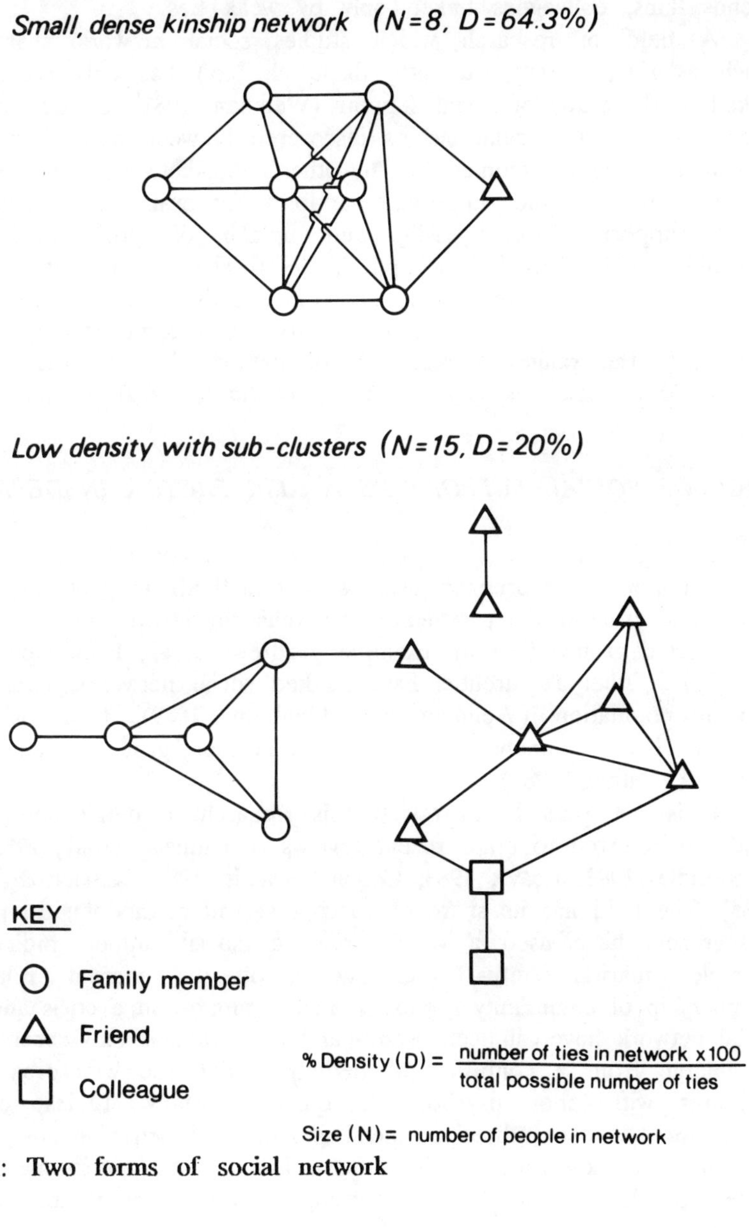

Figure 1: **Two forms of social network**

individual's personal network may or may not know each other. Two different types of network are illustrated in Figure 1. One is a small network, and most people within it know each other - this is characteristic of networks dominated by kinship. The second is not only larger but much less closely knit - there are several sub-clusters of friends, kins, colleagues linked only by weak ties.

A field of research which studies social network characteristics (such as size, density, strength, dispersal, etc.) has only recently been linked to the study of social support (Wellman, 1981). So far, there have been few consistent relationships discovered between network parameters and mental health outcomes. On the other hand, network structure appears to be related to other important variables, for example, satisfaction with social support (Stokes, 1983) and uptake of professional services (McKinlay, 1973; Birkel & Reppucci, 1983). There is also some evidence that although crisis support may be more speedy in small dense networks (Walker et al., 1977), when it comes to longer term adaptational tasks, these lack the range of resources of low density networks with sub-clusters and weak ties (Hirsch, 1981; Wellman, 1979).

LACK OF SOCIAL SUPPORT AS A RISK FACTOR IN DEPRESSION

Epidemiological research has yielded information about the relationship of social support to depression using survey methods in general population samples to examine the prevalence of psychiatric disorder in supported and unsupported groups (see for example, Andrews et al., 1978; Henderson et al., 1981). Other researchers have studied social networks, either in the general population (Wellman and Leighton, 1979), high risk groups (Hirsch, 1981; McLanahan et al., 1981) or in client groups (Hammer, 1981; Cuter & Tatum, 1983).

It is not possible to review this research in detail here and the reader is referred to other recent reviews (Broadhead et al., 1983; Heller & Swindle, 1983; Leavy, 1983; Cohen & Wills, 1985; Kessler & McLeod, 1985). The field has its share of conceptual and methodological problems. Researchers have used a wide variety of social support indices - for example, marital status, the quality of the marital relationship, membership of community groups, available support in a crisis and size of social network have all been used - and the field has only recently begun to emerge from a confusion of definitions and the widespread use of measures with poor psychometric qualities. Many studies report an association between indices of social support and better mental health in general population samples. Some have found that support has a stress-buffering role, so that the relationship between support and health is only observed among those who have suffered a stressful life event (Henderson et al., 1981; Brown & Harris, 1978). Others have reported that support can also be beneficial to mental health for those who have low levels of life event stress - that is, in routine circumstances as well as in a crisis (Aneshensel & Stone, 1982; Parry & Shapiro, 1986). One important conceptual distinction is that between global, diffuse or structural indices of support (such as membership of community groups) and specific, stress-related support, (such as the availability of a confiding person). The first is tapping social integration, contributes to the 'psychological sense of community' (to use S.B. Sarason's (1974) term), and tends to yield direct, independent effects; the second is differentially important following a stressful life event, and is more likely to act as a stress buffer (Cohen and Wills, 1985).

The way that crisis-related support can act to protect individuals from the mental health consequences of severe stress is not yet fully understood. Some authors have discussed the role of support in maintaining self-esteem and providing a sense of mastery over the environment (Pearlin, Lieberman, Menaghan & Mullan, 1981; Brown & Harris, 1978). Thoits (1986) argues that social support processes are a form of coping assistance, and like coping, can be conceptualized as problem an emotion focussed. Finally, it is possible that those who perceive themselves to be supported (which is what most studies have measured) have personalities which are more resilient to stress, whereas poor perceived support is associated with neuroticism and stress vulnerability (Henderson, 1984). This possibility must be examined carefully, since it has important implications for the cognitive behaviour therapist.

THE ROLE OF THE INDIVIDUAL IN SUPPORT MOBILIZATION

The epidemiological approach to the study of social support has tended to see it as an environmental factor acting upon individuals in a given population. This is unsatisfactory, although it may be a justifiable simplification in research using statistical techniques such as general linear modeling where reciprocal causes and feedback loops are difficult to test. The clinician requires a more realistic conceptualization of the support process (see Hobfoll, 1985 for a useful discussion of this issue). There is a good deal of evidence that whilst social isolation and the lack of confiding intimacy do affect mental health, so do mental health and personality affect the amount and quality of social support received. The degree to which this has been neglected in psychosocial stress research can be judged by the fact that Henderson (1984) found it necessary to remind his readers that "social support is obtainable only through social relationships which are themselves achieved only by having competence in establishing and maintaining them". Indeed, some authors have gone so far as to suggest that most of the social support findings could be accounted for by social competence (Heller, 1979; Hansson et al., 1984).

The majority of studies which have found associations between support and mental health outcomes have measured *perceived* social support rather than behavioural tallies of support received. This presents us with a problem, because it suggests either that social support outcomes are cognitively mediated or that correlations between perceived support and depression are spuriously high because the two measures are confounded. Of course, both possibilities could be true, and the clinician can have little doubt that all things being equal, depressed mood is likely to alter an individual's perception of how supported he or she is. However evidence from a prospective study (Henderson et al., 1981) where non-depressed individuals who perceive themselves to be poorly supported are subsequently more likely to become depressed, makes the first possibility worth considering.

Perceived support is, like 'loneliness', only partly accounted for by the actual support available to or received by an individual (Cutrona, 1982; Stokes, 1985). 'Feeling supported' is of course a *psychological* rather than a sociological phenomenon, based on an internal representation of self in relation to others. Where this self is perceived as unloved and unvalued, there may be a tendency to discount or devalue support. Here we can remember Cobb's (1976) definition of support as "information leading individuals to believe they are cared for and loved". When someone is clinically depressed, although their social environment may indeed be deficient in support, any supportive behaviours which do occur are likely to be interpreted negatively rather than to lead the person to believe they are loved and cared for. All support processes are linked to dependency relationships which have the potential for negative as well as positive messages about the self. I believe this is a fundamental issue too for the mobilization phase of the social support process.

A number of studies have investigated individual characteristics which are associated with perceived social support (Duckitt, 1984; Ganellen & Blaney, 1984; Sarason & Sarason, 1982; Stokes, 1985; Sarason, Sarason, Hacker & Basham, 1985). Unfortunately, these are correlational studies using student samples, and so lose generalizability compared to well-designed epidemiological surveys. In these studies, those who perceive themselves as lacking social support have been found to be less socially competent than 'high support' individuals, to be more introverted, to have higher trait anxiety, to be intolerant of psychological problems in others, to report unhappier experiences of their childhood relationships with parents, to have more pessimistic views about the benefits of social relationships with parents, to have a passive, uninvolved stance towards life events and to see these as a burden to be endured and to have external locus of control.

When facing a stressful life event of any severity, the belief that one is supported will, at some point, be tested. There is a great difference between believing you would be helped in a crisis and actually being helped in a crisis. The translation of potential support into mobilized support is likely to be influenced both by the individual and by characteristics of his or her network. We know that some socio-demographic variables affect the mobilization process; for example women may make more use of support following stress than men (Butler et al., 1985) and those with a higher level of education report more mobilized support following a stressful event (Eckenrode, 1983). We also need to understand why some individuals are less effective at mobilizing help than others. There may be two elements in this, help-*seeking* and help-*using*. It is in using help that the depressed person tends to have difficulties.

SELF REFERENT COGNITIONS AND SUPPORT DEFICITS

There is a body of social psychology research on recipient reactions to aid which, although isolated from the social support field, is relevant to understanding how help can be rejected. Fisher et al. (1983) discuss two clusters of reactions to aid, a negative, defensive reaction and a positive, accepting one. They review evidence from a range of sources illuminates the circumstances which elicit cluster 1 rather than cluster 2 reactions, showing that aid is more likely to be rejected when the recipient is unable to reciprocate, when the donor's motivation is negative, when it poses a threat to the autonomy of the recipient, when aid is requested rather than offered, and when aid is greatly needed rather than less needed.

Various theoretical frameworks have been used to make sense of these findings. Equity theory is based on the principle that there is a desire in social exchange relationships to maintain equity and that lack of equity causes distress. However, Fisher and Nadler argue that none of these account for the full range of findings as parsimoniously as the hypothesis that people reject aid when it poses a threat to their self esteem. If we link this to the social support and personality findings, we can hypothesize that individuals with vulnerable self-esteem are less likely to mobilize help effectively. When offers of support trigger negative self-referent cognitions, affects such as humiliation, embarrassment and shame are aroused. Exposure to these aversive states can be avoided by rejecting (or even sabotaging) offers to support. It should be clear that this approach has direct relevance for depression, because the depressed person is more likely to perceive (perhaps accurately, but certainly selectively) the negative implications of accepting help.

ASSESSMENT OF SOCIAL SUPPORT AND SOCIAL NETWORKS

Having outlined some of the theoretical principles which make a clinical intervention possible, I shall now describe their application within the framework of cognitive behaviour therapy. The first stage in any such therapy is assessment and problem formulation. If this is to be sensitive to the social context, it is essential to assess accurately the client's social relationships and problems in support mobilization. This includes mapping the network and its features (such as size, density, proportion of kin), assessing the frequency and type of helping behaviours that the client has experienced from others in the network, identifying areas of relative strength and deficit and discrepancies between the support available and the client's perceived social support. To upgrade one's technique in this field requires a knowledge of appropriate measures. These are essential in formulating the problem during assessment and in monitoring change. More than this, though, they are a central part of the intervention, since clients also learn to use these instruments. There are many published scales which measure different aspects of support. In practice the therapist needs use only three: a social network analysis, a measure of perceived support, and a measure of helping behaviours. These allow the therapist to 'triangulate' the social support process for a given individual.

Some of the principles and practicalities of social network analysis are described by Walker, MacBride and Vachon (1977), Hirsch (1981), Wellman (1981) and Maguire (1983). Typically, a list of primary group members is elicited by recording the names of all people the client meets to talk to regularly. Relatives, friends, neighbours, colleagues and professionals are included, but not those with whom there is only superficial contact (for example, nodding acquaintances, shopkeepers, etc.). People who are significant but are rarely seen can be included, for example, relatives and friends who are geographically distant and those with whom the client has lost touch as a result of the psychiatric episode. The 'map' of the social network is then drawn by establishing for each possible pair of people in the list, whether or not they have a personal relationship *independently of the client* (see Figure 1). The frequency of contact with each network member and its geographical dispersion, are also ascertained.

Next, the assessment moves from the structure of the social network to the social support mobilization within it. This aspect of the analysis is made more precisely by using the Inventory of Socially Supportive Behaviours (ISSB), as described by Barrera and Ainley (1983). In clinical practice it is best to modify the method from a retrospective one to a diary keeping format, where the client records each occasion on which a particular type of help is offered. Examples include 'Provided you with transport' (tangible assistance); 'Taught you how to do something' (directive guidance); 'Comforted you by showing you some physical affection' (non-directive support); 'Did some activity to help you get your mind off things' (positive social interaction).

The social network map is then examined in conjunction with the helping behaviour inventory to analyze how much of the network has been mobilized and in which areas, in order to pinpoint specific support deficits. Common dysfunctional patterns include a) very small networks, b) total lack of one or more types of support, and c) uneven mobilization, sometimes to the extent that all support is being received from one or two people. The network measure is then used to identify potential sources of help with the client's current problems and is the basis for planning behavioural assignments in support elicitation (described by Maguire, 1983). The method of using unexploited resources within the network to help the client solve problems can best be conceptualized as coping assistance (Thoits, 1986), and is the individual therapy equivalent to the community networking interventions I describe elsewhere (Parry, 1988).

In addition to the two assessment tools already described, a measure of perceived support is also of great value, and there are many available. The Perceived Social Network Inventory (Orritt, Paul, Stephen and Behrman, 1985) is a useful example, partly because it focusses on coping assistance and also because efforts have been made to establish its psychometric properties. This measure requires the individual to identify those people to whom he or she could turn when under stress or in need of help, then goes on to establish the type of support available from each, how often given, whether reciprocal and whether the relationship is characterized by negative feelings.

This type of questionnaire is primarily useful as a baseline measure of support perception. The cognitive behavioural intervention is aimed not just at altering the amount of support elicited from the network, but to alter the client's perception of that support. Hence an outcome measure is needed which taps this variable, ideally at the time of referral, as therapy starts, at the end of therapy and at follow up. In addition, a comparison of the perceptual measure with the ISSB can be the starting point for identifying dysfunctional cognitive processes about support. For example, the perceptual measure may reveal that the client perceives a particular network member as relatively unsupportive, when the ISSB shows that this person has been providing high levels of support which is cognitively devalued by the client. The systematic identification of such processes within cognitive therapy for depression is an important part of a socially oriented intervention.

SELF MONITORING SUPPORT-RELATED BEHAVIOUR

Therapy continues with a systematic examination of the indivdual's perception of being unsupported and identifies repetitive social interactions in which support is being devalued, rejected, abused or unmobilized. Fundamental to both aspects of the work is precision in identifying the specific ways, for this particular individual, that supportive acts are being interpreted as threatening self-esteem.

From the diary keeping format of the ISSB, the therapist is usually able to show the client that there are members of the network who are not providing support, or that all the supporting rests on one or two individuals. Gaps in the pattern of support (e.g. no companionship support) have also been identified. This leads easily to a self monitoring assignment where the frequency of specific problems is recorded. No behavioural change is asked for at this stage, but an accurate description of the behaviour is aimed for. Examples of this are as follows:

OFFER OF HELP	MY RESPONSE
My son J. did the washing up but he didn't do it properly.	I did it all again.
Mum asked if I needed anything from the shops whilst she was down there.	I said not to bother because it would make too much for her to carry.
Went to see M. (ex-colleague) & spoke about my problems since I lost my job. He said "It takes time you know".	I stopped talking about how I felt because he didn't understand.

The client will need guidance on how to record *all* instances of offered help, even if he or she perceived the 'offer' as unhelpful, insincere, inadequate etc. It also takes practice to write a clear description of one's own behaviour in these circumstances. Therapists are advised to complete the ISSB as a diary followed by this self-monitoring exercise in their own lives as this makes it easier to help clients learn to self-monitor.

CHALLENGING AUTOMATIC THOUGHTS ABOUT SUPPORT

The self-monitoring exercise will reveal a pattern of dysfunctional behaviours in response to potential support. These will be tackled by behavioural skills training, but in addition, dysfunctional beliefs about the social support process should be examined. It is logical for this work to be done prior to graded behavioural assignments, although in practice the two phases often overlap and proceed in parallel.

Statements such as these (taken from clinical material) will probably be familiar to most therapists:

" If he loved me, I wouldn't have to ask him to help me";

" I can't tell my (adult) children about my operation because it would worry them";

" Well, she did offer to babysit but I know she didn't really mean it";

" It's embarrassing to admit I can't cope";

" He only said he would take me out because he feels sorry for me";

" I feel bad going round to her house yet again because I can't give anything to her";

" You are only helping me because it's your job";

Here we see processes of attribution and equity beliefs which can be challenged successfully and the consequences of an alternative belief tested out. Each remark arises from a personal belief held by the patient about interpersonal relationships (see Ryle, 1982, for an account of these). All these beliefs lead to support being devalued or rejected, not out of wilful self-defeating wrongheadedness, but as a self-protective strategy. In my experience, the therapeutic alliance is strengthened if this is understood and acknowledged by the therapist. The messages about the self implied by admitting one cannot cope, accepting that someone feels sorry for one, or having to ask for help are identified, challenged, and alternatives tested. These alternatives may involve, for example, discovering the intrinsic value of the support regardless of the motives of the donor, accepting that less than perfect care is a normal aspect of reality, learning to tolerate self-consciousness and embarrassment, or the legitimate use of gratitude as 'payment' in social transactions.

The use of the self-monitoring exercise allows detailed examination of particular instances of dysfunctional support behaviour and the attendant cognitions. When the behavioural recording is established, the client is asked to record the automatic thoughts which precede the behaviour, as in Beck's method (Beck et al., 1979). The cognitive treatment for depression should precede the social support intervention, so that the client will already be familiar with the general technique. One of the examples from the section on self-monitoring can be used as an illustration of this:

OFFER OF HELP	MY AUTOMATIC THOUGHTS	MY RESPONSE
Went to see M. & spoke about my problems since I lost my job. He said "It takes time you know".	What the hell does he know about it? He just wants to shut me up. He thinks I'm a wisp.	I stopped talking about how I felt because he didn't understand.

Alternatives to these thoughts are then examined with the client, using conventional techniques of cognitive therapy.

DEVELOPING NEW SKILLS IN SUPPORT ELICITATION

As work on the individual's personal beliefs and automatic thoughts proceeds, new behaviours can be tested within the social network. An excellent discussion of this issue by Winefield (1984) is recommended, as she described ways in which new skills in eliciting support can be taught using behavioural assignments. She notes that traditional social skills teaching is unlikely to be helpful, and that behavioural interventions should focus on teaching patients a) the social norms for intimacy and its reciprocation, b) how much and when to complain, c) how to attend to and display interest in the other person and d) how to reward the other for helping by responding positively. It would be possible to do this in a group teaching format, although no reports of such an intervention are yet available.

In the individual therapy, the behavioural assignments are undertaken after behavioural self monitoring and examination of the cognitive basis of behaviour. I have found it best to introduce the points made by Winefield in the context of the examples brought by the client during self-monitoring. Rehearsal in alternative responses can take place in the session, first by the client (with prompts) thinking of an alternative, then acting it out in a role play with the therapist. Role reversal is useful here, with the therapist playing the client's part and the client acting as the would-be helper. Another of the examples given in the section on self-monitoring will serve as an illustration.

Offer of help:	Mum asked if I needed anything from the shops whilst she was down there.
My thoughts:	She doesn't really want to help me. She thinks I'm taking advantage of her. If she really means it she will insist that it's no trouble.
My response:	I said not to bother because it would make too much for her to carry.
Alternative thoughts:	She's offering me some help which I need. I would do the same for her.
Alternative response:	"Oh thanks Mum. I need some bread and vegetables."

This is a simple example and in practice most are more complex, but the same principles apply. It is better to start with simple examples so that the client can practice support elicitation responses, before giving more difficult assignments. Examples of these include judging when it is *not* appropriate to ask for support. This is an example of a support elicitation attempt which failed:

> *My sister said I was being very selfish not going to see Dad as I lived much nearer to him than she did and I was putting her in an impossible position. I said she didn't understand how upset she made me and I wish she would see my point of view.*

A simple acknowledgement of the sister's feelings would have been more useful as there is a request for expressive support in her statement. Instead the client responds with a counter-request, which violates the social norm of reciprocation.

GENERAL PRINCIPLES OF A SOCIAL SUPPORT AND SOCIAL NETWORK APPROACH

Two principles behind a social support intervention are first, that the individual, not the therapist, is to take responsibility for mobilizing the network and second, that behavioural assignments should take account of the social norms of the network. Although there is nothing intrinsically difficult about this form of work, it is an area where it is easy to make poorly focussed interventions due to ignorance about the ecological setting. Support cannot always be artificially 'grafted on' to an existing network; if it is inappropriate it may be rejected - just as a transplanted organ poorly matched for tissue type will be rejected by the living organism. This is what a social ecology is. Any such intervention must be planned carefully, on the basis of the social network analysis, to be a logical extension of natural support or a mobilization of existing support. For example, a therapist may be aware that the patient's network is small and restricted in friendship and sources of information. A recommendation about 'joining a club' or 'going to an evening class' is often entirely alien to the values of the network. In this case it is often better to examine the network for potential 'bridging ties' to other networks. These are weak ties which offer potential access to new friends and activities (Granovetter, 1973; Walker et al., 1977).

I have stressed the need to see the client within a social context, and the interventions discussed here are explicitly designed to alter the ecological system which the client inhabits. Willems (1973) has pointed out that there are significant dangers, when intervening in any ecological system, of setting up chains of events which lead to unpredicted and negative consequences[2]. This is demonstrably the case with biological systems, and equally possible within social systems. The approach described here has not yet been systematically researched, and the possibility of 'iatrogenic' problems developing within the network should be considered and any reported effects on other network members monitored carefully.

Notes

1. Some sections of this paper are drawn from Parry (1988).
2. I should like to thank Derek Milne for drawing my attention to this article.

REFERENCES

Andrews, G., Tennant, C., Newson, D.M. & Vaillant, G.E. (1978). Life event stress, social support, coping style and risk of psychological impairment. *Journal of Nervous and Mental Disease, 166*, 307-316.

Aneshensel, C.S. & Stone, J.D. (1982). Stress and depression: a test of the stress buffering model *Archives of General Psychiatry, 39*, 1392-1396.

Barrera, M. & Ainlay, S.L. (1983). The structure of social support: a conceptual and empirical analysis. *Journal of Community Psychology, 11*, 133-143.

Beck, A.T., Rush, A.T., Shaw, B.F. & Emery, G. (1979). *Cognitive Therapy for Depression.* New York: Guilford Press.

Birkel, R.C. & Reppucci, N.D. (1983). Social networks, information seeking

and the utilisation of services. *American Journal of Community Psychology, 11*, 185-205.
Broadhead, W., Kaplan, B., James, S., Wagner, E., Schoenbach, V., Grimson, R., Heyden, S., Tibblin, G. & Gehlbach, S. (1983). The epidemiologic evidence for a relationship between social support and health. *American Journal of Epidemiology, 117*, 521-537.
Brown, G.W. & Harris, T. (1978). *Social Origins of Depression: A Study of Psychiatric Disorder in Women*. London: Tavistock.
Caplan, G. (Ed.) (1974). *Support Systems and Community Mental Health*. New York: Basic Books.
Cobb, S. (1976). Social support as a moderator of life stress. *Psychosomatic Medicine, 38*, 300-314.
Cohen, S. & Wills, T.A. (1985). Stress, social support and the buffering hypothesis. *Psychological Bulletin*, 98, 310-357.
Coyne, J.C. & Gotlib, I.H. (1983). The role of cognition in depression: a critical appraisal. *Psychological Bulletin, 94*, 472-505.
Cuter, D.L. & Tatum, E. (1983). Networks and the chronic patient. *New Directions for Mental Health Services, 19*, 13-22.
Cutrona, C.E. (1982). Transition to college: Loneliness and the process of social adjustment. In: L.A. Peplau & D. Perlman (Eds.), *Loneliness: A Sourcebook of Current Theory, Research and Therapy*. New York: Wiley.
Duckitt, J. (1984). Social support, personality and the prediction of psychological distress: An interactionist approach. *Journal of Clinical Psychology, 40*, 1199-1205.
Eckenrode, J. (1983). The mobilisation of social supports: some individual constraints. *American Journal of Community Psychology, 11*, 509-528.
Fischer, J.D., Nadler, A. & De Paulo, B.M. (Eds.) (1983). *New Directions in Helping, Volume I. Recipient Reactions to Aid.* New York: Academic Press.
Ganellen, R.J. & Blaney, P.H. (1984). Hardiness and social support as moderators of the effects of life stress. *Journal of Personality and Social Psychology, 47*, 156-163.
Granovetter, M.S. (1973). The strength of weak ties. *American Journal of Sociology, 78*, 1360-1372.
Hammer, M. (1981). Social supports, social networks and schizophrenia. *Schizophrenia Bulletin, 7*, 45-57.
Hansson, R.O., Jones, W.H. & Carpenter, B.N. (1984). Relationship competence and social support. In: P. Shaver (Ed.), *Review of Personality and Social Psychology, Volume 5*. Beverly Hills: Sage.
Heller, K. (1979). The effects of social support. Prevention and treatment implications. In: A.P. Goldstein & F.H. Kanfer (Eds.), *Maximising Treatment Gains: Transfer Enhancement in Psychotherapy.*

New York: Academic Press.
Heller, K. & Swindle, R.W. (1983). Social networks, perceived social support and coping with stress. In: R.D. Feiner, L.A. Jason, J. Moritsugu & S.S. Farber (Eds.), *Preventive Psychology. Theory Research and Practice in Community Intervention*. Pergamon Press.
Henderson, S. (1984). Interpreting the evidence on social support. *Social Psychiatry, 19*, 49-52.
Henderson, S., Byrne, D.G. & Duncan-Jones, P. (1981). *Neurosis and the Social Environment*. Sydney: Academic Press.
Hirsch, B. (1981). Natural support systems and coping with major life changes. *American Journal of Community Psychology*, 7, 263-277.
Hobfoll, S.E. (1985). Limitations of social support in the stress process. In: I.G. Sarason & B.R. Sarason (Eds.), *Social Support: Theory, Research and Applications*. Dordrecht: Martinus Nijhoff Publishers.
House, J.S. (1981). *Work, Stress and Social Support*. Phillipines: Addison Wesley.
Kahn, R. & Antonucci, T. (1980). Convoys over the life course: Attachments, roles and social supports. In: P.B. Baltes & D. Brim (Eds.), *Life-span Development and Behaviour*. Boston: Lexington Press.
Kaplan, B.H., Cassel, J.C. & Gore, S. (1977). Social support and health. *Medical Care, 15*, 47-58.
Kessler, R.C. & McLeod, J. (1985). Social support and mental health in community samples. In: S. Cohen & L. Syme (Eds.), *Social Support and Health*. New York: Academic Press.
Leavy, R.L. (1983). Social support and psychological disorder. A review. *Journal of Community Psychology, 11*, 3-21.
McKinlay, J.B. (1973). Social networks, lay consultation and help-seeking behaviour. *Social Forces, 51*, 275-292.
McLanahan, S.S., Wedemeyer, N.V. & Adelberg, T. (1981). Network structure, social support and psychological well-being in the single parent family. *Journal of Marriage and the Family, 43*, 601-612.
Maguire, L. (1983). *Networking with individuals*. In: Understanding Social Networks. Beverly Hills: Sage Publications.
Orritt, E.J., Paul, S.C. & Behrman, J.A. (1985). The Perceived Support Network Inventory. *American Journal of Community Psychology, 13*, 565-582.
Parry, G. (1988). Mobilizing social support. Chapter in F.N. Watts (Ed.), *New Directions in Clinical Psychology, Volume II*. BPS Publications.
Parry, G. & Shapiro, D.A. (1986). Social support and life events in working class women. Stress buffering or independent effects ? *Archives of General Psychiatry, 43*, 315-323.
Pearlin, L.I., Lieberman, M.A., Menaghan, E.G. & Mullan, J.T. (1981). The

stress process. *Journal of Health and Social Behavior, 19*, 2-21.
Ryle, A. (1982). *Psychotherapy: A Cognitive Integration of Theory and Practice*. London: Academic Press.
Sarason, S.B. (1974). *The psychological sense of community*. San Francisco: Jossey Bass.
Sarason, I.G. & Sarason, B.R. (1982). Concomitants of social support: Attitudes, personality characteristics and life experiences. *Journal of Personality, 50*, 331-344.
Sarason, B.R., Sarason, I.G., Hacker, T.A. & Basham, R.B. (1985). Concomitants of social support: social skills, physical attractiveness and gender. *Journal of Personality and Social Psychology, 49*, 469-480.
Stokes, J.P. (1983). Predicting satisfaction with social support from social network structure. *American Journal of Community Psychology, 11*, 141-152.
Stokes, J.P. (1985). The relation of social network and individual difference variables to loneliness. *Journal of Personality and Social Psychology, 48*, 981-990.
Thoits, P.A. (1986). Social support as coping assistance. *Journal of Consulting and Clinical Psychology, 54*, 416-423.
Walker, K., MacBride, A. & Vachon, M. (1977). Social support networks and the crisis of bereavement. *Social Science and Medicine, 11*, 35-41.
Wellman, B. (1979). The community question. *American Journal of Sociology, 84*, 1201-1231.
Wellman, B. (1981). Applying network analysis to the study of social support. In: B.H. Gotlieb (Ed.), *Social Networks and Social Support*. Beverly Hills: Sage Publications.
Wellman, B. & Leighton, B. (1979). Networks, neighbourhoods and communities. *Urban Affairs Quarterly, 15*, 363-390.
Willems, E.P. (1973). Go ye into all the world and modify behavior: an ecologist's view. *Representative Research in Social Psychology, 4*, 93-105.
Winefield, H.R. (1984). The nature and elicitation of social support: Some implications for the helping professions. *Behavioural Psychotherapy, 12*, 318-330.
Wortman, C.B. (1984). Social support and the cancer patient. Conceptual and methodological issues. *Cancer, 53*, 2339-2360.

A COMPARATIVE EVALUATION OF COGNITIVE THERAPY AND PSYCHOPHARMACA IN THE TREATMENT OF DEPRESSION

S. Cayiroglu, E. Merkel, & H. Zapotoczky

University of Vienna, Department of Psychiatry, Austria

Evaluation of cognitive behaviour therapy in treatment of depressive patients suffers from the same problems as psychopharmacological studies: Subject variables are difficult to control, history of the affective disorder (i.e. number of previous episodes, duration of hospitalization, and previous treatment, type of depression etc.) is often unquantifiable; standardization of diagnostic procedures is difficult, individual differences cannot always be evaluated objectively, and the influence of sex, age, social data, as well as the number of drop outs has not always been taken into account.

Nevertheless there are a number of comparative studies on cognitive behaviour therapy and psychopharmacotherapy (Rush et al., 1977) that demonstrate the superiority of cognitive behaviour therapy over psychopharmacological treatment of depression. Furthermore patients participating in these studies show lower drop out rates and less relapses (Simmons et al., 1986).

The present paper compares three groups of patients that have been treated with a) cognitive behaviour therapy, b) a combination of cognitive therapy and a reversible MAO inhibitor (- of type A with a short biological half life, brand name Ro 11-1163) and c) a combination of cognitive behaviour therapy and placebo, using a randomized double blind procedure. Ro 11-1163 was chosen because of clinical considerations. The paper sets out to compare effectiveness of cognitive behaviour therapy with a new Mao inhibitor with both outpatients and inpatients, with the purpose of reinvestigating above mentioned findings in a controlled study.

The following hypotheses were tested:

1. In the course of therapy i.e. before commencement of therapy (T1) and after three weeks (T2) differences between the three groups will be found for the variables depression, self perception, dysfunctional beliefs and drive.
2. There will be differences over all groups at the three points in time T1, T2 and after six weeks (T3) on the measured variables.
3. In the course of therapy there will be differences between in- and outpatients on the 4 measured variables.
4. There will be sex differences in the results obtained.
5. During therapy, groups one and two, one and three as well as two and three will differ on the 4 evaluated variables.

METHOD

Subjects

32 patients suffering from "major depression" (DSM III) took part in the study. They were 19 female and 13 male patients; aged 19 to 52, the average being 35 years. 19 were inpatients at the ward for behaviour therapy. 13 outpatients participated in the study.

Patients with an indication of schizophrenic disorder, alcoholism, drug addiction, bi-polar manic depressive disorder, strong suicidal tendencies, florid psychotic disorders with delusion and/or hallucinations, neurotic disorders such as compulsive obsessive symptoms as well as patients who showed a contraindication for Ro 11-1163 were excluded from participation.

Included were patients showing endogenomorphic depressive patterns with sleeping disorder and disruption of biorhythm (Berner, 1975). Rather than a phasic process, patients showed a chronic depressive illness with an acute reactive phase due to life events.

Assessment

Psychopathological state was evaluated independent of the therapist using a clinical interview. In addition, before commencement of therapy (T1), after three week (T2), and after 6 weeks (T3) patients had to complete the following questionnaires:

Beck-Depression-Inventory (BDI)

Depressive Attitudes Scale (DAS): A questionnaire for depressive, negative and irrational views of oneself, the environment and the future as described by Beck.

Self Perception Scale: A questionnaire that measures self perception in personal and public aspects as well as social anxiety. The BDI and DAS are correlated, i.e. patients with high negative and dysfunctional perception usually score high on depression. Items O and Q from BDI were used for evaluation of drive. (Maximum score 12, minimum score 0).

Procedure

Therapy was largely based on Becks cognitive therapy of depression. Groups consisted of 5 to 7 patients and two therapists. Therapy lasted for 6 weeks, with 3 sessions that lasted for 1½ hours each. We evaluated scores at 3 points in time (T1, T2, T3) to be able to show onset and progress of effectiveness of treatment during the whole course of the study.

During the first session medication was distributed to groups one and two, using a doubleblind randomized procedure. The patients received two tablets Ro 11-1163 (100 mg each) or two tablets of placebo. Patients were divided into three groups:

Group one: 11 patients who were treated with cognitive therapy and Ro 11-1163.
Group two: 11 patients who received cognitive therapy and placebo.
Group three: 10 patients who received cognitive therapy only.

RESULTS

For the statistical evaluations SPSSX (Statistical Package for Social Sciences) was used. Friedman tests were used to test the second hypothesis, i.e. differences over the groups to the 3 different points in time.

Table 1: **Mean scores and Standard Deviation for Depression (BDI) and Dysfunctional Believes (DAS) (n = 32)**

	BDI		DAS	
	M	SD	M	SD
t_1	26,8	12,04	159,2	37,5
t_2	20,6	10,5	141,0	36,1
t_3	15,6	10,6	123,9	32,9

t_1 = start of therapy
t_2 = after 3 weeks
t_3 = after 6 weeks (end of therapy)

There are no significant differences among the three groups, i.e. in the evaluation of depression, self perception, dysfunctional beliefs and drive, no group was better than the other.

During therapy we could observe a statistically significant, progressive decline of depression and irrational beliefs from T1 over T2 to T3 in all patients (see table 1). Social anxiety does not decrease significantly between T1 and T2, but decreases significantly from T2 to T3. At the end of therapy all patients are significantly less anxious (see table 2).

Table 2: **Mean Scores and Standard Deviation for Drive (D) and Social Anxiety (SA) (n = 32)**

	D		SA	
	M	SD	M	SD
t_1	3,1	2	13,6	6,6
t_2	2,3	1,2	12,7	6,4
t_3	2,3	1,8	10,6	6,5

t_1 - start of therapy
t_2 - after 3 weeks
t_3 - after 6 weeks (end of therapy)

For all patients drive increases significantly from T1 to T2, and stays approximately the same from T2 to T3.

Concerning depression, dysfunctional beliefs, self perception and drive there are no significant differences between in- and outpatients: also no differences between the sexes. Only at the beginning of therapy, women show more irrational beliefs concerning the self, the environment and the future. However, this tendency is diminished as therapy progresses and at the end male and female patients show the same score.

Variables do not differ significantly between group 1 and 2 and 1 and 3 at any of the measured points in time T1, T2, T3. Between group two and three however (Placebo and cognitive therapy only) there is a slight, non significant increase related to social anxiety, i.e. in the course of therapy patients of group three cope better with social anxiety than patients of group two, but this tendency decreases towards the end of therapy. For most of the patients the depressive symptoms could be reduced using cognitive therapy only, without the need of medical treatment. For clinical considerations Ro 11-1163 was used as the comparative medication.

CONCLUSION

The aim of this controlled double-blind study was to compare the effectiveness of cognitive behaviour therapy to pharmacological treatment (MAO inhibitor, Type A) in the treatment of depressed patients. Some of the results obtained confirmed the hypothesis, that scores for the three variables depression, dysfunctional attitudes and self perception decrease during cognitive behaviour therapy, regardless of the use of pharmacological treatment. Thus our study confirms that cognitive therapy is helpful to improve the depressive state of patients. To strengthen these results however, further studies are needed.

REFERENCES:

Beck, A.T., Hollon, St.D., Young, J-E., Bedrosian, R.C., & Budenz, B. (1985) Treatment of Depression with Cognitive Therapy and Amitriptyline. *Archives of General Psychiatry*, 42, 142-148.

Berner, P. (1982) *Psychiatrische Systematik.* Verlag Hans Huber, 3. korr. Auflage.

Blackburn, I.M., Eunson, K.M., Bishop, S. (1986) A two Year-Naturalistic Follow-up of Depressed Patients treated with Cognitive Therapy, Pharmacotherapy and Combination of Both. *Journal of Affective Disorders*, 10, 67-75.

Gasic, S., Korn, A., Eichler, H.G., Oberhummer, J., Zapotoczky, H.G. (1983) Cardiocirculatory Effects of Moclobemide (Ro 11-1163), a New Reversible, a Short-Acting MAO-inhibitor with Prefential Type A Inhibition, in Healthy Volunteers and Depressive Patients. *European Journal of Clinical Pharmacology,* 25, 173-177.

Mc Lean, P.D., Hastian, A.R. (1979) Clinical depression: Comparative efficacy of outpatient treatments. *Journal of Consulting and Clinical Psychology,* 47, 818-836.

Rush, A.J., Beck, A.I., Kovacs, M., Hollon, S.D. (1977) Comparative efficacy of cognitive therapy and pharmacotherapy in the treatment of depressed outpatients. *Cognitive Therapy and Research,* 1, 17-37.

Simmons, A., Murphy, G.E., Levine, J.L., Wetzel, R.D. (1986) Cognitive Therapy and Pharmaco-therapy for Depression. *Archives of General Psychiatry*, 43, 43-49.

PART IV:

ADDICTIVE DISORDERS

BEHAVIORAL HOSPITAL TREATMENT OF BULIMIA: "OUTCOME AND REVISION"

S. Bossert, E. Schnabel, B. Dippel, M. Berger, & J.C. Krieg

Max Planck Institute, Department of Psychiatry, Münich, F.R.G.

INTRODUCTION

Several psychological, mainly behavioral and cognitive-behavioral, and pharmacological, predominantly antidepressant, treatment-approaches have been proposed for bulimia and were reviewed by Johnson, Connors, Beaumont, and Casper (1987), Wilson (1985) and Griffiths, Touyz, Mitchell, and Bacon (1987). It is not yet known whether the long-term outcome of the disturbance is influenced by any intervention and, if so, by which treatment modality. The majority of psychological treatments, however, was applied on an outpatient basis and the rarity of treatment studies as well as clinical reports from bulimic inpatients is surprising. Problems such as suicidality, (severe) medical complications, impulse-related behavior and diagnosis in addition to the eating disorder or an impaired life adjustment were frequently reported in bulimia and often made hospital admission necessary.

The present study was based on the pragmatic assumption that the treatment concepts utilized in bulimic outpatients using cognitive behavioral interventions as suggested by Fairburn (1981) are transferable to bulimic inpatients.

We also hypothesized that a treatment program focusing especially on bulimic behavior is more effective than nonspecific therapy in terms of reduction of bulimic symptoms and, as a consequence, also in the improvement of associated depressive symptomatology.

METHOD

Patients

All 14 patients were female and met the DSM-III diagnostic criteria for bulimia. Clinical characteristics of patients in the self-management group are presented in Table 1. Except for a history of previous anorexia nervosa, which was present in all six patients in the nonspecific therapy group (X^2 = 4.2; df = 1; p = 0.04), there were no statistically significant differences regarding these clinical variables between the self-management and the nonspecific treatment group.

Table 1: **Clinical characteristics of the 8 patients having had management therapy.**

Pat. no.	Age at admission (years)	Previous hospital treatment	Duration of bulimia (years)	History of anorexia nervosa	Additional diagnosis (DSM-III)
1	27	0	2	absent	PD, MD, SUD
2	25	4	3	absent	PD, MD, SUD
3	10	1	4	present	-
4	18	1	3	present	PD
5	22	0	5	absent	PD, SUD
6	23	0	10	present	-
7	20	2	3	present	PD, MD, SUD
8	18	2	1	absent	MD
Mean	21.6	1.25	3.9		
SD	3.2	1.4	2.7		

PD - Personality Disorder (histrionic, borderline, dependent personality)
MD - Major Depressive Disorder
SUD- Substance Use Disorder (drug- or alcohol abuse)

Treatment

Patients were admitted consecutively to the hospital and randomly assigned to the *self-management* treatment condition or to the *nonspecific therapy* condition: In both treatment conditions patients received weekly three 40-minute sessions of individual therapy. Patients were all treated on the same ward. Participation in therapeutic groups and ward activities as well as other nonspecific influences from the hospital milieu were similar for both groups.

In *nonspecific therapy* non specific self-control techniques were used. In a supportive therapeutic relationship emphasis was placed on understanding one's bulimia by fostering introspection.

The *self-management* program included the following main components and phases:

1. Self-monitoring
2. Training of alternative modes of behavior
3. Written-contract system, including self-administered response prevention
4. Breaks from hospital treatment
5. Problem-solving approach.

All components were characterized by a high degree of personal control and responsibility. Self-management as a therapeutic procedure in the sense of Kanfer (1970) was practiced, however, in form of the written-contract system.

1. *Self-monitoring*

During the first ten days after hospital admission patients were requested to fill out sheets in order to monitor and analyze eating habits, emotions and thoughts as well as circumstances which elicit bulimic behavior.

Patients monitored themselves in the hospital and later also on weekends in their natural social environment. Sheets were reviewed and discussed in detail in the treatment sessions. The first aim was to get information on eating patterns and to give advice on their control (functional behavior analysis); the second aim was to sensitize the patient to the antecedents and consequences of binges.

2. *Training of alternative behaviors*

During the first two weeks of treatment patients were instructed in the progressive relaxation training (Jacobson) in order to modify negative emotion associated with the body and to establish a stress- and anxiety-reducing alternative behavior, incompatible with bingeing and vomiting. Possible reinforcers and pleasurable events were assessed by the reinforcement survey schedule (Cautela & Kastenbaum, 1967) in order to develop alternative modes of behavior and possible sources for self-reinforcement.

3. *Contract system and self-administered response prevention*

The written contract signed by the patient and therapist, which was employed in the third week of treatment, contained the following rules:

- -- Maintenance of actual body weight with a maximum weight fluctuation of two kilograms. The body weight range should not decrease below 85% ideal body wight (IBW), which was calculated according the tables of the Metroplitan Life Insurance Statistical Bulletin (1959). The median of body weight at admission was 101% IBW.
- -- Body weight was measured twice a week.
- -- Three regular hospital meals plus two snacks had to be consumed together with the other patients.
- -- Patients were asked to abstain from hiding, hoarding or bartering food as well as from storing it in the room.
- -- Patients were asked to engage in pleasurable activities incompatible with bingeing and vomiting.
- -- For the most critical time, i.e. after meals, patients stayed together with other patients or a nurse for one to two hours in order to prevent self-induced vomiting.
- -- Random samples of serum potassium and serum chloride had to produce values within the normal range.

Adherence to the contract was positively reinforced only by the use of individualized rewards which the patients had specified in the reinforcement survey schedule (Cautela & Kastenbaum, 1967).

4. *Breaks from hospital treatment / partial hospitalization*

After reaching a stable improvement in bulimic behavior "intermittent vacation from treatment" was introduced step by step in order to test the stability and generalization of self-management outside the hospital and to enhance treatment transfer to natural conditions of living.

In the beginning of this phase patients were allowed to leave the hospital only for weekends. As a next step, time intervals outside the hospital were prolonged until two to three weeks before discharge, when the patient spent only evenings and nights in the hospital. "Partial hospitalization" enabled the therapist to discuss the problems in eating behavior occurring in the natural environment and the difficulties in the application of self-management skills.

5. *Problem-solving approach*

During the stage of "vacation from treatment", problems in the areas of work, school, or current living arrangement, as well as conflicts in close relationships, e.g. the patient's family or friends, became more apparent. Therefore occasional joint interviews with the family and/or friends of the patient were arranged.

This treatment program outlined so far was standardized and applied to eight patients.

Assessment

1. *Body weight*
   The patient's body weight was recorded twice a week in the morning after voiding, before breakfast.
2. *Distress and depressed mood*
   The AMS-self-rating measurement of well-being, von Zerssen (1986); original version: "Befindlichkeits-Skala" Bf-S, von Zerssen (1976a), measuring general distress, was filled out daily by the patients. The PDS (Paranoid-Depression-Scale, von Zerssen (1986)); original version: "Paranoid-Depressivitäts-Skala", von Zerssen (1976b), was used by the patients for self-evaluation on admission and at discharge. In addition, the IMPS (Inpatient Multidimensional Psychiatric Scale, Lorr & Klett, 1967) measuring the general psychopathology was administered. On admission and at discharge the IMPS factors relevant for depression ("anxious depression", "intropunitiveness", "retardation/apathy") were analyzed.
3. *Bulimic behavior*
   Information regarding the frequency of bingeing and vomiting was gathered from three different sources:
   (a) by medical records;
   (b) by semi-standardized interview on admission and at discharge, which was conducted by a psychologist who was blind regarding treatment conditions;
   (c) by the self-monitoring sheets used in the self-management training.

RESULTS

The mean hospital stay was 90 days in the self-management group and 101 days in the control group. Table 2 shows the individual raw data for the self-management group.

Table 2: **Treatment duration, distress and depressed mood in patients during self-management therapy (N = 8)**

Pat. no.	Duration of hospital stay (days)	Distress and depressed mood (% max) AMS A	AMS D	PDS-D A	PDS-D D	IMPS-D A	IMPS-D D
1	83	76.2	54.4	50.0	41.7	36.5	11.1
2	165	86.0	50.5	50.0	33.3	21.2	18.8
3	42	50.0	30.8	43.8	16.7	37.0	36.5
4	62	44.1	46.9	31.3	12.5	31.7	17.8
5	51	36.4	25.0	8.3	8.3	21.6	15.9
6	90	19.6	45.1	18.8	45.8	24.0	13.9
7	151	71.7	91.0	43.8	50.0	28.4	25.0
8	83	50.3	29.4	31.3	8.3	25.0	7.2
mean	90.9	54.3	46.6	34.7	27.1	28.2	18.3 *
SD	44.8	22.2	20.9	15.2	17.5	6.3	9.1

* $p < 0.01$
A - Admission
D - Discharge

Body weight

In the self-management group body weight of seven patients was within a range of 87-123 % IBW and remained quite constant during hospital treatment. One patient (no. 3) remained underweight (79 % IBW).

In the control group body weight ranged from 82-115 %, it was rather stable until discharge and did not differ significantly from body weights measured in the self-management group.

Distress and depressed mood

Table 2 indicates that during self-management training scores in the self-rated distress (AMS) and depressed mood (PDS) had decreased in five patients and increased in three patients at discharge. A significant decrease in IMPS factors relevant for depression reflects the improvement according to the clinical rating in all patients in the self-management group ($p \leq .01$, Wilcoxon-test for paired differences, one-tailed). There was no significant change in any of these variables in the control group.

Table 3: **Changes in bulimic behavior during self-management therapy (N = 8)**

Pat. no.	Bulimic Behavior Admission	Discharge
1	-	+
2	-	-
3	-	+
4	+ +	+ +
5	-	+
6	-	+
7	-	-
8	-	+

+ = improvement, i.e. up to one bulimic episode per week.
- = deterioration.

Bulimic behavior

On admission there was no significant difference in the frequency of bulimic attacks between the two groups. At discharge, as presented in Table 3, bulimic behavior in the self-management group improved significantly ($X^2 = 3.2$; $p < .05$, one-tailed) in five of seven patients. In one patient bulimic attacks ceased shortly after hospital admission (patient no. 4) and in two patients (patient no. 2 and patient no. 7) bulimic behavior persisted during the whole hospital stay, whereas only two patients in the control group had improved. Bulimic behavior was regarded as improved when the patient reported a frequency of less than one bulimic attack per week. A deterioration or persistence of bulimic symptomatology was defined when bulimic attacks occurred more frequently. During break from treatment, which was meant to foster treatment transfer, bulimic symptoms reoccurred in three patients (no. 2, 4, 7) under the natural conditions of daily living.

Four patients with a history of anorexia nervosa (patients no. 3, 4, 6, 7) showed a tendency towards a shift from vomiting to fasting. In two of them (patient no. 3 and patient no. 4) an operant reinforcement program for gaining weight (Bossert, Schnabel, Krieg & Berger, 1988) was administered, since their body weight was at or had decreased below 85% IBW, respectively.

DISCUSSION

In contrast to patients who did not receive self-management training, in six of eight patients in the self-management group bulimic attacks and vomiting decreased significantly during hospital treatment and, in one patient, ceased at the time of hospital admission. In two patients an operant reinforcement program for gaining weight (Bossert et al., 1988) was applied. Whereas the loss of control during previous binges was very distressing to these patients, motivation to gain weight as well as to abolish starvation-related symptoms was low. Treatment of these two cases of "demasked anorexia nervosa" was difficult and the response to treatment was rather low, especially in terms of weight gain.

The self-rated depressed mood improved in both treatment groups, but still remained high after hospital treatment. For the self-management training group the clinical rating of depressive symptoms revealed contradictory results, which have to be interpreted with caution, since the clinical rating was not carried out blind and was, therefore, possibly biased. The finding of a rather stable dysphoric state is confirmed by the often reported close relationship between bulimic and depressive symptoms (Hudson, Laffer & Pope, 1982; Hatsukami, Mitchell & Eckert, 1984; Swift, Andrews & Barklage, 1986; Lacey, 1985). Some studies (Norman & Herzog, 1986; Swift, Kalin, Wambolt, Kaslow & Rithoz, 1985), however, revealed contradictory results and the persistence of depressive symptoms in bulimia has to be assessed in long-term follow-up studies.

In contrast to the treatment results for bulimic patients, the behavioral hospital treatment of patients with anorexia nervosa led to a significant improvement in terms of depressive mood as well as weight gain (Bossert et al., 1987).

Most of the variables that have been found associated with a poorer treatment outcome, i.e. anorectic tendencies, severity of the personality disorder, major depression and continuing to live at home throughout treatment, were met in the patient sample investigated. Therefore, taking the general level of psychopathology into account, self-management training might be a useful additional therapeutic tool in order to achieve an improvement of the eating disorder. It was disappointing, however, that the effects of this specific, symptom-oriented treatment were rather modest and only slightly superior to a treatment condition, which did not provide any behavioral strategies to the patients in order to control symptoms. This finding, however, does not yet support the precaution of Andersen for instance that "outpatient programs designed especially for mild, monosymptomatic, normal weight bulimia may not work for more ill patients" (Andersen, 1985, p.117). The treatment recommendations given by Johnson (1985) are underscored by our findings: Johnson suggests that patients with a personality disorder, suffering from a polysymptomatic disturbance and having an impulse-dominated life history may require hospitalization. Since the transfer to a natural environment was only fostered in the self-management group we suppose, however, that the improvement in this group is more generalized and stable. This assumption, however, has to be proven by a two-year follow-up study in preparation.

Intervention aimed at life management, social integration and interpersonal problem solving were not the primary focus of the reported self-management treatment. Among the problems in living arrangements of the patients, material and financial dependence on others - mainly the parents - and an ambivalent attitude towards living at home seemed to be the most prominent areas of conflict. The significance of these factors regarding the prognosis of bulimia is further underscored by the results of the studies of Norman and Herzog (1984), Schwartz, Barrett, and Saba (1984) and Johnson and Berndt (1983). In this context, it can also be speculated that persistent depressive symptoms in the majority of patients studied might be attributed to the difficulties in life adjustment.

The fact that the self-management program only resulted in a modest therapeutic effect provided support for a more directive treatment, focusing on external control of bulimic behavior outlined below:

In the *preadmission interview* the treatment program is described and handed out in written form to the future patient. The future patient is requested to monitor eating and purging behavior for one week before hospital admission by using a special self-monitoring sheet. In addition to the recording of mood and physical activity, an eating diary is handed out to the patient in order to get information about the quality and quantity of food intake.

Besides stimulus narrowing and stimulus control, exposure plus response prevention is the main focus in the *first week* after hospital admission: The patient is requested to eat three regular hospital meals in the presence of the nursing staff in the dining room on the ward. In order to prevent purging behavior the patient is asked to remain in the company of a nurse for at least two hours after meals.

During the first week in hospital the patient leaves the hospital only accompanied by a nurse. The patient takes part in a relaxation training group in order to establish anxiety and tension-reducing behavior incompatible with purging (especially vomiting) and participated in an informal group for bulimic patients, which mainly serves modeling, mutual feedback exchange and motivational functions. Daily weight control has primarily anxiety-reducing functions and additionally serves as a precondition for correcting cognitive distortions about eating and weight.

In the *second week* external control of eating behavior is reduced by structuring the day by participation in different therapeutic groups.

Besides recreational and ergotherapeutic activities, perceptions and sensations related towards the own body are sensitized and modified in a "body-awareness training" group. Together with depressed patients the bulimic patients take part in a structured group therapy for three weeks with six 90-minute sessions focusing on activity planning, establishment of self-reinforcing behaviors (other than eating), training in alternative behaviors and adequate coping skills in situations which used to elicit binges or uncontrolled eating. Social counseling is offered to the patients already in the second week after hospital admission. In order to prevent avoidance behavior and a possible maintaining effect of social maladjustment on the eating disorder, an early analysis of psychosocial problems seems unavoidable, otherwise hospital stay is unnecessarily prolonged. From the *second week* on weight is only controlled on a weekly basis in order to enhance the tolerance of delayed feedback while food-intake during a structured timetable for meals is continued.

Vacation from hospital therapy is introduced stepwise, lasting from one afternoon to several days and, finally, partial hospitalization, when the patient only spends the night in the clinic, is implemented. This intermittent treatment is practiced from the *third week* onward in order to test the stability of eating behavior and to foster generalization and transfer of treatment effects to the natural conditions of living. This component seems to be crucial for the effect of an inpatient treatment program. Therefore the self-monitoring procedure applied during the preadmission phase is repeated during every break from hospital therapy and after discharge.

The revised behavioral treatment concept outlined so far was applied to more than 20 patients with bulimia. Although no empirical data are available up to now, the first experiences made with this approach seem quite promising.

REFERENCES

Andersen, A.E. (1985). *Practical comprehensive treatment of anorexia nervosa and bulimia*. London: Edward Arnold.

Bossert, S., Schnabel, E., Krieg, J.-C. & Berger, M. (1988). Modifications and problems of behavioural inpatient management of anorexia nervosa: A "patient-suited" approach ? *Acta Psychiatrica Scandinavica, 77*, 105-110.

Bossert, S., Schnabel, E, Krieg, J.-C., Molitor, P., Kemper, J. & Berger, M. (1987). Integratives stationär-ambulantes Therapiekonzept bei Patienten mit Anorexia nervosa: ein revidierter Therapieansatz. *Psychotherapie, Psychosomatik, Medizinische Psychologie, 37*, 331-336.

Cautela, J.R. & Kastenbaum, M.R. (1967). A reinforcement survey schedule for use in therapy, training and research. *Psychological Reports, 10*, 1115-1130.

Fairburn, C.G. (1981). A cognitive behavioral approach to the treatment of bulimia. *Psychological Medicine, 11*, 707-711.

Griffith, R.A. Touyz, S.W., Mitchell, P.B. & Bacon, W. (1987). The treatment of bulimia nervosa. *Australian and New Zealand Journal of Psychiatry, 21*, 5-15.

Hatsukami, D.K., Mitchell, J.E. & Eckert, E.D. (1984). Eating disorders: a variant of mood disorders ? *Psychiatric Clinics of North America, 7*, 349-365.

Hudson, J.I., Laffer, P.S. & Pope, H.G. (1982). Bulimia related to affective disorder by family history and response to the dexamethasone suppression test. *American Journal of Psychiatry, 137*, 695-698.

Johnson, C. (1985). Initial consultation for patients with bulimia and anorexia nervosa. In: D.M. Garner & P.E. Garfinkel (Eds.), *Handbook of psychotherapy for anorexia nervosa and bulimia* (19-51). New York: Guilford Press.

Johnson, C. & Berndt, D. (1983). Preliminary investigation of bulimia and life adjustment: a preliminary investigation. *American Journal of Psychiatry, 140*, 774-777.

Johnson, C., Connors, M., Beaumont, P.J.V. & Casper, R.C. (1987). *Handbook of eating disorders*. Amsterdam: Elsevier.

Kanfer, F.H. (1970). Self-regulation: Research, issues, and speculations. In: C. Neuringer & J.L. Michael (Eds.), *Behavior modification in clinical psychology* (178-220). New York: Appleton-Century-Crofts.

Lacey, J.H. (1985). Time-limited individual and group-treatment for bulimia. In: D.M. Garner & P.E. Garfinkel (Eds.), *Handbook of psychotherapy for anorexia nervosa and bulimia* (pp.431-457). New York: Guilford Press.

Lorr, M. & Klett, C.J. (1967). *Inpatient multidimensional psychiatric scales (IMPS)* (rev. ed.). Palo Alto/California: Consulting Psychologists Press.

Norman, D.K. & Herzog, D.B. (1984). Persistent social maladjustment in bulimia: a 1-year follow-up. *American Journal of Psychiatry, 141*, 444-446.

Norman, D.K. & Herzog, D.B. (1986). A 3-year outcome study of normal-weight bulimia: Assessment op psychosocial functioning and eating attitudes. *Psychiatry Research, 19*, 199-205.

Schwartz, R.C., Barrett, M.J. & Saba, G. (1984). Family therapy for bulimia. In: D.M. Garner & P.E. Garfinkel (Eds.), *Handbook of psychotherapy for anorexia nervosa and bulimia* (281-307). New York:

Guilford Press.
Metropolitan Life Insurance Co. (1959). *Statistical Bulletin of the Metropolitan Life Insurance Co.* (40, 1).
Swift, W.J., Andrews, D. & Barklage, N.E. (1986). The relationship between affective disorder and eating disorder: A review of the literature. *American Journal of Psychiatry, 143*, 290-299.
Swift, W.J., Kalin, N.H., Wambolt, F.S., Kaslow, N. & Rithoz, M. (1985). Depression in bulimia at 2- to 5-year follow-up. *Psychiatry Research, 16*, 111-122.
Wilson, G.T. (1985). Cognitive-behavioral and pharmacological therapies for bulimia. In: K.D. Brownell & I.P. Foreyt (Eds.), *Physiology, psychology and treatment of eating disorders* (pp. 60-94). New York: Basic Books.
Zerssen, D. von, with the assistance of Koeller, D.-M. (1976a). *Die Befindlichkeits-Skala-Parallelformen Bf-S und Bf-S'*. Weinheim: Beltz Verlag.
Zerssen, D. von, in collaboration with Koeller, D.-M. (1976b). *Klinische Selbstbeurteilungs-Skalen (KSb-S) aus dem Münchener Psychiatrischen Informations-System (PSYCHIS München), Manuale. a) Allgemeiner Teil: b) Die Beschwerden-Liste; c) Paranoid-Depressivitäts-Skala. Depressivitäts-Skala; d) Die Befindlichkeits-Skala*. Weinheim: Beltz Test.
Zerssen, D. von (1986). Clinical self-rating scales (CSRS) of the Munich Psychiatric Information System (PSYCHIS, München). In: N. Sartorius & T.A. Ban (Eds.), *Assessment of depression* (pp.270-303). Berlin: Springer.

ANALYSIS OF RELAPSE IN ALCOHOL ADDICTS

R. De Jong-Meyer, W. Brodd, & T. Heyden

Westfälische Wilhelms-Universität, Münster, F.R.G.

The relapse process of alcohol addicts is seen as a highly relevant but largely neglected research field. Marlatt & Gordon (1985), Cronkite & Moos (1980), Litman et al. (1979) and a few other researchers in this field have outlined behavioral-oriented multifactorial models, in which " ... relapse is viewed as a transitional process, a series of events that may or may not be followed by a return to baseline levels ... " (Marlatt & Gordon, 1985, p.32) of drinking. They recommend research focussing both on the immediate precipitating circumstances as well as on the longer chain of external and internal events preceding "High Risk Situations" (HRS). These are defined as situations, in which the probability of lapses ("any discrete violation of a self-imposed rule ...", Marlatt & Gordon, 1985, p.36) is heightened and which may eventually lead to a full return to the old drinking habits (relapse).

Comparing samples of relapsed and not (yet) relapsed alcoholic addicts, our findings so far (de Jong-Meyer et al., 1988) supported the model and previous findings on immediate precipitation circumstances. We found the following characteristics of "High Risk Situations" to be prominent subjects: Place of HRS was primarily "home", where the addicts had been drunk before, and where discriminative stimuli reminded at earlier drinking episodes. Alcohol was not easily available but there was a stock for 25% to 50% of the relapsed samples. Of the HRS, 3/4 occurred in the second half of the day with no preference of a particular day of the week.

One third of the relapsed addicts drank alone, the others with 1 to 5 persons mostly familiar to them. In 3/4 of the cases these other persons consumed alcohol too, but did barely exert any pressure on the addicts, neither positive nor negative.

As to *intrapsychic context*, the most prominent emotional states were anxious and depressive, and barely others like furious, annoyed or joyful. Thoughts were characterized primarily as depressive, worrisome or selfdevaluative. Nearly half of the relapsed subjects and one third in a not yet relapsed group reported thoughts circulating around the decision to drink or not to drink. Around one third of the relapsers admitted that alcohol consumption in the HRS was started as an attempt to controlled drinking. Only 30% of both types of addicts reported physical complaints and a third to a half had experienced craving sensations.

As relapse situations and "High Risk Situations" of not yet relapsed alcoholics didn't seem to differ much in their precipitating circumstances, we turned to the second set of assumptions concerning the longer chain of external and internal events, which may act as "covert" antecedents of relapses (Marlatt & Gordon, 1985).

The aims of the pilot investigations to be reported here were to accumulate in Germany empirical support for these covert antecedents, and to add and assess three new ones, namely patterns of irrational beliefs, drinking motives, and degree of self-communication.

METHOD

We compared two groups of *subjects*: alcohol addicts, who experienced a recent full-blown relapse (R), and, as "not yet" relapsed group, alcoholic addicts who managed a critical time period after discharge from inpatient treatment - at least three months - without a relapse (NR).

Several R-groups are studied by now (see de Jong-Meyer et al., 1988). The results of three of them are reported here, each consisting of 22 to 29 patients, 2/3 male. Their socioeconomic level was medium, with a high percentage (about 50%) of unemployment. Their addiction histories dated back 11 years on the average, with 3 or 4 inpatient treatments and a lot more relapse episodes in between. As we recruited them in inpatients programs, their last alcohol consumption was six to seven weeks ago. Two-third reported contacts to self-help-groups.

The NR-addicts (3 samples of 22 to 32 individuals) were recruited via clinics, self-help-groups or counseling personnel. They did not differ in most sample characteristics from the R-subjects, except that their unemployment rate was lower (25%), they had less inpatient treatments in their history, and their last alcohol consumption was more than four months ago. Nevertheless they all agreed (that was an entrance criterium) having experienced "High Risk Situations" in the recent past, which were defined as "situations that posed a problem in terms of heightened risk for relapse".

In addition one sample was recruited, where patients had to be abstinent for at least three months, then had a lapse incidence (following Marlatt & Gordon (1985), in the differentiation between lapses and relapses), but without developing their old drinking patterns again.

Assessment

The variables subsumed under covert antecedents of relapses were daily hassles, daily uplifts, should/want ratio, general coping repertoire, general and alcohol specific irrational belief style, drinking motives, self-communication, and apparently irrelevant decisions. These variables were either proposed by Marlatt & Gordon (1985) or introduced by us because of theoretical assumptions or previous work.

Most of the "covert antecedents of relapse" were assessed by reliable and valid scales chosen from the literature:

-- General coping: Stress Management Inventory, SVF (Janke et al., 1984)
-- Lifestyle variables: Daily Hassles Scale (Kanner et al., 1981); Daily Uplifts Scale (Kanner et al, 1981)
-- Irrational Beliefs: General and Alcoholic Specific Irrational Belief Scale, FID, consisting of 10 main irrational beliefs by Ellis (see Rohsenow & Smith, 1982), plus 9 alcoholic specific irrational beliefs (Brodd & Schimm, 1986)
-- Drinking motives: Drinking Motives Inventory (Antons & Schulz, 1976, adapted by Riedesel, 1987)
-- Self-communication: Inventory of Self-Communication for Adults, ISE (Tönnis, 1982)

The "Should/Want Ratio" was calculated from half standardized diary ratings (Farke, 1987, adapting the procedure proposed by Marlatt & Gordon, 1980). "Apparently Irrelevant Decisions" were assessed by a half-standardized inventory (Farke, 1987, using items from previous studies and from Marlatt & Gordon, 1985).

In addition a "High Risk Situation" inventory (Brodd et al., submitted, 35 items with precoded answer categories) developed in previous studies was used to gather information on HRS specific coping, substance effect expectancies as well as self-efficacy ratings.

RESULTS

Daily hassles, daily uplifts, should/want ratio (Sample 3)

Daily hassles (summary scale of the German version of the "Daily Hassles Scale" (Kanner et al., 1981), translated by Farke, 1987) were significantly more frequent in the relapsed group (N = 22) and they tended to be experienced more stressful than in the NR-group (N = 32). There were no qualitative differences concerning types of hassles, with one exception: "Having to wait" was reported as a hassle by 59% of the R- as compared to 27% of the NR-subjects.

There were no differences in the amount and experienced intensity of *daily uplifts* (summary scores of the German version of the "Daily Uplifts Scale" (Kanner et al., 1981), translated by Farke, 1987).

Table 1: **Means, standard deviations, significance level of t-tests-differences between R- and NR-subjects (Sample 1) in the factors of the SVF.**

Subtest	R (N = 22)		NR (N = 22)		
	M	SD	M	SD	p <
(1) Positive self instruction	15.82	3.9	19.23	3.9	.01
(2) Social withdrawal	11.55	6.0	4.68	3.4	.01
(3) Resignation	11.05	4.4	6.14	2.9	.01
(4) Selfpity	12.82	4.8	7.18	3.3	.01
(5) Selfattribution of guilt	15.36	4.2	9.59	3.1	.01
(6) Medication	8.18	5.5	2.95	1.8	.01
(7) Flight tendency	14.27	5.5	8.05	2.9	.01
(8) Avoidance tendency	14.23	5.3	10.64	5.1	.05
(9) Search for substitutes	9.14	6.1	13.95	5.1	.05
(10) Stimulus control trials	15.14	5.9	18.27	3.5	.05
(11) Denial	12.18	4.3	14.18	3.6	n.s.
(12) Minimization	8.73	4.9	10.45	4.0	n.s.
(13) Defense	11.14	4.8	12.45	3.2	n.s.
(14) Distraction	12.64	6.2	13.72	4.6	n.s.
(15) Search for self-reinforcement	12.45	5.6	13.95	4.8	n.s.
(16) Response control trials	15.41	5.0	17.13	4.1	n.s.
(17) Demand for social supp.	11.95	7.0	15.50	5.3	n.s.
(18) Thinking it over & over	15.86	4.0	12.64	5.3	n.s.
(19) Aggression	9.82	6.1	9.27	4.0	n.s.

Should/want ratios were assessed by diary rating scales. R-subjects (N = 22) did not differ in these ratios from NR-subjects (N = 22). One has to keep in mind here, however, that the days were not in relation to relapses or "High Risk Situations". Both groups were presumably abstinent during these days.

General coping repertoire (Sample 1)

The results in the coping repertoire factors of the "Stress Management Inventory" (SVF, Janke et al., 1984) are shown in table 1. A series of significant differences were found between the 22 Rs and 22 NRs addicts of this study (Runde & Skaletz, 1986). The NRs scored higher in "positive self-instruction", "search for substitutes" and "stimulus control attempts". The Rs scored higher in presumably more dysfunctional coping alternatives, like "social withdrawal", "resignation", "self-pity", "self-attribution of guilt", "medication" as well as "flight" and "avoidance-tendencies".

Asked about their *coping alternatives in the HRS* more than half of the R-subjects had no coping alternative available (a significant difference to the NR-subjects). Retrospectively the Rs thought primarily of the contacts to self-help-groups (SHG) as an alternative to drinking. The NRs responded more specifically, writing down the names of persons (instead of SHG in general) and in addition they reported intrapsychic coping strategies, too, which were similar to the general coping strategies (see above).

General and alcohol specific irrational belief style (Sample 1 + 2)

General as well as alcohol specific irrational belief style (Irrational Belief Scale, FID, following the "Ellis-items" by Rosenow and Smith, 1982, added by alcohol specific items, Brodd & Schimm, 1986) lead to the most replicated significant differences between our groups (see table 2).

The differences in the more general beliefs were consistently significant on the 5% level, the differences in alcohol specific irrational beliefs were even stronger in both samples.

Drinking Motives (Sample 2).

Drinking motives (here conceived as generalized positive substance effect expectancies) tended to be agreed by large percentages of both relapsed (N = 29) and non-relapsed addicts (N = 22, data from Riedesel, 1987). No significant differences emerged in the most prominent motives, which were: "Distracts from work, family problems" (93% versus 81%), "Makes one feel less shy" (89.7% versus 71.4%), "Makes loneliness/not being understood more bearable" (89.8% versus 71.4%), "Helps to cope with blueness/depressive feelings" (86.2% versus 71.4%), "Feeling more at ease

Table 2: **Means, standard deviations and significance level of t-test-differences between R and NR (Sample 1 + 2) in the scores of FID**

	Relapsed addicts (R) M	SD	Not-relapsed addicts (NR) M	SD	p <
General irrational beliefs (Sample 1: R=22, NR=22)	40.8	7.0	35.0	7.0	.05
General irrational beliefs (Sample 2: R=22, NR=27)	36.2	6.9	37.7	5.8	.05
Alcohol specific irrational beliefs (Sample 1: R=22, NR=22)	27.7	8.6	17.2	3.3	.01
Alcohol specific irrational beliefs (Sample 2: R=22, NR=27)	23.2	5.7	18.0	3.9	.01

at social gatherings" (82.8% versus 81%). Two motives were significant more frequent in the relapsed group: "Drives away boredom" (79.9% versus 31.5%) and "Enhancement of calmness and tranquility" (58.6% versus 23.8%).

As to substance effect expectancies in HRS, there were no differences in expected *behavioral effects*. These expected effects were positive, like "self-competent behavior" and "facilitation of social contacts". Differences emerged in some expected *cognitive and emotional substance effects*: The NRs anticipated more frequently to be confronted with "old problems" again if they would drink (a significant difference of 62% versus 28% of the R-subjects).
Significantly more R- than NR-subjects had expected to become relaxed if yielding to alcohol in the HRS (45% versus 9% of the NRs). More than half of both groups of subjects expected the dampening of negative feelings as the most prominent consequence of drinking.

Self-communication (Sample 2).

As a potential mediation variable between dysfunctional attitudes and life style (operationalized here with "daily hassles", "daily uplifts" and the "should/want ratio") we introduced self-communication in one of the studies (Riedesel, 1987). The "Self-Communication-Inventory" (ISE, Tönnis, 1982) allows to compute degree of total self-communication as well as degree of positively and negatively tuned self-communication separately.

Neither total self-communication scores of the R- and the NR-groups nor the scores in the subscales reflecting degree of positive self-communication did differ between the groups. The relapsed alcoholics did show a significant more pronounced negative self-communication than the NR-subjects.

Table 3: **Medium rank sums and significance level of z-test-differences between R (N=27) and NR (N=19) subjects in the ISE-subscales (Sample 3).**

	R (N=27)	NR (N=19)	
	mrs	mrs	p <
Dissatisfaction with oneself	27.0	18.5	.05
Selfresignation (self-effic. neg.)	27.8	17.3	.01
Negative mood states	27.7	17.5	.01
Total negative self-communication	28.1	17.0	.01
Satisfaction with oneself	23.5	23.5	n.s.
Selfmotivation (self-effic. pos.)	22.8	23.4	n.s.
Positive mood states	23.6	24.5	n.s.
Total positive self-communication	23.7	23.3	n.s.
Selfcommunication Total	26.7	18.9	n.s.

Apparently irrelevant decisions (Sample 3)

It is hypothesized by Marlatt & Gordon "that a person who is headed for a relapse makes a number of mini-decisions over time, each of which brings the individual closer to the brink of the triggering "High Risk Situation"" (Marlatt & Gordon, 1985, p.49). The findings of one investigation (Farke, 1987) supported the potential significance of these "covert antecedents". The R-subjects (N = 22) reported significantly more apparently irrelevant decisions (Mean number of irrelevant decisions of Rs: M = 7.73, mean number of irrelevant decisions of NRs (N = 32): M = 4.13, $p < .01$) and estimated their risk higher than the addicts without relapse ($U = 3.41$, $p < .001$).

Some items occurred significantly more often in the relapse group: "Reduction of social contact", "irregular visits at SHG-meetings", "not to admit addiction", "convinced of being able to drink moderately and give a try", "retreat within SHG" and "others".

DISCUSSION

In the investigation reported here, we compared samples of alcohol addicts, who recently experienced a full-blown relapse, with abstinent former addicts in a series of variables termed "covert antecedents". In our model derived from Marlatt & Gordon (1985) and other relapse concepts and findings, "covert antecedents" are seen as determinants of potential significance in the prediction of "High Risk Situations" and lapse/relapse chains of events.

Our findings empirically supported the "covert antecedents" proposed by Marlatt & Gordon and included hints to specify future concepts. Addicts with a recent relapse did not differ in number of daily positive events nor in their ratio of "should" to "want" activities but in number and subjective impact of "daily hassles". In addition they differed in their general ways of coping. They reported less "positive self-instruction", less "search for substitutes" or "stimulus control attempts", and more "social withdrawal", "resignation", "flight" as well as "avoidance tendencies", "self-pity", "self-attribution of guilt", and "medication". Concerning "High Risk Situations" for alcohol intake, they had less coping alternatives available, relying in a rather unconcrete way on self-help-group assistance. Furthermore they reported more apparently irrelevant decisions, characterized mainly by "social withdrawal" activities on the one hand and on the conviction, that they could manage moderate drinking on the other hand.

The addicts, who had successfully abstained for longer times, and who reported less hassles, a more active coping repertoire and less "irrelevant" mini-decisions, might be seen as models for designing relapse prevention strategies. Implications are, that relapse prevention strategies should focus on the assessment of "daily hassles", and on the teaching of coping strategies to deal with negatively tuned daily events, and on the assessment and change of mini-decisions prior to risk situations. Beyond these general implications, the findings suggest specific contents of the intervention procedures.

The three "covert antecedents" we added to existing relapse models, namely patterns of irrational beliefs, drinking motives and self-communication, all three turned out to be relevant, at least as far as differences between our samples are concerned. Parallel to the lifestyle balance findings discussed above, relapsed and not relapsed addicts did not differ in their degree of total nor in the degree of positively tuned self-communication, but only in the degree of negatively tuned self-communication. Together these findings lead to the speculative assumption that degree of negatively tuned arousal state may be the critical chain link towards "apparently irrelevant decisions" and to "High Risk Situations".

In the area of motives and substance effect expectancies, we found that not only relapsed alcoholics but even the abstinent ones still strongly believe in many positive functions of alcohol. Alcohol specific as well as general irrational beliefs, however, were shared by significantly more relapsed addicts.

Again, the findings on the nearly added "covert antecedents" have potential significance in tailoring relapse interventions. They call for implementing and evaluating behavior-cognitive components (e.g. restructuring of overgeneralized beliefs) in combination with interventions aimed at focussing perception away from negatively tuned inner states towards realistic perception of the self-environment-interactions.

The findings encourage replicative studies and further research efforts in the area of relapse analysis and prevention.

REFERENCES

Antons, K. & Schulz, W. (1976). *Normales Trinken und Suchtentwicklung.* Göttingen: Hogrefe.

Brodd, W. & Schimm, A. (1986). *Rückfall bei Alkoholabhängigen. Empirische Rückfallanalyse und Vergleich von rückfälligen und nicht-rückfälligen Alkoholabhängigen.* Unpublished diploma thesis. Westf. Wilhelms-Universität, Münster.

Brodd, W., Schimm, A., Runde, H., Skaletz, R. & de Jong-Meyer, R. (1987). *Analyse von Rückfällen bei Alkoholabhängigen.* Submitted.

Cronkite, R.C. & Moos, R.H. (1980). Determinants of the posttreatment functioning of alcoholic patients: A conceptual framework. *Journal of Consulting and Clinical Psychology, 48*, 305-316. Washington.

Farke, M. (1987). *Rückfall bei Alkoholabhängigen: Eine empirische Vergleichstudie unter besonderer Berücksichtigung von Lebensfaktoren.* Unpublished diploma thesis. Westf. Wilhelms Universität, Münster.

Janke, W., Erdmann, G. & Kallus, W. (1985). *Stressverarbeitungs-fragebogen (SVF).* Göttingen: Verlag für Psychologie.

de Jong-Meyer, R., Heyden, T., Schierik, H. & Skaletz, R. (1987). *Vergleich rückfälliger und nicht-rückfälliger Alkoholiker*. In press.

Kanner, A.D., Coyne, J.C. Schaefer, C. & Lazarus, R.S. (1981). Comparison of two models of stress management: Daily hassles and uplifts versus major life events. *Journal of Behavioral Medicine, 1*, 1-39.

Litman, G.K., Eiser, J.R., Rawson, S.B. & Oppenheim, A.N. (1979). Differences in relapse precipitants and coping behavior between alcoholic relapsers and survivors. *Behavior Research and Therapy, 17*, 89-94.

Marlatt, G.A. & Gordon, J.R. (1980). Determinants of relapse: Implications for the maintenance of behavior change. In: Davidson, P.O. & Davidson, S.M. (Eds.), *Behavioral Medicine: Changing health lifestyles*. New York: Bruner/Mazel.

Marlatt, G.A. & Gordon, J.R. (1985). *Relapse prevention. Maintenance strategies in the treatment of addictive behaviors*. New York, London: the Guilford Press.

Riedesel, D. (1987). *Der Rückfall bei Alkoholabhängigen. Eine Vergleichstudie unter der besonderer Berücksichtigung kognitiver Faktoren*. Unpublished diploma thesis. Westf. Wilhelms-Universität, Münster.

Rohsenow, D.J. & Smith, R.E. (1982). Irrational beliefs as predictors of negative affective states. *Motivation and Emotion, 6*, 299-314. New York.

Runde, H. & Skaletz, R. (1986). *Rückfall bei Alkoholabhängigen. Ein Vergleich rückfälliger und abstinent lebender Alkoholabhängiger*. Unpublished diploma thesis. West. Wilhelms-Universität, Münster.

Tönnis, S. (1982). *Inventar zur Selbstkommunikation (Testhandbuch)*. Weinheim: Beltz.

PART V:

BEHAVIOURAL MEDICINE

GROUP TREATMENT FOR ESSENTIAL HYPERTENSIVE PATIENTS IN GENERAL MEDICAL PRACTICE

H.D. Basler & B. Beisenherz

Institute for Medical Psychology, Marburg, F.R.G.

INTRODUCTION

According to the stress-hypothesis on essential hypertension psycho-social strains ("stress"), among other factors, play an important role in the development and maintenance of high blood pressure (Shapiro and Goldstein, 1980; Hodapp and Weyer, 1982; Linden, 1983). Although further research is needed to clarify the physiological links between psychological stress and long-range blood pressure elevations, animal experiments show the dependence of blood pressure regulation on the activity of the endocrine glands. Hormones produced in the tissue of the brain, e.g. angiotensin, seem to have a mediating function. In borderline hypertensive patients, blood pressure reactivity was connected in a specific way to stress-stimuli on a psychological, not a physical level (Weder and Julius, 1985). So, in the treatment of high blood pressure, training to improve stress management seems advisable for those subjects whose increase in blood pressure can be seen to be related to their life style.

The first studies on stress management with essential hypertensive subjects were carried out by Jorgenson et al. (1981), Haag et al. (1982) and Crowther (1983). In a carefully planned study, Kallinke et al. (1982) found clinically relevant reductions in blood pressure of 19/10 mmHg with a starting level of 154/102 mmHg after a one year follow-up. Recent studies focussed on relaxation training, which usually is a part of a comprehensive stress-management programme, and found relaxation to be superior to a waiting-list condition (Hatch et al., 1985), or to mild exercise (Irvine et al., 1986).

Blanchard et al. (1986) reported a significant reduction in medication as a consequence of relaxation treatment. Hatch et al. (1985) did not find subsequent blood pressure elevations in subjects who showed medication reductions after psychological treatment. In a review, Johnston (1985) found evidence that relaxation and stress management can lower blood pressure by useful amounts in mild primary hypertension although the mechanisms underlying these reductions are unclear. Meanwhile, essential hypertensives in a study of Zurawski et al. (1987), who participated in a multimodal stress management training, exhibited reliably lower resting diastolic blood pressure and tended to exhibit lower systolic pressures than GSR-feedback controls. Effects remained stable through a 6-month follow-up period. Knox et al. (1986) found a stress management training to be an effective alternative to medication treatment in mild hypertensives in the Swedish primary health care system. In a pilot study with 13 subjects, the mean blood pressure level could be lowered from 151/96 mmHg to 125/89 mmHg. Their sample, however, was very small and controls were lacking. Anyway, if behavioural treatment of hypertensive patients shall gain broader efficacy, it must be introduced into a primary care setting. In the FRG, most hypertensives are discovered and treated by general practitioners. This is the reason why general physicians should be offered a training in stress management procedures.

In a pilot stage we first examined the implementation of a stress-coping programme in two general practices with a total of 41 essential hypertensives being treated with medication. Patients of each practice were assigned either to a treatment or to a waiting-list control group. Treatment was conducted by clinical psychologists on a group outpatient basis and resulted in significant blood pressure reductions (Jaekel and Basler, 1985).

After a revision and standardization of the treatment programme, we conducted the main study described here, in which now specially trained general practitioners themselves worked as therapists. We are testing the assumption that improvements on the psychological level (emotional state, complaints, increase in the ability to cope with stress, behavioural changes), as well as on the medical level (changes in the medication, reduction in blood pressure) can be proven to result from participation in a standardized group treatment programme for the promotion of stress management.

PROGRAMME DESCRIPTION

The programme "Relaxation and Stress-Management for Essential Hypertensives" is based on Lazarus' (1967) transactional stress model according to which stress reaction occurs in the interaction of stressful events and individual coping processes. Cognitions related to the character of the stress agent as well as to the availability of coping strategies determine whether potentially stressful events take effect as actual stress agents, which then cause stress-reactions at somatic, cognitive-emotional, and behavioural levels, and through which coping attempts are introduced (Basler, 1986a).

In this context, the patients learn the Jacobson method of progressive muscle relaxation, where a tape with a relaxation text is made available to them as an aid to home practice. Further, the patients are taught to concertedly balance out strain through activities which they find pleasurable and which increase their quality of life.

To make the connection between stress of living and blood pressure level clear to the patients, they measure their own blood pressure and complete a measurement protocol. This protocol also serves as a report on the success of the treatment during the group work.

Parallel to this, the patients are given information about the causes and risk of high blood pressure, the effects of the medication, and of sodium chloride consumption. The possibilities of reduced salt diets are repeatedly stressed, where particular value is placed on the motivation to change behaviour.

The programme is conducted in standardized form from a manual in which 12 group meetings of 90 minutes each are planned. There is also a theoretical manual for the group leader, in which the concept of the programme is explained. The programme is offered in the waiting room of the doctor's practice to essential hypertensives of normal weight who are under stress. To make it possible for every patient to actively take part in the group discussion, no more than 6 patients should make up a group.

General physicians in the WHO community intervention area near Heidelberg (Malchow et al., 1984), who before had participated in various intervention programmes on a community basis, cooperated in the study. A group leader training was offered to them which involved 20 hours on a weekend (Friday to Sunday). Special emphasis was laid on trial therapy sessions and behavioural training. During the practical work with the groups further individual counselling was offered.

DESIGN

Eight general practitioners in individual conversations motivated 10 - 12 patients each to participate in the stress management programme and the associated scientific research. Besides essential hypertension and existing stress-load, the criteria for patient selection were normal weight, since there is another version of the programme available for over-weight patients (Basler, 1986b). In each practice the patients were divided alternatively, in the order of being selected for the programme, into a test- and waiting-control group. However, in certain cases the group assignment had to be corrected because of scheduling difficulties for the patients.

After the patients had agreed to the associated scientific research and to the recording of their personal data, all of them had to participate in an half an hour interview and had to answer standardized questionnaires. After a rest period at the end of the interview, the patients' blood pressure was measured with an electronic device (Visocor from the Hestia Company) while sitting, as well as the body size and weight recorded on the office scales.

Apart from a specification of the stress-load and the medication, the interview also included questions about hypertension-related health knowledge, health behaviour including sodium chloride consumption, and sociodemographic details. In recording the sodium chloride consumption, we concentrated on the habitual amount of salt added at the table, particularly with specific foods such as tomatoes, radishes, or eggs. We also concentrated on the habitual consumption of foods with a high salt content, for instance, salted nuts, smoked ham, or instant soups.

We used the following standardized questionnaires:

-- Emotional-State Scale (BF-S version from von Zerssen, 1976a). This consists of a list of items registering the subjective mood between the depressive and the manic pole. An increase in the values indicates greater depressive disorder.
-- List of Complaints (B-L version from von Zerssen, 1976b). Common physical and general complaints are registered here.
-- Stress-Coping questionnaire (SVF) from Erdmann, Janke and Boucsein (1978).

With the help of the latter questionnaire, the form of individual coping styles in stress situations was explored in which a total of 17 different coping styles are analyzed (for example: aversion, the need to talk, the consumption of medications and stimulants). Instead of the original 128 items, we used a shortened version of the test developed by Knispel (1982) in our study, which we expanded on a scale for "active problem-solving" developed by Küchler (1984). After conclusion of the pre-test (t1), group treatment, lasting for 12 weeks, began.

Subsequently, the practitioners had to check the medication for the test and waiting-control groups and adjust it to the expected change in blood pressure level. The adjustments in medication were recorded.

Two to three months after the conclusion of the group treatment the patients were contacted again (t2). An interview and a questionnaire study were again conducted, the content of which was identical to that of the first measurement. Moreover, an additional measurement instrument was also introduced:

-- Questionnaire on the change in well-being and behaviour (Zielke and Kopf-Mehnert, 1978).

The questionnaire measures the degree and direction of the changes in experience and behaviour of patients after the conclusion of psychotherapy; the poles being "relaxation, calmness and optimism" versus "tension, insecurity, and pessimism".

Three months later, experimental subjects were again sent a questionnaire in which they were asked to evaluate the treatment programme (t3).

DESCRIPTION OF THE SAMPLE

First interviews were conducted with 41 patients from the test group and with 38 patients from the waiting-control group. Second interviews with 31 patients from each group have been carried out. Those patients had to be excluded who did not meet the criteria for patient selection or who missed the second interview. Only one patient dropped out of treatment.

The proportion of women in the test group totals 41.9 %, in the control group 35.9 %. The difference was not significant ($Chi^2 = 0.2719$; df = 1; n.s.). The test group (M = 44.7 years, sd = 11.1) appeared to be somewhat younger than the control group (M = 48.8 years, sd = 8.1). This difference was also not statistically significant (t = 1.78; df = 60; n.s.). Asked about their stress-load, 17.7 % reported personal relation problems at work, 58.1 % work itself. A proportion of 48.4 % of the patients were convinced that their occupational stress was detrimental to their health. Financial strains were mentioned by 17.7 %. Strains in the family due to conflicts with the partner, parents, or children were mentioned by 48.4 %; 43.5 % felt stressed because of the state of their health. The stress from the household, i.e. the household and profession, played a role in 52.2 % of the reasons given by women.

RESULTS

State of Health, Health Behaviour, and Health Knowledge

Where at first interview, 41.4 % of the patients in the experimental group rated their state of health as good or very good, this was 71.0 % at the second interview. This change was significant (Wilcoxon: z = 2.86; $p < 0.01$). The control group exhibited a change from 35.5 % to 38.7 %. This change was not significant (Wilcoxon; z = 0.47; n.s.).

The health knowledge of the patients improved significantly in the experimental group (Wilcoxon: $z = 4.78$; $p < 0.01$) as well as in the control group (Wilcoxon: $z = 2.99$; $p < 0.01$). Salt consumption was reduced in the experimental group only. Thus, the proportion of those patients in the experimental group who do not add salt at the table increased from 45.2 % to 64.5 % (Wilcoxon: $z = 2.72$; $p < 0.01$). A tendency in the opposite direction was observed in the control group from 51.6 % to 41.9 % ($z = 1.14$; n.s.). General health behaviour (physical activity, smoking) remained unchanged in the experimental group and the control group.

Change in Well-Being and Behaviour

A score on the questionnaire of change in well-being and behaviour over 192 means a significant improvement at the one percent level (Zielke and Kopf-Mehnert, 1978). It is shown that 64.5 % of the patients in the experimental group is above this value as opposed to 18.2 % in the control group. The difference was statistically significant ($Chi^2 = 11.15$; $df = 1$; $p < 0.01$). Significant deteriorations were not reported in either the experimental group or the control group.

Change in Complaints, Emotional State, and Stress-Coping

Since the single scales of the stress-coping questionnaire seemed to measure either stress-intensifying or stress-minimizing strategies (face validity), we asked four psychological experts to categorize all scales into those which are stress-intensifying and those which are stress-minimizing. The following strategies measured by the questionnaire were rated being stress-intensifying: self-accusation, social isolation, resignation, avoidance, self-pity, physical symptoms, medication and stimulant usage, and brooding. Projection, bagatellization, substitutive gratification, the need to talk, outwardly directed aggression, distraction, intellectualization, self-evaluation through comparison with others, and active problem solving were categorized to be stress-minimizing. In processing the data, together with the information from the complaint questionnaire and the state of health scale, only two coping variables are to be used in the multivariate analysis of variance.

Before the effects of individual variables are analyzed, it should first be examined whether the effects are significant in multivariate comparison. A significant interaction was shown here between group and time ($F = 3.60$; $df = 4.43$; $p < 0.01$) as well as a significant effect of time ($F = 5.75$; $df = 4.43$; $p < 0.01$). A group effect could not be shown ($F = 1.27$; $df = 4.43$; n.s.).

Table 1 presents the effects of the individual variables included in the analysis. Results show the following:

-- a reduction of the stress-intensifying coping styles in the experimental group
-- a significant increase in the stress-minimizing coping styles in the experimental group
-- a significant drop in complaints to the same degree in both the experimental group and the control group.

The change in emotional state is not significant. Only the change in the coping strategies can be assessed as an effect of the programme.

Analysis of Changes in Stress-Coping

Since it could be proved that the coping style changes as a result of the programme, it seems justifiable, using a univariate analysis, to examine which of the strategies measured by the coping questionnaire were influenced by the programme. For this reason we tested the average changes in coping styles for significance using t-tests for paired samples.

Table 1: **Means (M) and Standard Deviations (sd) in Stress-Coping, Emotional State, and Complaints for the Experimental Group (n=27) and the Control Group (n=21) as well as the results of the univariate variance analyses.**

	Exper. Group		Control Group			Effects	
	t1 M (sd)	t2 M (sd)	t1 M (sd)	t2 M (sd)	Grp	Grp x Time	Time
Stress-intensifying Coping Styles	53.3 (15.8)	40.3 (14.5)	55.5 (19.9)	54.9 (23.4)	n.s.	<.01	<.01
Stress-minimizing Coping Styles	72.1 (18.0)	78.1 (12.0)	72.5 (15.2)	70.1 (15.8)	n.s.	<.05	n.s.
Emotional State Scale	13.0 (9.2)	9.6 (9.2)	15.1 (10.1)	14.5 (9.9)	n.s.	n.s.	n.s.
Complaint List	25.5 (10.4)	19.7 (9.5)	24.3 (10.0)	22.0 (9.9)	n.s.	n.s.	<.01

It can be concluded from the analysis that on a 1 % level of significance absolutely no changes in coping styles can be determined for the control group. The following coping styles changed in a positive way as a result of the programme: self-accusation, resignation, physical symptoms, medication and stimulant usage as well as brooding on some stressful event. Only bagatellization increased in the stress-minimizing coping styles.

MEDICAL SUCCESS CRITERIA

Medication

After completion of the group treatment, the doctors examined whether the medication should be changed as a result of the changed blood pressure values for the patients in the experimental group and the control group. At the time t2, the experienced changes were recorded.
There were significant differences between experimental group and control group in the termination and reduction of medication as compared to the change of the medication, unaltered medication and medication increase ($Chi^2 = 3.923$; $df = 1$; $p < 0.05$).

Table 2: **Changes in Medication for the Experimental Group and Control Group**

	Experimental n	Group %	Control n	Group %
Termination of Medication	8	30.8	2	8.0
Reduction of the Dosage	4	15.4	3	12.0
Medication unaltered	11	42.3	16	8.0
Change in the Medication	3	11.5	1	4.0
Dosage increased or newly prescribed Medication	0	0.0	3	21.0
No Medication at t1 & t2	5		6	

Blood Pressure

Considering the hypothesis of a blood pressure reduction in addition to the reduction of the medication, a multivariate analysis of variance was conducted, in which the systolic and diastolic blood pressure levels were included. In the experimental group mean blood pressure values changed from 146.3/92.3 mmHg (sd = 17.1/10.8) to 138.2/88.4 mmHg (sd = 17.0/14.1). In the control group there was a change from 143/96.1 mmHg (sd = 18.8/12.0) to 139.2/89.0 mmHg (sd = 16.4/8.7).

The multivariate comparison shows exclusively an effect of time ($F = 5.57$; $df = 2.59$; $p < 0.01$), but not a group effect ($F = 1.10$; $df = 2.59$; n.s.) or interaction ($F = 1.87$; $df = 2.59$; n.s.).

FOLLOW-UP

Three months after the second interview was conducted, the patients from the experimental group were asked to evaluate the programme by a questionnaire and indicate the practical use of what they had learned under every day conditions.

To the question what in the programme had helped them the most, 15 people mentioned the relaxation exercises and 12 the training to cope with problems. Only 3 mentioned the search for a counterbalance to strains. These statements are supplemented with spontaneous remarks. Accordingly, 17 patients stressed the importance of the group discussions with patients with similar problems.

On the whole, the course was judged as good. Twenty-five patients will empathically recommend it to other patients without reservations. Only one patient will not express such a recommendation.

DISCUSSION

The stress management programme resulted in an improvement of the observed state of health, a reduction in stress-intensifying coping styles and an increase in stress-minimizing coping styles, a change of attitude towards the pole "relaxation, calmness and optimism" and a reduction of the medication. However, therapy and control group did not differ in changes of general health behaviour, emotional state, physical complaints, and blood pressure. Obviously the programme was successful in influencing subjective state of health and stress-coping strategies.

Effects on the blood pressure level specifically due to the programme cannot be proved since the blood pressure drops equally in both the experimental group and the control group. It should be noted, however, that apart from five subjects in the therapy group and eight subjects in the control group, all of them had initially been treated by various drugs and their blood pressure consequently had dropped to borderline values so that a further drop would be difficult to detect.

The most striking effect on the programme seems to be the fact that the medication could either be discontinued or essentially reduced for more than 40% of those patients who had been initially treated by drugs. No similar effect can be shown in the control group. Blanchard et al. (1986) also report medication reductions in subjects whose blood pressures were controlled on a regimen of at least two drugs. After thermal feedback relaxation training, 35% of the patients remained off the second-stage medication for over 12 months. In a study on the effects of a behavioural training for obese essential hypertensives, we found that 30% of the patients could reduce their drug consumption after a weight-loss of 5-6 kg (Basler, 1987). Since many patients fear potential damage of a long-term medication, these findings should reinforce the integration of adequate coping into every-day living. Follow-up data one year after treatment will allow to test the stability of the reported results.

In a randomized controlled trial, Patel and Marmot (1987) showed that relaxation and stress-management training were associated with a reduction in blood pressure maintained over four years of observation. Patients who practiced relaxation in everyday life and used cognitive reappraisal in coping with stress, showed greater reductions in blood pressure than those who did not. Subjects in the treatment group reported significant improvements regarding their relationships at work, general health, enjoyment of life, and personal and family relationships as compared to controls at a 4-year follow-up.

There is considerable evidence that relaxation and stress-management not only are effective in enhancing the quality of life, but they also contribute significantly to a better control of blood pressure with smaller doses of drugs, thus reducing the chances of side-effects.

This study was conducted in cooperation with GALENUS MANNHEIM company.
The following general practitioners took part in the study: H. Bergdolt (Wiesloch), W. Billich (Hockenheim), K. Ebschner (Eberbach), B. Müller-Wittig (Brühl), H. Ruck (Rheinstetten-Forchheim), M. Stafunsky (Marburg), K. Uffelman (Gemünden), and A. Wiesemann (Odenheim).

REFERENCES

Basler, H.D. (1986a). Entspannung und Stressbewältigung ein Trainingsprogramm für essentielle Hypertoniker. *Allgemeinmedizin, 15*, 187-193.

Basler, H.D. (1986b). Die Prävention von Koronarer krankungen in der allgemeinärztlichen Praxis - ein gesundheitspolitisch relevantes

Kooperationsmodell zwischen Universität und Industrie. In: K. Nöldner & H. Kreuter (Eds.), *Medizin - Gesundheit - Politik. Prävention als interdisziplinäre Aufgabe* (155-170). Köln: Deutscher Ärzte-Verlag.

Basler, H.D. (1987). "Hypertonie im Gespräch" - Ergebnisse eines bundesweiten Einsatzes des Gruppenprogramms für adipöse essentielle Hypertoniker. *Münchener Medizinische Wochenschrift, 129*, 703-705.

Basler, H.D., Brinkmeier, U., Buser, K., Haehn, K.D. & Mölders-Kober, R. (1985). Psychological group treatment of obese essential hypertensives by lay therapists in rural general practice settings. *Psychosomatic Research, 29*, 383-391.

Crowther, J.H. (1983). Stress management training and relaxation imagery in the treatment of essential hypertension. *Journal of Behavioural Medicine, 8*, 169-187.

Erdmann, G., Janke, W. & Boucsein, W. (1987). Der Stressverarbeitungsfragebogen. *Ärztliche Praxis, 15*, 1208-1210.

Haag, G., Larbig, W. & Birbaumer, N. (1982). Psychologische Verfahren zur Behandlung der essentiellen Hypertonie. In: D. Vaitl (Ed.), *Essentielle Hypertonie* (203-223). Berlin: Springer.

Hatch, J.P., Klatt, K.D., Supik, J.D. & Rios, N. (1985). Combined behavioral and pharmacological treatment of essential hypertension. *Biofeedback and Self Regulation, 10*, 119-138.

Hodapp, V. & Weyer, G. (1982). Zur Stress-Hypothese der essentiellen Hypertonie. In: D. Vaitl (Ed.), *Essentielle Hypertonie* (112-139). Berlin: Springer.

Hoelscher, T., Lichstein, K.L. & Rosenthal, T.L. (1986). Home relaxation practice in hypertension treatment: Objective assessment and compliance induction. *Journal of Consulting and Clinical Psychology, 54*, 217-221.

Irvine, M.J, Johnston, D.W., Jenner, D.A. & Marie, G.V. (1986). Relaxation and stress management in the treatment of essential hypertension. *Journal of Psychosomatic Research, 30*, 437-450.

Jaekel, H. & Basler, H.D. (1985). Verhaltenstherapie mit Gruppen normalgewichter essentieller Hypertoniker in der Allgemeinpraxis. *Psychotherapie Psychosomatik Medizinische Psychologie, 35*, 219-224.

Johnston, D.W. (1985). Psychological interventions in cardiovascular disease. *Psychosomatic Research, 29*, 447-456.

Jorgensen, R.S., Houston, B.K. & Zurawski, R.M. (1981). Anxiety management training in the treatment of essential hypertension. *Behaviour Research and Therapy, 19*, 467-474.

Kallinke, D., Kulick, B. & Heim, P. (1982). Psychologische Behandlungsmöglichkeiten bei essentiellen Hypertonikern. In: K. Köhle (Ed.), *Zur Psychosomatik von Herz-Kreislauf-Erkrankungen* (p.75-93). Berlin: Springer.

Kaluza, G. & Basler, H.D. (1986). *Entwicklung und Evaluation eines Programms zur Stressbewältigung*. Abschlussbericht an die Bundeszentrale für gesundheitliche Aufklärung in Köln.
Knispel, M. (1982). *Vegetative Labilität, subjektives Belastungserleben und Möglichkeiten der Stressbewältigung bei Migränikern - eine vergleichende Studie*. Unveröffentliche Diplomarbeit, Marburg.
Knox, S., Thorell, T., Malmberg, B.G. & Lindqvist, R. (1986). Stress management in the treatment of essential hypertension in primary health care. *Scandinavian Journal of Primary Health Care, 4*, 175-181.
Küchler, P. (1984). Stressbewältigung bei Migräne. Unveröffentlichte Diplomarbeit, Marburg, FRG.
Lazarus, P.S. (1967). Stress theory and psychophysiological research. In: L. Levi (Ed.), *Emotional stress*. Basel: Karger.
Linden, W. (1983). *Psychologische Perspektiven des Bluthochdrucks*. Basel: S. Karger.
Malchow, H., Neumeister, H., Nüssel, E., Bergdolt, H. & Ebschner, K.J. (1984). *Prävention in der Praxis*. München: Münchner wissenschaftliche Publikationen.
Patel, E. & Marmot, M.G. (1987). Stress management, blood pressure and quality of life. *Journal of Hypertension* (Suppl.), 5, 21-28.
Shapiro, D. & Goldstein, I.B. (1980). Verhaltensmuster und ihre Beziehung zur Hypertonie. In: J. Rosenthal (Ed.), *Arterielle Hypertonie* (12-25). Berlin: Springer.
Weder, A.B. & Julius, S. (1985). Behavior, blood pressure variability and hypertension. *Psychosomatic Medicine, 47*, 406-412.
Von Zerssen, D. (1976a). *Die Befindlichkeits-Skala*. Weinheim: Beltz.
Von Zerssen, D. (1976b). *Die Beschwerde-Liste*. Weinheim: Beltz.
Zielke, M. & Kopf-Mehnert, C. (1978). Veränderungs-fragebogen des Erlebens und Verhaltens. Weinheim: Beltz.
Zurawski, R.M., Smith, T.W., & Houston, B.K. (1987) Stress management for essential hypertension: comparison with a minimally effective treatment, predictors of response te treatment, and effects on reactivity. *Journal of Psychosomatic Research*, 31, 453-462.

THE EFFECTS OF A PSYCHO-EDUCATIONAL GROUP INTERVENTION PROGRAMME ON THE REHABILITATION OF CORONARY HEART PATIENTS

T. van Elderen, & S. Maes

Tilburg University, Department of Psychology, The Netherlands

THE TRADITIONAL REHABILITATION PROGRAMME

Apart from pharmacological therapy and medical advice concerning specific life-styles, the hard core of the traditional rehabilitation programme is physical training. Physical training is initiated during hospitalization and intensified after the patient is dismissed from hospital. On average, the frequency and duration of the physical training given in the Netherlands is 2 to 5 times a week for a period of 2 to 3 months.

In addition to physical training, physicians prescribe medication and give advice with respect to specific health behaviours. It is often their opinion that it is the patients own responsibility to comply with this medical advice.

The traditional rehabilitation programme, consisting of physical training and "standard medical care" aims mainly at the recovery of physical functioning. The idea behind this being that physical recovery will, among other things, enhance psychosocial functioning and self confidence and reduce anxiety and depression (Wenger, 1979). Research has demonstrated, however, that the traditional physical training programme for coronary heart patients has limited physical and psychosocial effects.

Firstly, experimental studies only show short-term successes on physical condition (De Backer, 1980; Vermeulen et al., 1978; Mayou, 1981; Mayou et al., 1981). There are also no indications for mortality and morbidity (reinfarct rate within one year) to reduce in short-term physical training groups compared to non-training groups (Commission for the Rehabilitation of Heart Patients of the Dutch Heart Foundation, 1977; International Society and Federation of Cardiology Scientific Councils, 1981).

Secondly, the psychosocial effects of the traditional rehabilitation programme are also limited. Experimental studies have shown no stable significant differences in psychological functioning between patients after short-term physical training and patients who did not receive physical training (McPherson et al., 1967; Mayou, 1981; Mayou et al., 1981; Erdman et al., 1984). Although some research has demonstrated positive effects of physical training on re-employment (Erdman et al., 1984; Kellerman et al., 1968), most studies fail to find any effects (Diederiks, 1982).

Thirdly, physical training is characterized by a drop-out phenomenon, which may range from approximately 30% to 70% (Martin & Dubbert, 1982).

Fourthly, the traditional rehabilitation programme has a limited impact on specific health behaviours. Whereas individuals who quit smoking exhibit lower morbidity and mortality than those who continue to smoke, Burling et al. (1984) showed in a review study that only one third to one half of the smokers reduced or quit smoking following myocardial infarction. Ley (1976), the US Food and Drug Administration (1979), and Barofsky (1980) provided reviews on percentages of patients complying with medication regimens. They found a range of non-compliant percentages from 39 to 61% for different types of patients, including for hypertensive patients. Heller et al. (1982) reported adherence percentages on behaviour risk factors 3½ years after coronary artery bypass surgery. With respect to diet prescriptions, only 22% said to be fully compliant. With respect to physical exercise, only 38% followed medical advice fully. As these data are derived from self-reports, real adherence percentages may be even lower. It can, therefore, be concluded that adherence with medical advice can be improved.

Summarizing the effects of the traditional rehabilitation programme (physical exercise, pharmacological therapy and medical advice concerning specific health behaviours) the conclusion is justified that:

1. There are temporary effects on physical condition.
2. There are temporary effects and/or limited results on psychosocial recovery.
3. Adherence with medical advice concerning smoking cessation, diet, physical exercise, and medication regimens can be improved.
4. Long-term physical rehabilitation programmes seem to have more favourable effects, but are characterized by high drop-out rates.

Considering these conclusions, the literature was reviewed on the physical and psychosocial effects of health education and counseling (also called 'psycho-educational' interventions) on the rehabilitation of coronary heart patients, in order to see whether such programmes could enhance the attainment of rehabilitation objectives.

STUDIES ON HEALTH EDUCATION AND COUNSELING

Studies on psycho-educational interventions during cardiac rehabilitation can be divided into two groups: (a) studies investigating the effects of a combination of physical training and health education (Kallio et al., 1979; Roviaro et al., 1984) and (b) studies investigating the effects of health education programmes exclusively (Ibrahim et al., 1974; Rahe et al., 1979; Dracup et al., 1984; Horlick et al., 1984; Thockloth et al., 1973).

In two experimental studies a combination of physical exercise training and health education was investigated. Kallio et al. (1979) found significant differences on mortality, weight reduction, serum cholesterol level, level of serum triglycerides, systolic and diastolic blood pressure and compliance with medication regimens, in favour of the intervention group. Roviaro et al. (1984) found that patients in the experimental group had significantly more knowledge about coronary heart diseases, were more compliant with medication regimens, diet and physical exercise prescriptions, had a higher level of physical activities, had a more positive self-perception, participated more in social and leisure activities, had a slower heart rate and a lower systolic blood pressure than patients in the control group. Although the results of these studies were favourable, it is not clear which part of the intervention (physical training, health education, or the combination of the two) was responsible for these effects.

Intervention studies, which investigated the effects of health education programmes exclusively, found positive effects on the mortality rate (Ibrahim et al., 1974; Rahe et al., 1979), reinfarct rate (Rahe et al., 1979), period of rehospitalization (Ibrahim et al., 1974), body-fat (Dracup et al., 1984), reemployment (Rahe et al., 1979; Thockloth et al., 1973), working overtime and time-pressure (Rahe et al., 1979), social alienation (Ibrahim et al., 1974) and depression (Thockloth et al., 1973). Although different programmes seem to have differential effects, there is a trend in the results for the programmes to be more successful when patients focus on modification of risk behaviours than for programmes with unstructured free discussions between patients and/or their partners (Maes et al., 1987). As a consequence of this literature review, we constructed a psycho-educational group intervention programme.

PSYCHO-EDUCATIONAL GROUP INTERVENTION

This psycho-educational group intervention has the following characteristics:

a. The training is *complementary* to the standard medical rehabilitation programme;
b. The training involves two components. Information is given about crucial aspects of coronary heart disease. Besides *information* provision, *rational emotive behaviour modification* aiming at the alteration of cognitions inhibiting somatic and psychosocial recovery is also a corner stone of the programme;
c. The training is *multidisciplinary*. As an integrated team disciplines involved in the treatment of patients with coronary heart disease bring a coherent message to patients and partners;
d. For reasons of efficiency, the training is given in *groups* of five to eight patients.
e. *Partners* are invited not only because they have their own problems, but also because the objectives are reached a lot easier if partners support compliance with medical advice and healthy life-styles.
f. Patients are encouraged to be responsible for their own health, to *actively participate* in the programme in order to benefit fully from it.

The main objectives of this psycho-educational group intervention are: (a) to increase compliance with medical advice concerning: medication, smoking, diet, physical exercise and type A behaviour, and (b) to reduce emotional distress, i.e. anxiety, anger, vital exhaustion and depression, feelings of invalidity, displeasure and social inhibition.

The effects of the programme were assessed by means of a randomized pretest-posttest control group design, which is described below.

THE EFFECT STUDY

Method

Subjects

51 male and 4 female coronary heart patients between the ages of 37 and 72 took part in the study. These patients were referred to us by two rehabilitation physicians one month after the first myocardial infarction or coronary bypass grafting.

Design

Patients were randomly assigned to an experimental group of 33 patients and a control group op 22 patients. In groups of 5 to 8 patients and their partners, experimental patients received a psycho-educational group intervention programme in addition to standard medical care including physical exercise. The control group received standard medical care including physical exercise only. A pretest-posttest control group design (Campbell and Stanley, 1963) was used in order to evaluate the effects of the group intervention. Assessment took place in both groups immediately before and after the group intervention (about one and four months after the incident). A third measurement took place one year after the incident (28 experimental patients and 20 control patients).

Procedure

The psycho-educational intervention programme was conducted in eight weekly two-hour sessions for groups of 5 to 8 patients and their partners. During the first session, principles of Rational Emotive Therapy (Ellis, 1962) were explained by a health psychologist. Ellis (1962) assumes that a change in the cognitive, perceptual processes results in a change in man's emotional and behavioural reactions. He suggests that when a person experiences unadjusted emotional consequences (C) as a result of certain events or situations (A), he has made use of a series of irrational beliefs (B). It is these irrational ideas that lead directly to unadjusted emotions or behaviour. Disputing (D) the mediating irrational beliefs results in more adjusted emotions and behaviour (E). This 'ABCDE'-model is used as a guide to alter risk behaviour and reduce emotional distress.

In the first half of the following sessions, health professionals, involved in the standard care of coronary heart patients, gave relevant information about a specific topic concerning heart disease. Medical issues and medication were discussed by a rehabilitation physician and a cardiologist in two sessions, diet by a dietitian in one session, physical exercise by a physiotherapist in one session, working situation and social security by a social worker in one session, and risk behaviour, psychological reactions, sexual behaviour, leisure and professional activities by a health psychologist in the remaining sessions. As much as possible an attempt was made to discuss these topics in an interaction with patients and partners. Health professionals answered questions which had emerged from a prior need assessment among patients. In the second half of these sessions, patients and partners tried, under the supervision of a psychologist, to discover and discuss irrational beliefs concerning the topic of the session. By means of the ABCDE-scheme irrational beliefs inhibiting specific health behaviours and/or psychosocial recovery with reference to the topic of the session were discovered and discussed. An irrational belief is, for example: "I have smoked for a long time, it doesn't make any sense to change my behaviour. Its too late anyway". Such an irrational idea will probably not result in smoking cessation. At the end of each session, the session was evaluated and homework was given. Additionally, written information was given with reference to both rational emotive behaviour modification and the specific topics mentioned above.

Instruments of Measurement

a. *Health promoting behaviour* was assessed by means of:
   - The General Questionnaire for Heart Patients (GQH, Maes et al., 1984).
   - The type A behaviour pattern by the Dutch Version of the Videotaped Structured Interview (VSI, Van Elderen, 1984) and the Dutch Version of the Jenkins Activity Survey (Appels, 1985).

b. *Emotional distress*:
   - State and Trait Anxiety were assessed by means of the Dutch version of the STAI (Van der Ploeg et al., 1981).
   - State and Trait Anger were assessed by means of the Dutch version of the STAS (Van der Ploeg et al., 1982).
   - Vital Exhaustion and Depression were assessed by means of the Questionnaire for Vital Exhaustion and Depression (Appels, 1979).
   - Well-being, Feelings of Invalidity, Displeasure and Social Inhibition were assessed by the Medical Psychological Questionnaire for Heart Patients (MPQH, Erdman, 1982).

RESULTS

Short-term and long-term effects with reference to compliance with diet and medication prescriptions were determined by means of a chi-square test or a Fisher's exact test. There proved to be only a significant intervention effect for the increase of compliance with diet prescriptions in the long-term (Fisher's exact test, $p < 0.029$).
Short-term and long-term effects on the other variables were determined by means of covariance analyses (SPSS-X), using pretest scores as a covariate.

Table 1: **Results of analyses of covariance on health behaviour scores with the pretest scores as covariate on posttest and follow-up scores (M2 and M3) in the experimental group compared to the control group.**

Variables	Experimental			Control			F	F
	M1	M2	M3	M1	M2	M3	Short-term	Long-term
Smoking	2.61	4.42	5.30	1.91	2.73	3.55	0.79	0.40
Physical exercise	8.42	7.24	7.89	5.41	6.55	4.35	0.18	3.45*
Type A (JAS)	12.50	11.76	11.46	12.36	12.25	11.79	1.13	0.55
Type B (JAS)	29.00	23.88	-	26.16	25.20	-	2.84*	-

* $p < 0.05$

Table 2: **Results of analyses of covariance on emotional distress scores with the pretest scores as covariate on posttest and follow-up scores (M2 and M3) in the experimental group compared to the control group.**

Variables	Experimental			Control			F	F
	M1	M2	M3	M1	M2	M3	Short-term	Long-term
S-Anxiety	39.83	37.90	37.07	37.77	37.14	35.22	0.12	0.38
T-Anxiety	37.52	36.03	37.00	37.50	34.67	37.17	0.00	0.02
S-Anger	12.33	12.39	12.22	11.14	11.55	11.67	0.01	0.07
T-Anger	18.19	18.59	17.30	15.05	14.71	15.88	0.81	0.91
Depression	84.97	77.30	73.96	78.00	79.86	81.61	3.07**	1.45
Well-being	26.21	28.44	29.52	26.55	27.29	29.25	0.48	0.53
Feelings of invalidity	25.42	24.77	22.54	25.86	26.60	25.75	0.50	7.51**
Displeasure	17.59	16.76	15.26	15.67	17.05	15.35	0.51	0.80
Social inhibition	12.59	11.76	10.93	12.00	12.14	12.55	3.36*	4.12*

* $p < 0.05$; ** $p < 0.01$

As can be derived from Table 1, in the short-term the intervention resulted in a significant decrease in type A behaviour assessed by the Videotaped Structured Interview. In the long-term, the intervention proved to increase compliance with medical advice concerning physical exercise.

Table 2 shows that in the short-term the intervention resulted in a significant reduction of vital exhaustion and depression and social inhibition. In the long-term, there was a significant decrease in feelings of invalidity and social inhibition. Both short and long-term effects were in favour of the experimental group.

DISCUSSION

With reference to health behaviour the short-term intervention effects are limited. The only change appears to be a change in type A behaviour. Other health behaviours seemed not to be affected in the short-term. This is not surprising, since virtually all patients were compliant with medical advice concerning medication, diet, physical exercise and smoking cessation at the time of the posttest, there was virtually no room for improvement in the experimental groups. In order to understand this phenomenon one should keep in mind that the first posttest takes place three to four months after the threatening incident, which seems to be recent enough to motivate all patients to behave in a healthy way.

As far as emotional distress in the short-term is concerned, the programme proves to have beneficial effects on vital exhaustion and depression and social inhibition. Expected effects on anxiety and anger did not occur. Further inspection of the data revealed that patients in both the experimental and the control group had (for a clinical population) very low pretest scores on these scales, which points at possible effects of denial at the first measuring point. Such a phenomenon may mask a significant decrease in favour of the experimental group. The lack of significant effects on other distress variables may also be due to this phenomenon. In further studies we will, therefore, try to assess (and control for) approach/avoidance strategies at the different measuring points in order to control for the possible influence of tendencies.

In the long-term (one year after the incident) the picture becomes quite different. In contrast to the first posttest, significant effects on health behaviour could be noted in favour of the experimental group with respect to compliance with diet prescriptions and physical exercise. Lack of possible significant effects on compliance with medication is again due to the fact that virtually all patients in both the experimental and control group were compliant with advice concerning medication. However, biomedical assessment of compliance with medication might very well show other results. We are, therefore, currently investigating other ways of assessing medication compliance. As far as smoking is concerned, one may not forget that smoking is an addictive behaviour, which can probably not be affected by one session. Even long lasting comprehensive programmes have limited effects on smoking cessation (Lichtenstein, 1980). As such, it is probably more advisable to offer separate smoking cessation programmes parallel to our programme to smokers.

There are also noticeable effects on emotional distress variables in the long-term. Patients in the experimental group reported significantly less feelings of invalidity and social inhibition. Apart from being beneficial for psychological functioning, these effects can be considered as important for mediating social reintegration in work, family and leisure settings. In order to test this hypothesis, we will pay more attention to these social consequences in future research. Apart from the fact that it is quite possible that the average patient does not need extra programmes to enhance psychological recovery, the lack of effects on anger and anxiety may be due to the remarks made above.

In conclusion, the psycho-educational intervention proves, especially in the long-term, to have beneficial effects on compliance with diet prescriptions and physical exercise, and on feelings of invalidity and social inhibition. As such these findings may motivate researchers into being cautious with the interpretation and generalization of results from studies with short-term posttests only, which are rather the rule than the exception in this area of research (Maes et al., 1987).

As these results are encouraging, we will continue our research during the next few years. There is, however, still a long way to go: (a) as we did not measure irrational beliefs, we do not know whether the observed treatment effects are parallelled by changes in beliefs. Assessment of the beliefs and related coping behaviour is essential to relate the observed effects to our cognitive theory and intervention strategy (Maes, 1987); (b) we must find a solution for the measurement of denial and its effects on different measuring points; (c) the effects must be replicated in larger groups of patients in different settings; (d) the effects on other relevant variables (overweight, alcohol abuse, social variables) must be assessed; (e) we must control for possible attention placebo effects and last but not least (f) for reasons of efficiency, we must try to identify groups of patients who would benefit most from the intervention in order to be able to develop a relevant screening instrument.

* This study was supported by a research grant from the Dutch

Prevention Fund (PREVENTIEFONDS).

REFERENCES

Appels, A. (1985). *J.A.S., Jenkins Activity Survey, Handleiding*. Lisse: Swets & Zeitlinger.

Appels, A., Pool, J., Lubsen, J. & Does, E. van der (1979). Psychische prodromen van het hartinfarct. *Nederlands Tijdschrift voor de Psychologie, 34*, 213-223.

Backer, G. de (1980). Revalidatie van hartpatiënten. *Tijdschrift voor Geneeskunde, 36*, 719-726.

Barofsky, I. (1980). *The chronic psychiatric patient in the community*. New York: Plenum.

Burling, T.A., Singleton, E.G., Bigelow, G.E., Baile, W.F. & Gottlieb, S.W. (1984). Smoking following myocardial infarction: A critical review of the literature. *Health Psychology, 3*, 83-96.

Campbell, D.T. & Stanley, J.C. (1963). *Experimental and quasi-experimental designs for research*. Chicago: Rand McNally.

Diederiks, J.P.M. (1982). Herstel en revalidatie na het hartinfarct. Deel I: Aard en omvang van het probleem. *Keesing Medisch Archief, 1788*, 12271-12284.

Dracup, K., Meleis, A.I, Clark, S., Clyburn, A., Shields, L. & Staley, M. (1984). Group counseling in cardiac rehabilitation: Effect on patients compliance. *Patient Education and Counseling, 6* (4), 169-177.

Dutch Heart Foundation (1977). *Rehabilitation of Heart Patients*, 's-Gravenhage.

Elderen, T. van (1984). *De Nederlandse versie van het Videotaped Structured Interview van Friedman & Powell*. Tilburg: Subfaculteit Psychologie.

Ellis, A. (1962). *Reason and emotion in psychotherapy*. New York: Lyle Stuart.

Erdman, R.A.M. (1982). *M.P.V.H., Medisch Psychologische Vragenlijst voor Hartpatiënten, Handleiding*. Lisse: Swets en Zeitlinger.

Erdman, R.A.M., Duivenvoorden, H.J., Verhage, F., Kazemier, M. & Hugenholtz, P.G. (1984). Hartrevalidatie: Een vervolgonderzoek over 5 jaar naar psychisch functioneren, werkhervatting, rookgewoonten en sportieve activiteiten. *Nederlands Tijdschrift voor de Geneeskunde, 128*, 846-851.

Food and Drug Administration (1979). Prescription drug products: Patient labelling requirements. *Federal Register, 44*, 40016-40041.

Heller, St.S., Frank, K.A., Kornfeld, D.S., Wilson, S.N. & Malm, J.R.

(1982). *Psychological and behavioural responses following coronary artery bypass surgery*. In: Becker et al. (Eds.). Berlin Heidelberg: Springer Verlag.
Horlick, R., Cameron, R., Firor, W., Bhalerao, U. & Baltzan, R. (1984). The effects of education and group discussion in the post-myocardial infarction patient. *Journal of Psychosomatic Research, 28*, (6), 485-492.
Ibrahim, M.A., Feldman, J.G., Sultz, H.A., Staiman, M.G., Young, L.J. & Dean, D. (1974). Management after myocardial infarction: A controlled trial of the effect of group psychotherapy. *International Journal of Psychiatry in Medicine, 5* (3), 253-268.
International Society and Federation of Cardiology Scientific Councils (1981). Secondary Prevention in survivors of myocardial infarction. *British Medical Journal, 282*, 849-986.
Kallio, V., Hämäläinen, H., Hakkila, J. & Luurila, O.J. (1979). Reduction in sudden deaths by a multifactorial intervention programme after acute myocardial infarction. *The Lancet, 2*, 1091-1094.
Kellerman, J.J. & Kariv, I. (1968). *Rehabilitation of coronary patients*. Tel Aviv: Segal Press.
Ley, P. (1976). Towards better doctor-patient communication: Contributions from social and experimental psychology. In: A.E. Bennett (Ed.), *Communication between doctors and patients*. London: Nuffield Provincial Hospitals Trust.
Lichtenstein, E. & Brown, R.A. (1980). Smoking cessation methods: Review and recommendation. In: R.W. Miller (Ed.), *The Addictive behaviors*. New York: Pergamon Press.
Maes, S. (1987). Reducing emotional distress in chronic patients, a cognitive approach. In: M. Boekaerts & S. Maes (Eds.), *Emotion and cognition* (pp.261-276).
Maes, S., Bruggemans, E. & Elderen, T. van (1984). *De Algemene Vragenlijst voor Hartpatiënten*. Tilburg: Subfaculteit Psychologie.
Maes, S., Elderen, T. van & Bruggemans, E. (1987). Effecten van voorlichting aan coronaire hartpatiënten. *Gezondheid en Samenleving, 8* (2), 60-76.
Martin, J.E. & Dubbert, P.M. (1982). Exercise applications and promotion in behavioral medicine: Current status and future directions. *Journal of Consulting and Clinical Psychology, 50* (6), 1004-1017.
Mayou, R. (1981). Effectiveness of cardiac rehabilitation. *Journal of Psychosomatic Research, 25*, 423-427.
Mayou, R., MacMahon, D., Sleight, P. & Florencio, M.J. (1981). Early rehabilitation after myocardial infarction. *The Lancet, 26*, 1399-1401.
McPherson, B.D., Paivio, A., Yuhasz, M.S., Rechnitzer, P.A., Pickard, H. &

Lefcoe, N. (1967). Psychological effects of an exercise program for post infarct and normal adult men. *J. Sports. Med. Phys. Fitness, 7*, 95-102.

Ploeg, H.M. van der, Defares, P.B. & Spielberger, C.D. (1981). *Handleiding bij de Zelf-Beoordelings Vragenlijst, Z.B.V.. Een Nederlandstalige bewerking van de Spielberger State-Trait Anxiety Inventory, S.T.A.I. -DY.* Lisse: Swets & Zeitlinger.

Ploeg, H.M. van der, Defares, P.B. & Spielberger, C.D. (1982). *Handleiding bij de Zelf-Analyse Vragenlijst, Z.A.V.. Een Nederlandstalige bewerking van de Spielberger State-Trait Anger Scale*. Lisse: Swets & Zeitlinger.

Rahe, R.H., Ward, H.W. & Hayes, V. (1979). Brief group therapy in myocardial infarction rehabilitation: Three to four year follow-up of a controlled trial. *Psychosomatic Medicine, 41*, 229-242.

Roviaro, S., Holmes, D.S. & Holmsten, R. (1984). Influence of a cardiac rehabilitation program on the cardiovascular, psychological and social functioning of cardiac patients. *Journal of Behavioural Medicine, 7* (1), 61-81.

Thockloth, R.M., Ho, S.C., Wright, H. & Seldon, W.A. (1973). Is cardiac rehabilitation really necessary ? *Medical Journal of Australia, 2*, 669-674.

Vermeulen, A., Heijboer, C. & Lie, K.I. (1978). Een vergelijkend onderzoek naar de invloed van een revalidatieprogramma bij hartinfarctpatiënten. *Nederlands Tijdschrift voor de Geneeskunde, 112*, 1737.

Wenger, N.K. (1979). Research related to rehabilitation. *Circulation, 60*, 1636-1639.

BIOFEEDBACK AS PAIN CONTROL STRATEGY IN EXPERIMENTAL PAIN

W. Larbig, W. Miltner, & Ch. Braun

University of Tuebingen, Departments of Clinical and Medical Psychology, F.R.G.

INTRODUCTION

Biofeedback has been defined as a system that allows for the self-modification of biological responses within the patient's body (Hatch et al., 1987). Biofeedback training plays an important role in the treatment of chronic pain. Various kinds of biofeedback modalities have been applied in the achievement of voluntary control of different physiological processes contributing to pain: electromyographic (EMG), temperature, skin conductance, electroencephalographic (EEG) biofeedback procedures.

The purpose of this chapter is to describe an experimental EEG biofeedback paradigm within a standardized laboratory setting employing event-related potentials (ERP) evoked by phasic painful electrical stimulation. Only a few studies so far have investigated methods of operant conditioning of ERP's within a latency range up to 800 ms. Finley (1984) reported positive behavioral effects to a biofeedback-training with quadriplegic subjects showing improved sensory functioning after early components of cervical somatosensory evoked potentials (N14) have been conditioned. Additionally he has shown that brain stem auditory evoked potentials are amenable to operant control (Finley et al., 1981). Roger (1984) demonstrated biofeedback-induced modifications of the amplitudes of visual ERPs. Miltner et al. (1986) investigated an operant control paradigm to modify the P300 of the visual ERP and showed that an increase of the positivity of P300 was associated with a decrease in reaction time.

Most of the work on the operant control of somatosensory evoked potentials within the latency range up to 500 ms was done by Rosenfeld

(1984) indicating that both humans and animals may regulate the amplitude of the nociceptive evoked potential (P200). Furthermore this modification was associated with changes in the perception of pain.

In algesimetric studies using somatosensory evoked potentials (SEPs) as quasi objective parameters of pain perception some research groups have substantiated that the N150-P260 complex of SEP responds very sensitively to different intensities of nociceptive stimuli and that the size of this complex correlates relatively high with the subjective pain report (Chapman and Jacobson, 1984; Bromm, 1984; Miltner et al., 1988). Furthermore it was shown repeatedly that analgesics not only reduce the verbal pain reports but also the size of this complex (Bromm, 1984; Chapman and Jacobson, 1984).

On the background of the algesimetric importance of this complex and the successful modification of visual and somatosensory ERPs by means of operant conditioning the present study investigates whether the N150-P260 complex of SEP may be influenced by a biofeedback paradigm and whether this leads to a concurrent modification of the perception of phasic pain.

METHODS

Subjects

10 male healthy volunteers aged between 21 and 46 participated as paid subjects. Subjects were informed about the course of the experiment and gave written informed consent according to the Helsinki convention. No subject was under current medication and none suffered from any disease.

Procedure

For each subject the experiment took one session lasting about 2 hours. During the first part of the session both the individual pain threshold (ITP) and a threshold of 20% above the individual pain threshold (ITP20) were measured. During a second part of the session the baseline ERPs and subjective pain reports according to ITP20 were recorded. The last part of the session was devoted to the feedback training. To elicit the ERP during feedback training the stimulus intensity of ITP20 was used.

Pain threshold measurement

A standardized method of intracutaneous electrical stimulation (IES) was employed (Miltner et al., 1988) using weak electrical currents with an intensity between 70 and 900 μA applied to the subcutaneous layers of a finger tip on the non-dominant hand. The anode was an isolated golden pin of 1 mm length and .9 mm diameter inserted into a prepared epidermal cavity and properly fixed. The cathode consisted of a flexible steel electrode worn by the subject on the same finger. Preparation of the cavity was done carefully preventing bleedings but deep enough that the skin resistance fell below 10 K.Ohms. Subjects were grounded with a flexible bandlike and humid electrode fixed around the wrist. The IES consisted of a bipolar square pulse of 10 ms duration. During the part 1 (individual pain threshold measurement) subjects were stimulated with two consecutive series of about 80 IES totally. Each series starts with an intensity of zero being increased stepwise to a maximal intensity of about 40% above individual pain threshold. Then the intensity was decreased stepwise back to zero. Each IES was indicated by a visual warning stimulus presented at a video screen 1000 ms prior to its occurrence. The warning stimulus consisted of a light square of 24.4 cm^2. Interstimulus interval of IES was randomized varying between 9 and 12 s. After presentation of each stimulus subjects were asked to rate the intensity of the actual sensations by using a visual analogue scale (VAS) presented on a video screen placed 3 m in front of the subject. Its height was to increase by pressing a micro-switch. The VAS contained three lines, one at the bottom of the scale indicating "no sensation", one 10% below the midline "just perceivable pain" and one at the top of the scale "unbearable pain". Actual number of IES within this part of experiment was depending on the level of the individual pain threshold and ranged between 30 and 36 stimuli per series. This procedure of approaching the individual pain threshold four times by two increasing and two decreasing stimulus runs resulted in a relative precise estimation of the pain threshold and ITP20.

Pre-training baseline

During this part of the experiment 100 IES with an intensity of ITP20 were applied to each subject. The method of stimulation (warning signal and IES), the time course of one trial and the inter-trial intervals were the same as during the first part of the experiment. Again the VAS was presented 3 s after each single IES and the subjective pain report was taken after each block of 10 trials. Furthermore several physiological parameters were recorded before and after stimulation, including EEG, EOG, EMG. Artifactfree EEGs of this period were averaged for the mean peak-to-peak size of the N150-P260 complex of ERP (SEP) from each subject, serving as reference values for the amount of reinforcement given to each subject during both training sections.

Feedback training

During the feedback training a series of 300 IES were applied to each subject. The intensity of training stimuli was identical to that of ITP20 from pre-training baseline. Each IES and the training task were indicated by a warning signal presented 1000 ms before IES application. Two tasks were differentiated: one in which the subjects were requested to increase the peak-to-peak size of the N150-P260 complex of SEP (up-training) and one in which this complex should be decreased (down-training). Up- and down-training conditions were changed randomly from trial to trial. According to the up- and down-training condition the warning signal was either a symbolized male or a female figure. Subjects were not informed about the relationship between style of figures and the kind of task. They only were instructed to fixate the warning figure and try to produce as many figures as possible to the video screen after the application and perception of the IES (ITP20). After presentation of a male warning figure their behavioral response should affect an increase of the number of male figures; after a female warning signal the task was to increase the female figures. Association of male and female figures to either up-training or down-training was matched among subjects.

The number of figures displayed on the screen was calculated by dividing the amount of the actual peak-to-peak size of the N150-P260 complex through the individual mean of its pretraining baseline value. I.e., the more the actual size of this complex exceeded or fell below the baseline reference (i.e. the averaged N150-P260 size of pre-training ITP20s), the more respectively the less figures were displayed. When the actual size exceeded the baseline for more than one standard deviation 3 figures were displayed. Maximum number of figures were 11, minimum was 1. In addition to the number of figures a monetary bonus was displayed at the top of the video screen after each trial.

After each block of 50 trials the VAS was displayed twice and the subject was requested to rate the intensity of the mean pain sensations experienced during both the up- and down-training condition respectively.

RESULTS

Table 1 summarizes the means and standard deviation of the peak-to-peak N150-P260 amplitudes according to the 6 blocks of trials and the two feedback-training conditions. As can be seen there is a significant difference in the size of the N150-P260 complex between the up- and down-training condition ($F\ (1.9) = 10.42$; $p = 0.01$). Furthermore there is a systematic decrement of the size of this complex from block 1 to block 6, indicating habituation (F (5.45) = 7.03; p < 0.01).

Table 1: **Mean peak-to-peak size and standard deviation of N150-P260 complex of SEP during 6 consecutive blocks of biofeedback training related to up- and down-training conditions.**

BLOCK	TRIALS	UP-TRAINING Mean (μV)	UP-TRAINING SD	DOWN-TRAINING Mean (μV)	DOWN-TRAINING SD
1	1 - 50	13.39	3.28	10.64	4.04
2	51 - 100	13.10	4.23	10.08	3.41
3	101 - 150	11.70	3.37	8.21	3.12
4	151 - 200	10.37	2.70	9.04	2.78
5	201 - 250	10.90	3.48	7.64	2.97
6	251 - 300	8.82	2.83	7.58	2.85

Analysis of variance:

Factor	Degrees of freedom	F-value	p	
BLOCKS	(5.45)	7.03	0.0001	ss
TRAINING CONDITIONS	(1.9)	10.42	0.0104	ss
BLOCKS x TRAINING CONDITIONS	(5.45)	1.18	0.3321	ns

Furthermore the data show that the acquisition of self-control was achieved very rapidly after a few trials (Fig. 1).

Figure 1 displays the effects of the feedback training of the peak-to-peak size of the N150-P260 complex of single trials SEPs elicited by an intracutaneous electrical stimulus of 10 ms duration. The left group of 6 columns indicates the mean peak-to-peak sizes of all up-training trials, the right group of 6 colums those of down-training trials within 300 trials of stimulation. Up- and down-training trials have changed randomly from trial to trial. One single column comprises up- resp. down-training trials within 50 consecutive trials starting with trial one and ending with trial 50 for the black column etc.

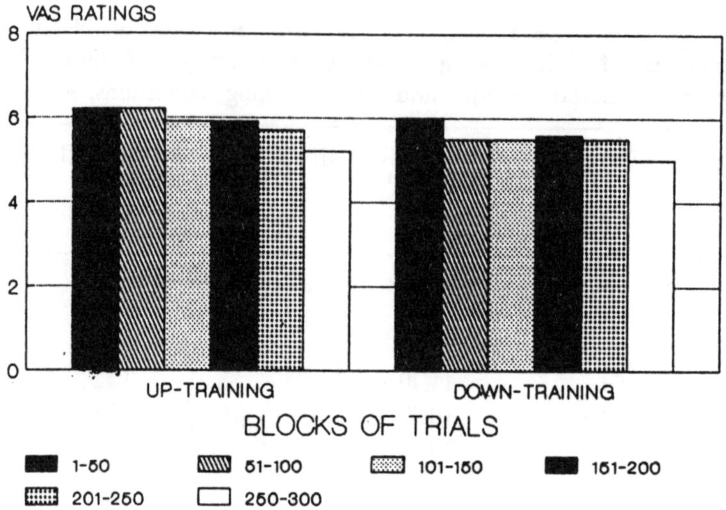

Figure 1: **Effects of feedback-training on the subjective pain rating**

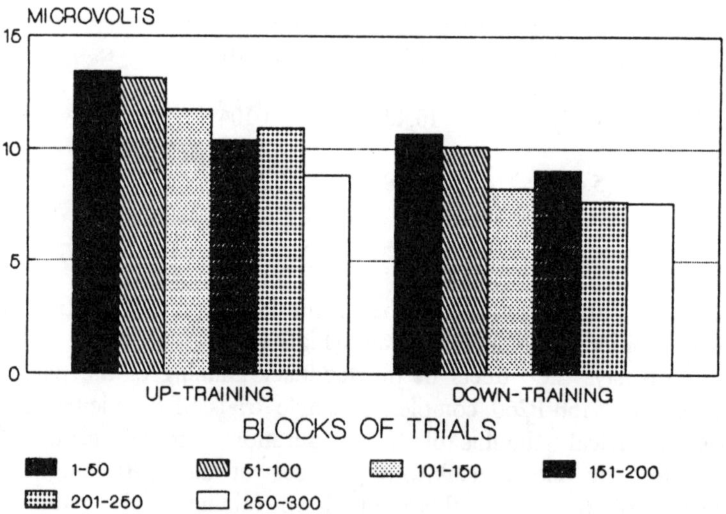

Figure 2: **Effects of feedback-training on the size on N150-P260 complex**

The data of the mean peak-to-peak size of the P500 complex of the SEP revealed no significant difference between the up- and down-training conditions.

The Chi-square test on the distribution of up- and down-training trials with either high or low negativity of pre-stimulus CNV-levels revealed a significant difference between the four cells tested (CHI-Square according to Yates correction $p = 0.044$). However the data suggest that the significant effect is mainly due to trials with the most negative pre-stimulus CNV-levels, not to those with low negativity pre-stimulus CNVs. Feedback trials of the down-training condition show significantly more pronounced negative pre-stimulus CNV-levels than trials of the up-training condition.

According to the ERP changes the subjective pain reports show significant differences between up- and down-training (table 2). Throughout the training stimuli of up-training trials were rated more painful than those of down-training trials ($F (1.9) = 5.71$, $p < 0.05$). In contrast to the ERPs the subjective pain report did not show habituation, i.e. there was no significant decrease of the ratings over time independent of the training conditions. The lack of any significant interaction between BLOCKS and TRAINING CONDITION indicates that the subjective effects mainly have to be assigned to the training procedure and not to other sources of variance (Fig. 2).
However, only some subjects were able to increase the N150-P260 complex above the baseline level. In most cases the N150-P260 complex remained smaller under both conditions than under baseline condition. Training effects of both conditions therefore cannot be considered in relation to baseline but only in relation to each other, indicating that up-training trials result in larger N150-P260 amplitudes than down-training trials. As far as we understand this effect the reason has to be discussed in terms of the biofeedback paradigm used and in terms of different task conditions.

DISCUSSION

The study confirms earlier findings by Rosenfeld and coworkers (Rosenfeld, 1984), demonstrating that ERPs evoked by nociceptive stimuli may be brought under biofeedback control both in humans and animals. In contrast to Rosenfeld's findings in our study subjects were rather rapidly able to control the size of the N150-P260 complex provided that they got contingent reinforcement on their brain responses. According to the differential effects of the up- and down-training conditions on the size of the N150-P260 complex of SEP the subjective pain report was increased

Table 2: **Changes of subjective pain report. Mean pain ratings (VAS) and standard deviation at the end of 6 blocks related to up- and down-training conditions. VAS ranged from 0 (no sensation), 4 (pain threshold) to 8 (unbearable pain).**

BLOCK	END OF TRIAL	UP-TRAINING MEAN	UP-TRAINING SD	DOWN-TRAINING MEAN	DOWN-TRAINING SD
1	50	6.2	0.82	6.0	0.71
2	100	6.2	1.10	5.5	0.75
3	150	5.9	1.16	5.5	1.18
4	200	5.9	1.37	5.6	1.16
5	250	5.7	1.41	5.5	1.43
6	300	5.2	1.63	5.0	1.62

Analysis of variance:

Factor	Degrees of freedom	F.value	p	
BLOCKS	(5.45)	2.23	0.07	ns
TRAINING CONDITIONS	(1.9)	5.71	0.04	s
BLOCKS X TRAINING CONDITIONS	(5.45)	1.45	0.22	ns

under up- and decreased under down-training condition (Fig. 1 and 2).

Though this effect was small the study emphasizes the strong relationship between the size of the N150-P260 complex and the subjective pain experience as it was found in many other analgesic studies before (Bromm, 1984; Chudler and Dong, 1983; Chapman and Jacobson, 1984). The study too replicated some earlier findings revealing different habituation processes for ERPs and the subjective pain report (Chapman et al., 1984). As ERPs show habituation even when evoked by randomly presented painful stimuli of different intensity, the subjective ratings did not.

The differences of the pre-stimulus CNV-levels within up- and down-training trials may point to the fact that our feedback paradigm not only was affecting the peak-to-peak size of the ERP but also the preceding CNV. Our data might suggest that our subjects were conditioned to increase the negativity of the CNV-level in order to fulfil the task requested. This could be interpreted that the changes in peak-to-peak size are by no means specific but only the result of a preceding CNV change. However, a number of studies have shown that an increase in negativity of the pre-stimulus CNV leads to larger post-stimulus ERP amplitudes. In our experiment just the opposite relationship was found, i.e. the most negative CNV-levels are followed by the smallest ERP amplitudes and the less negative CNV-levels by the largest ERPs. These effects indicate that the speculation of a conditioned CNV change influencing the ERP cannot be maintained and objectified by the CHI-square procedure used. We rather suggest that the difference in the N150-P260 size between up- respectively down-training trials was influenced by the arrangement and timing of the feedback procedure. The assumption of a specific conditioning process is supported by the ANOVA of those components of the EEG which were not contingently reinforced (P500 of SEP). They showed no change in relation to the different training conditions.

The peak-to-peak size of the N150-P260 complex was usually smaller under both biofeedback conditions compared to baseline. Interviews at the end of the session revealed that it was difficult for all subjects to exceed the baseline level of the N150-P260 complex when requested to do so during up-training trials. It is difficult to decide whether an increase is generally more difficult to achieve than a decrease or whether this is rather a result of the reinforcement procedure used. Due to the difficulty to comply with this task most subjects therefore did not invest much energy to fulfil the up-training task after some trials of training. To get reinforcement most of them paid attention primarily to down- and not to up-training trials. This strategy was facilitated by the fact that they were not "punished" for false responses but only positively reinforced for correct responses. By conditioning our subjects to pay more attention to down-training trials our biofeedback paradigm in this experiment led to the fact that an increase in negativity is associated with a decrease and a less negativity with an increase of the size of the N150-P260 complex.

The fact that the baseline N150-P260 complex commonly exceeded the training size requires further consideration in so far as it indicates that the baseline condition was not adequate compared to the biofeedback conditions. During baseline stimulation subjects had to perform one single task, i.e. to concentrate on the warning stimulus and the painful stimulus impended. During feedback, subjects tasks were more complex: here they had to distinguish between two warning signals indicating different tasks, process the painful stimulus and finally prepare and comply with the requested response cued by the warning signal. Stated in another way, subjects not only had to process two stimuli but also to prepare different responses (up- vs. down-response) and different consequences of these responses. Therefore the baseline in this experiment may be considered as a task mainly affording attention to the painful stimulus. In contrary the feedback task afforded selective attention to two different warning stimuli and probably less attention to the painful stimulus.

A number of studies have shown that attention to stimuli results in an increase of the power of ERP amplitudes. Non-attention to stimuli however decreases its power (Rhodes et al., 1987; Näätänen et al., 1980; Hillyard, 1984; Miltner et al., 1988).

Taken all these findings together our data support the idea that the N150-P260 size does not solely reflect neurophysiological aspects of stimulus processing but complex psychological aspects, i.e. attentional aspects as pain control strategies, variables of pain perception and processings of painful stimulus and response preparation.

Research was supported by the Deutsche Forschungsgemeinschaft (DFG) SFB 307 B2.

REFERENCES

Bromm, B. (1984). Pain-related components in the cerebral potential. Experiment and multivariate statistical approaches. In: B. Bromm (Ed.), *Pain measurement in man. Neurophysiological correlates of pain* (pp.257-290). Amsterdam, New York, Oxford: Elsevier.

Chapman, C.R. & Jacobson, R.C. (1984). Assessment of analgesic states: Can evoked potentials play a role. In: B. Bromm (Ed.), *Pain measurement in man. Neurophysiological correlates of pain* (pp.233-255). Amsterdam: Elsevier.

Chudler, E.H. & Dong, W.K. (1983). The assessment of pain by cerebral evoked potentials. *Pain*, 16, 221-244.

Finley, W. & Johnson, G. (1981). Biofeedback of brainstem auditory evoked potentials. *Proceedings of the 12th Annual Meeting of the Biofeedback Society of America*, 15-18.

Finley, W.W. (1984). Biofeedback of very early potentials from the brain stem. In: T. Elbert, B. Rockstroh, W. Lutzenberger & N. Birbaumer (Eds.), *Self-regulation of the brain and behavior* (pp.143-163). Berlin, Heidelberg, New York, Tokyo: Springer-Verlag.

Hatch, J.P., Fisher, J.G. & Rugh, J.D. (1987). Biofeedback: Studies in clinical efficacy. New York, London: Plenum Press.

Hillyard, S.A. (1984). Event-related potentials and selective attention. In: E. Donchin (Ed.), *Cognitive psychology: event-related potentials and the study of cognition* (The Carmel Conferences, Vol. 1, pp.51-72). Hillsdale, London: Lawrence Erlbaum Ass.

Miltner, W., Larbig, W. & Braun, C. (1986). Biofeedback of visual evoked potentials. *International Journal of Neuroscience, 29*, 291-303.

Miltner, W., Larbig, W. & Braun, C. (1988). Tooth pulp and intracutaneous electrical stimulation. Major properties and differences. *In press.*

Näätänen, R., Gaillard, A.W.K. & Mäntysalo, S. (1980). Brain potential correlates of voluntary and involuntary attention. In: H.H. Kornhuber & L. Deecke (Eds.), *Motivation, motor, and sensory processes of the brain. Electrical potentials, behavior, and clinical use* (pp.343-348). Amsterdam: Elsevier.

Rhodes, D.L., Buffington, V. & Chapman, C.R. (1987). Effects of attention/distraction on evoked potentials to painful and nonpainful gingival stimulation. *Pain*, 183.

Roger, M. (1984). Operant control of evoked potentials: some comments on the learning characteristics in man and on the conditioning of subcortical responses in the curarized rat. In: T. Elbert, B.

Rockstroh, W. Lutzenberger & N. Birbaumer (Eds.), *Self-regulation of the brain and behavior* (pp.180-197). Berlin, Heidelberg, New York, Tokyo: Springer-Verlag.

Rosenfeld, J.P., Dowman, R., Silvia, R., & Heinricher, M. (1984). Operant controlled somatosensory brain potentials: specific effects on pain processes. In: T. Elbert, B. Rockstroh, W. Lutzenberger & N. Birbaumer (Eds), *Self-regulation of the brain and behavior* (pp.164-179). Berlin, Heidelberg, New York, Tokyo: Springer-Verlag.

TREATING CHILDREN WITH ENCOPRESIS AND CONSTIPATION: AN EVALUATION BY MEANS OF SINGLE CASE STUDIES

J.D. Bosch

Free University, Amsterdam, The Netherlands

INTRODUCTION

Encopresis is a problem of faecal incontinence. In the literature different names are used to describe this problem: "soiling" is one of them. There are several types which can be distinguished within the group of children suffering from encopresis. Encopresis with and without constipation, is in our opinion diagnostically the most important distinction which can be made.

Encopresis is a behavior problem which is predominantly found amongst children. The frequency of soiling declines with the age to the point of almost total non-existence during adolescence (Bellman, 1966; Bosch, 1986; Largo et al., 1978).

In a pilot study (Bosch et al., 1984), an outpatient treatment program for encopresis was devised and subsequently tested on ten children. This program was based on the one, described by Neale (1963), which was used in the case of 4 boys in a child psychiatric clinic. The pilot study produced a scenario for a combined group parent training and individual mediation therapy program, which has been described elsewhere (Bosch, 1984). This behavior modification program was improved and evaluated with 21 children.

In this article the results of our behavioral intervention program will be presented. In addition to the discussion of the results obtained with these 21 children we will illustrate the evaluation procedure in more detail with a case report of an eight year old boy with encopresis and chronic constipation.

A combined approach of behavior modification and medical treatment is necessary in those cases where encopresis is accompanied by serious constipation complaints. Incontinence, however, should remain the primary objective of treatment. It is remarkable that within the medical setting "soiling" is considered much more frequently as a constipation problem than as a problem of incontinence. Medical treatment of constipation only creates the conditions necessary for a toilet training.

BEHAVIOR-PROGRAM EVALUATION

Treatments were evaluated by means of the quasi-experimental AB-design, a so-called N = 1 design. The main objective was the evaluation of the following target behaviors: soiling behavior as well as adaptive toileting behavior. The decreases and increases in both types of behavior - expressed in terms of weekly frequencies - were visualized in graphs. The base-line phase (A) was thus compared with the intervention phase (B).

Behavioral intervention program

The behavior modification program consisted of the following components:

1. Manipulation of the adaptive (appropriate) behavior of going to the toilet by means of *stimulus control* (cuing, prompting, fading) and *contingency management procedures*. Verbal cues and prompts were withdrawn as quickly as possible. The desired responses were reinforced socially as well as materially. The central technique used here was the 'token economy'. Sometimes the technique of *shaping* was used as well.
2. Manipulation of the undesired (soiling-)behavior by means of *extinction*: inquiries were made tactfully with regard to the condition of clothing (soiled or unsoiled) and no reprimands were given in the case of soiling. In the case that this procedure proved to be insufficient the technique of '*response cost*' (RC) was applied. Mostly RC was fitted into the token-economy procedure. RC-contingencies were introduced only after the attainment of positive reinforcement contingencies.
3. The parents were instructed to observe and record the target behaviors daily. They were also trained to modify their reactions to the child's behavior by administering the above mentioned interventions. If necessary, the arrangements and agreements arrived at between parents and child were laid down in writing: '*contracting*'. The written contract provides greater specificity and clarity than do oral contingency agreements. The most important steps to be taken during the course of the treatment are summarized in table 1.

Evaluation

All of the single-case studies were evaluated in a visual-descriptive manner. When necessary, a statistical evaluation was carried out as well. In this article we will restrict ourselves to the visual-descriptive evaluation procedure. This evaluation was carried out on the basis of a priori criteria described by Kazdin (1981). The five evaluation dimensions and application of them in this study, can be summarized as follows:

(1) *Type of data / Objective data*
Discrete categories are used in the evaluation of the toileting behaviors:- defecation in toilet or not
- soiling or not soiling
In other words: the requirement of objectivity can be met, with hardly any exceptions.

(2) *Assessment occasions / Continuous assessment*
This means to say, no 'one-or-two-shot' assessments. In the treatment of encopresis observations are made every day. A negative score is given when the observations are stopped and a plus/minus score when the observations are irregular.

(3) *Past and future projections / Stability of the problem*
Encopretic complaints are usually quite stable. When in doubt, the

---

Table 1: **Therapeutic steps**

1. *Interviewing* of parents (anamnesis)
2. *Monitoring* (the parents observe and make record of the target behaviors on a daily basis)
3. *Training* in the application of learning principles
4. *Application* of techniques
   - in the case of young children (up to 12 years of age) usually via the parents: mediation therapy
   - in the case of older children (or in exceptional cases with younger children): self control procedures.
5. *Evaluation* during the entire treatment
6. *Termination* of the program

TABLE: OVERVIEW RESULTS OF EVALUATION BEHAVIOUR MODIFICATION PROGRAMME

Child Number ▶ ▼ Measures	1	2	3	4	5	6	7	8	9	10	11	12	13	14	15	16	17	18	19	20	21	
	−	+	−	−	+	+	−	+	+	+	−	+	+	+	+	+	+	+	+	+	+	Elimination Encopresis
1. Obj. Data		+		+	+	+		+	+	+		+/−	+	+	+	+	+	+	+	+	+	Kazdin Criteria
2. Cont. Assessm.		+		+	+/−	+		+	+	+		−	+	+	+	+	+	+	+	+	+	
3. Stability		−		+	+	+		+	+	+		+	+	+	+	+	+	+	+	+	+	
4. Marked Effects		−		+	+/−	+/−		+/−	+	+		+/−	+	−	+/−	+	+/−	+/−	+/−	+	+	
5. Multiple Cases		+		+	+	+		+	+	+		+	+	+	+	+	+	+	+	+	+	
1. History		−		+	−	+/−		+	+	+		+	+	+	+/−	+	+	+	+	+	+	Campbell & Stanley Criteria
2. Maturation		+/−		+	+	+		+	+	+		+	+/−	+/−	+/−	+/−	+/−	+/−	+/−	+	+	
3. Testing		+		+/−	+	+/−		+/−	+	+		+	+	+	+	+	−	−	+	+	+	
4. Instrumentation		+		+	+	+		+	+	+		+/−	+	+	+/−	+	+	+	+	+	+	
5. Stat. Regression		+		+	+	+		+	+	+		+	+	+	+	+	+	+	+	+	+	
	−	+/−	−	+	+/−	+/−	−	+/−	+	+	−	+/−	+	+/−	+/−	+	+/−	+/−	+	+	+	Treatment Effects

base-line phase may be extended. When the pattern of complaints is cyclic, which can be related to the season of the year in some cases, a plus/minus score should be given.

(4) *Type of effect / Immediate and marked effects*
Large and abrupt changes between the A- and B-phase make the assumption of "treatment effects" more plausible. Alternative explanations can be ruled out more easily. If the toileting behavior remains unchanged during the first intervention-period, a negative score should be given. Very gradual changes should receive a plus/minus score.

(5) *Number of heterogeneity / Multiple cases*
The presumed efficacy will be all the more plausible, in the case that the same intervention has the same favourable result in several clients and in clients who differ from one another (in different situations).

In summary: A positive score is given when the requirement is met; a plus/minus score is given in case of doubt and a negative score when the requirement has not been met.

In addition, five other evaluation criteria pertaining to possible threats to internal validity as formulated by Campbell & Stanley (1966), were used.
On the basis of these, one can evaluate whether alternative explanations may have contributed to the beneficial changes which have taken place. For example, it is quite possible that specific life events (history) coincide with the sudden favorable changes or that maturational variables (*maturation*) are responsible for the positive changes.
Reactive observation effects (*testing*) or changes in assessment criteria (*instrumentation*) can also be a threat to internal validity (see Gelfand & Hartmann, 1984). *Statistical regression*, the fifth criterion by means of which one can assess internal validity, does not play a role if complete elimination of encopretic behavior is reached.
In summary: A positive score is given when alternative explanations are ruled out: a plus/minus score is given in case of doubt and a negative score when alternative explanations are plausible (Bosch, 1984).

Results of the program evaluation

At the end of the treatment, one out of two scores could be given with regard to the encopretic complaint: removed/cured (plus) or unimproved (minus).

The therapeutic results and assessment scores are summarized in table 2.

Sixteen of the 21 children (= 76%) had no complaints after treatment. In the first row (elimination of encopresis) the therapeutic failures are shown: case numbers 1, 3, 4, 7 and 11. In order to clarify table 2 we will first give an example, case number 12.

Inspection of the column referring to this case reveals that a negative score and three plus/minus scores were given. Continuous assessment received a negative score in this case, because the parents of the child discontinued the observation and recording of target-behavior during the intervention phase. The objectivity of the data was therefore doubted. Aside from the elimination of encopresis it was uncertain whether positive scores could be given with regard to immediate and marked effects and with regard to instrumentation. In this case elimination of encopresis is not entirely attributed to the effectiveness of the method. This case was therefore given a 'plusminus' score in the last row, referring to treatment effects.

In nine of the cases the elimination of encopresis cannot be ascribed to the intervention alone. Reasons for this are uncertain factors (the "plus/minus scores"), in particular with regard to possible maturation variables and history as alternative explanations for success. Furthermore, when treating encopresis, one will often find a very gradual improvement, so that the requirement of Kazdins third assessment criterion could not be met entirely. The treatment effect was judged positively, when there were two or less plus/minus scores present. In this conservative manner of evaluation the treatment effect was demonstrated as being positive in seven out of sixteen cases. In one extra case, case number 4, a treatment-effect could also be demonstrated. However, the parents relapsed twice into their old inadequate behavior. This is an unintended example of an experimental ABABA-design. Therefore this case was in the end evaluated as negative (see the first row, table 2): at the termination of treatment the child relapsed for the second time in encopretic behavior. Paradoxically, there was no doubt with regard to the efficacy of the behavior modification program; the duration of the intervention, however, was too short.

CASE ILLUSTRATION

We would like to illustrate the treatment approach with a case description. John is an eight year old boy with continuous encopresis and severe chronic constipation for which he has been under medical supervision since he was four. His problems with toilet-training (and constipation) date back to when he was a year and a half. A premature attempt at toilet-training failed. John does however have appropriate control over the elimination of urine since he was four years old. John is an anxious child: he is afraid of being alone; he has nightmares about ghosts who want to drag him away along tubes. His relationship with his mother has its problems. John has temper tantrums. His mother does not dare to make demands anymore. She is constantly irritated by his disobedience and the fact that he never listens. His relationship with friends is also problematical. During the last two years John has received play-therapy. During this period the parents received counseling. There was no improvement however, and the treatment was discontinued.

Toilet behavior: John only uses the toilet in order to urinate; he holds his urine as long as possible and runs away once he has flushed the toilet. He never goes to the toilet in order to defecate, but defecates in his clothes. Our behavioral diagnosis concerning this case was: a form of toilet phobia.

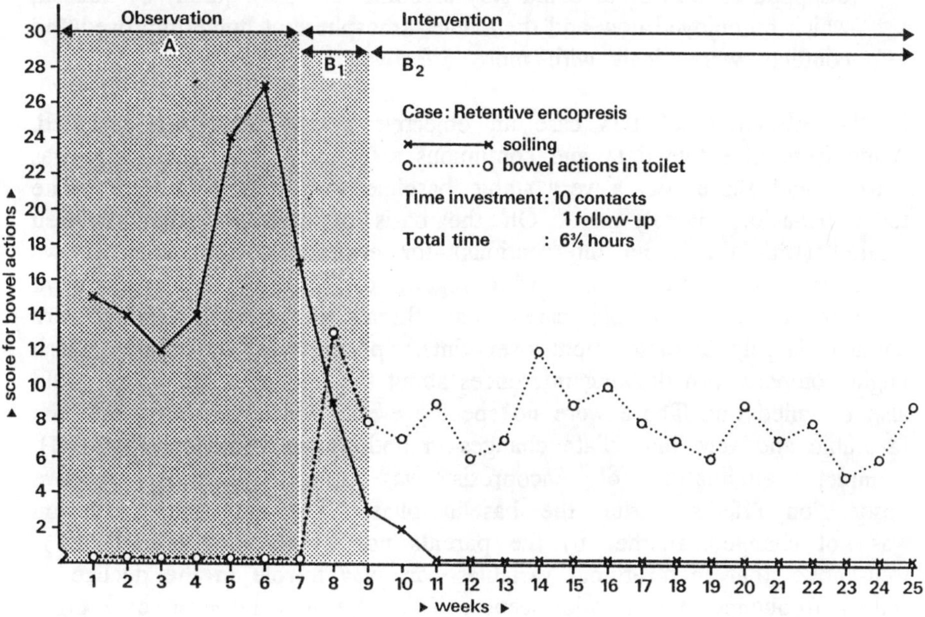

Figure 1: **Case John**

The duration of the baseline was 7 weeks. The various toilet behaviors which were recorded daily by the parents were plotted in weekly totals in a graph. From the beginning John's parents had him participate in the monitoring of the target behaviors and keeping the graph up to date. John was very motivated.

B 1: With a minimal Systematic Desensitization-procedure and with the help of the parents it was achieved that John could sit on the toilet without being afraid and without having temper tantrums (In this period medication was also introduced).

B 2: After two weeks a token economy procedure was implemented. Five weeks later things went so well that the parents stopped the systematic checking of soiling: John stayed clean and went to the toilet on his own initiative. The anxiety and sleeping problems decreased and his contacts with other children improved. The frequency of the treatment contacts was very low.

At the termination of therapy this positive result was maintained. The token economy program was not necessary anymore. Furthermore, the parents also reported improvements in other areas. John had become more open, talkative, independent and less anxious. The nightmares disappeared and John could stay at home and play quietly by himself, which he enjoyed now and then. The atmosphere at home improved and conflicts were dealt with more effectively.

In the evaluation of this case an objective measurement was included. Aside from objective data and continuous assessment, soiling behavior was chronic and there was a very stable baseline with regard to appropriate toilet behavior, namely zero. On the basis of data on other children treated (with the same interventions) for encopresis (see table 2), we could give a positive score with regard to Kazdin's fifth assessment criterion as well: multiple cases. The threats to internal validity were handled largely by assessment over time. Specific rival hypotheses which might compete with drawing inferences about the impact of treatment could also be ruled out. There were no specific events which coincided with the favorable and very immediate changes in both target behaviors (figure 1). Complete elimination of encopresis was attained, without reactive observation effects during the baseline-phase. The assessment criterion was not changed, neither by the parents nor by the boy himself. It is well-known that maturational variables can play a role in the decline of soiling frequency during adolescence. This boy was however only eight years old and the treatment duration very short; so, we may safely conclude that maturational effects were not present.
In sum, the evaluation criteria could be scored positively. This case study provides very strong evidence for the impact of the treatment.

CONCLUSIONS

In our opinion the method of treatment evaluation, as described above, is extremely well suited for clinical practice. This form of evaluation is also more feasible for the clinician than evaluation by means of group designs. The threats to internal validity can be assessed quite well on the basis of case records. The requirements with regard to observation (Kazdin, 1980; 1981) are really a rephrasing of the traditionally dictated requirement of objectivity in behavior therapy. The possibility of generalization is usually considered to be the greatest advantage of group designs. However, when individually successful treatments are repeated, with the same interventions and in totally different situations, generalization should be possible in the long run. Therefore, when individual cases are aggregated, the resulting information is more convincing than information obtained from a single case.
We entirely agree with Kazdin when he states that: (1) The case study occupies an extremely important place in clinical work. The intensive study of the individual tends to magnify details about a client that otherwise would be lost. (2) It is possible to include features in the case that help to decrease the plausibility of specific rival hypotheses. However, treatment that is accompanied by a rapid change in behavior provides a convincing demonstration, particularly where repeated attempts to alter that behavior by means of other treatments have failed consistently. (3) It is important to regard the case study as a potential source of scientifically useful information and to adopt procedures in order to increase the strength of case demonstrations in clinical settings. The single-case study can therefore be a very good clinical and experimental method by which to test one's ideas directly.
The total number of successfully treated encopretic children, whose problems differed greatly in nature and severity and who were treated under different circumstances as well as in different treatment settings, leaves no doubt as to the efficacy of this applied behavior modification program. Finally, it should be noted that because of the flexibility with which this program fits into medical settings - this form of therapy contributes to 'behavioral medicine' (Bosch, 1984).

REFERENCES

Bellman, M. (1966). Studies on encopresis. *Acta Paediatrica Scandinavica*, Suppl. 170.

Bosch, J.D. (1984). *Gedragsmodificatie van encopresis*. (Ph.D. Dissertation), Lisse: Swets & Zeitlinger.

Bosch, J.D. (1986). Behandeling van encopresis in de adolescentie:

literatuur en casuïstiek. *Gedragstherapie, 19*, 2, 109-124.
Bosch, J.D., Dik, M.I., Douwes, A.C., Jongenelen, E & Kerstens, T., (1984). *Kinderen met vieze broeken (2)*: Begeleiding van ouders en kinderen. Lisse: Swets & Zeitlinger.
Campbell, D.F. & Stanley, J.C. (1966). *Experimental and Quasi-Experimental Designs for Research*. Chicago: Rand McNally College Publ. Comp.
Gelfand, D.M. & Hartmann, D.P. (1984). *Child Behavior Analysis and Therapy*. Second Edition, New York: Pergamon Press.
Kazdin, A.E. (1981). Drawing valid inferences from case studies. *Journal of Consulting and Clinical Psychology, 49*, 183-192.
Kazdin, A.E. (1980). *Research Design in Clinical Psychology*, New York: Harper & Row, Publ.
Largo, R.H., Gianciaruso, M. & Prader, A. (1978). Die Entwicklung der Darm- und Blasenkontrolle von der Geburt biszum 18. Lebensjahr: Longitudinale Studie. *Schweizerisches medizinische Wochenschrift, 108*, 155-160.
Neale, D.A. (1963). Behaviour therapy and encopresis in children. *Behaviour Research and Therapy, 1*, 139-149.

DIFFERENTIATION IN PRODROMAL AND ACUTE SYMPTOMS OF PATIENTS WITH CARDIAC AND NON-CARDIAC CHEST PAIN

R. Beunderman, H. Van Dis, R.W. Koster, E. Boel, C. Tiemessen & J. Schipper

University of Amsterdam, Departments of Psychology and Cardiology, The Netherlands.

INTRODUCTION

For some years, our research group at the Academic Hospital of the University of Amsterdam (AMC) has studied ways of recognizing myocardial infarction (MI) sýmptoms in both the acute and the prodromal (preliminary) phases.
It has been assumed that of all patients dying of a heart attack, 40 to 75 percent do so within an hour after the onset of the acute symptoms. For effective action to be taken, it is important that both patient and doctor act as promptly as possible (Beunderman and Duyvis, 1983). The low specificity of ischemic symptoms in the prodromal but even in the acute phase interferes with their prompt recognition and may delay due action on the part of both patient and doctor. Among the patients admitted to a coronary care department with suspected myocardial infarction, on account of symptoms of cardiac origin as for instance angina pectoris (AP), there are some who have a pain on the chest for which no somatic cause can be found. In the literature on related subjects this diagnosis is given several names like "cardiac neurosis", "pseudo-angina", "angina innocens". In cardiology cardiac phobia/neurosis is often mistaken for a heart complaint of cardiac origin. For the cardiologist, it is a form of diagnostic noise and thus poses a differential diagnostic and therapeutic problem (Blacklock, 1977; Wilcox et al., 1981; Bennett, 1983; Todd, 1983; Schutz, 1987). The result is a large number of unnecessary visits to the emergency coronary care unit (ECCU) or the cardiology outpatient department.
Cardiac neurosis or phobia can, however, be taken as a separate diagnostic

entity which may be distinguished from cardiac disorders, other somatic illnesses and other psychiatric conditions (Nutzinger and Zapotoczky, 1985). If clearly identified, the disorder may be effectively treated by methods of behavioral medicine. Early "positive" diagnosis of cardiac phobia as against cardiac complaints of non-cardiac origin (in the absence of cardiac pathology) should lead to better referrals of patients to behavior therapeutic and/or psychopharmacological treatment. This could help to prevent cardiac phobia patients from paying unnecessary visits to the cardiologist (i.e. to prevent somatic fixation) and should contribute to a higher quality of life for these patients.
In this study these patients are referred to as "non-cardiac chest pain" (NCCP) patients.

An earlier study focussed on the identification of a detailed pattern of pain localization (Beunderman, Van Dis & Duyvis, 1987). The present study made a further investigation into the pain and other symptoms related to NCCP disorders. MI patients and AP patients were used as comparison groups. In our interviews we asked the patients about the acute symptoms that had made them decide to present at the cardiac emergency department and also about the prodromal symptoms.
Our statistical analysis aimed at finding criteria other than ECG and biochemical tests which would enable us to differentiate between NCCP, MI and AP patients.

Method

Patients

All patients had attended the ECCU of the department of cardiology in the AMC Academic Hospital of the University of Amsterdam and the Department of Cardiology of the Onze Lieve Vrouwe Gasthuis, Amsterdam. They had been referred by their GP or presented of their own accord. The ECCU is a specially equipped outpatient clinic for the diagnosis of acute cardiac conditions.
Acute MI was diagnosed on the basis of ECG and the usual biochemical tests (LDH, CPK-MB, and SGOT). Diagnoses of AP were based upon patients' medical histories and supplementary diagnostic examination. A diagnosis of NCCP was made if somatic pathology was excluded.
Three groups of patients were interviewed:
(a) 53 who had been classed as NCCP patients;
(b) 39 who had been classed as AP patients;
(c) 53 who had been classed as MI patients.
The acute phase was defined as the period between the onset of the acute symptoms and arrival at the ECCU. The prodromal phase was defined as the three weeks preceding the acute phase.

Interview

The investigation was conducted by means of a semi-structured interview. If possible, MI and AP patients were interviewed within the first seven days after admission to the ECCU. The NCCP patients were interviewed at home, one to three months after admission (the delay owing to technical and administrative causes).
Patients were asked about pain symptoms in the acute phase and invited to indicate the whereabouts of their pain on a chart outlining a human figure. Questions were asked concerning the qualitative aspects of the pain and other somatic and/or psychological complaints accompanying the cardiac emergency state and the prodromal phase.

RESULTS

In the MI and AP groups, more patients were males (77% and 82%, respectively) than in the NCCP group (45%) ($p < .05$). The average age was lower in the NCCP group than in both other groups ($p < .05$) (Table 1).

Table 1: **Age and sex distribution**

	Non-cardiac chest pain (N=53)	Angina pectoris (N=39)	Myocardial infarction (N=53)
Men	24	32	41
Women	29	7	12
< 50 years	33	2	6
50 - 65 years	15	20	30
> 65 years	5	16	17

Acute phase

In the acute phase the pattern of somatic and psychological complaints in the NCCP group differed distinctly from that in the MI group (Table 2). In the acute phase, pain on the center of the chest was reported by 81% of the MI, 67% of the AP and only 56% of the NCCP patients. The difference between the MI and the NCCP patients was significant ($p < .01$). This fact is further illustrated by figure 1 showing the distribution of pain symptoms as indicated by the members of each group. This figure shows that pain on the center of the chest is typical of the MI condition.
As to pain quality (categories were nagging, piercing, stinging, burning, oppressive and convulsive pain) no significant differences could be

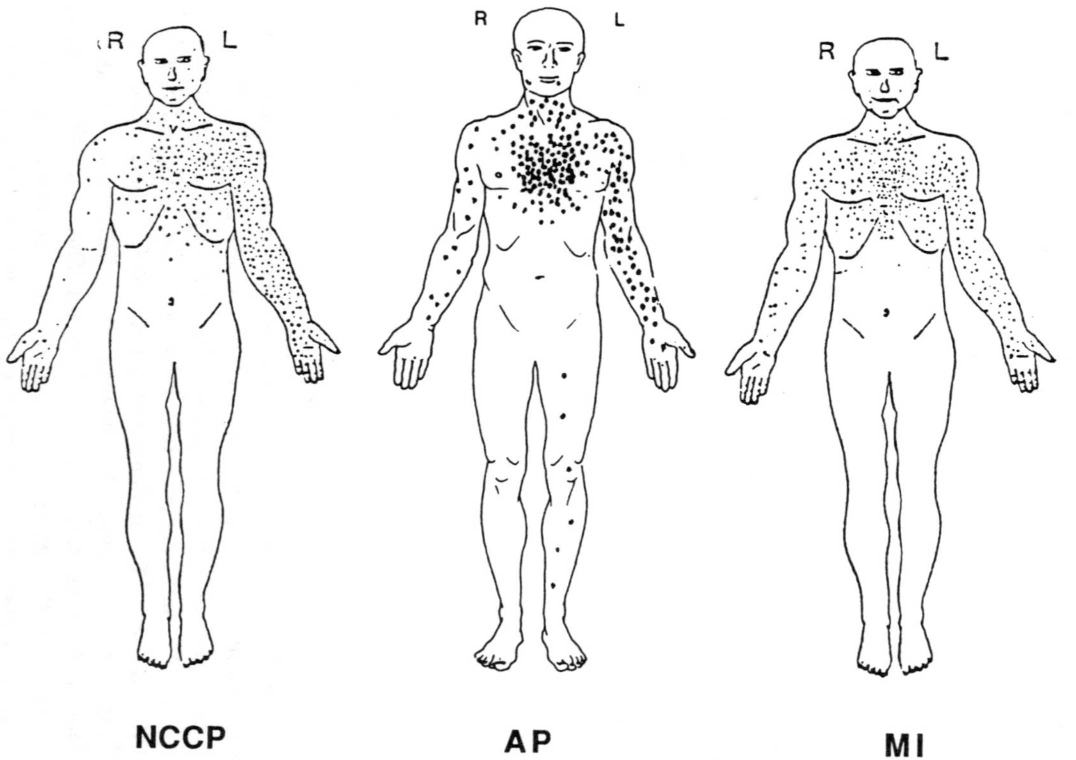

FIG 1: PAIN SYMPTOMS IN ACUTE PHASE: VENTRAL SIDE

established.
The groups also differed in their reports of non-pain symptoms.
In the NCCP group, palpitations, tiredness, dizziness and/or limpness, paresthesias and numb feelings in arms and legs were reported more frequently than in the AP group, whereas nausea proved less frequent. Symptoms reported more frequently in the NCCP group than the MI group ($p < .05$) were palpitations, paresthesias, numbness of the arms and legs; less frequent was, again, nausea ($p < .05$).

Table 2: **Somatic and psychological complaints in the Non-Cardiac Chest Pain group, the Angina Pectoris group and the Myocardial Infarction group (ACUTE PHASE).**

Symptoms	% NCCP N=53	% AP N=39	% MI N=53	p NCCP AP	p AP MI	p NCCP MI
Pain left	62	33	64	++	++	-
Pain center	56	67	81	-	-	++
Palpitations	45	21	13	+	-	+++
Tightness	58	51	56	-	-	-
Tiredness	41	21	43	++	+	-
Stiff/numb fingers	11	5	5	-	-	-
Dizziness/limpness	47	18	40	++	-	-
Paresthesias	39	15	11	+	-	+++
Numb feelings	47	23	19	+	-	++
Anxiety	69	51	58	-	-	-
Nausea	17	41	41	+	-	++
Perspiration	28	10	38	+	+	-

X^2-test + $p < .05$
++ $p < .01$
+++ $p < .001$

The prodromal phase

As to the perception of chest pain, no statistical differences could be established between the NCCP group and both other groups, The three groups could be differentiated as to non-chest pain prodromata (Table 3).

More NCCP patients than MI patients ($p < .05$) reported the following symptoms: palpitations, stiff and/or numb fingers, dizziness and/or limpness, paresthesias, numbness of arms and legs, feelings of anxiety. The NCCP group differed greatly from the AP group in its reports of palpitations, dizziness, limpness and paresthesias ($p < .05$).

Table 3: **Somatic and psychological complaints in the Non-Cardiac Chest Pain group, the Angina Pectoris group and the Myocardial Infarction group (PRODROMAL PHASE).**

Symptoms	% NCCP	% AP	% MI	p NCCP AP	p AP MI	p NCCP MI
Pain left	39	23	38	-	-	-
Pain center	41	41	51	-	-	-
Palpitations	39	10	4	++	-	+++
Tightness	41	28	34	-	-	-
Tiredness	32	26	28	-	-	-
Stiff/numb fingers	13	3	0	-	-	++
Dizziness/limpness	32	5	6	++	-	+++
Paresthesias	30	8	6	++	-	+++
Numb feelings	24	15	8	-	-	++
Anxiety	36	28	13	-	-	++
Nausea	111	3	15	-	+	-
Perspiration	21	13	15	-	-	-

X^2-test + $p < .05$
++ $p < .01$
+++ $p < .001$

To summarize the results: in the acute phase significantly more MI patients reported a pain on the center of the chest than did NCCP patients and AP patients. In both the acute and the prodromal phases, NCCP patients reported significantly more, and more frequent, non-pain symptoms than did MI and AP patients.

DISCUSSION

As reported in our earlier study on NCCP and MI patients, more than 90% of these could be correctly classified on the basis of sex, age, subjective symptoms and help-seeking behavior, in both the acute and the prodromal phases (Beunderman, Van Dis & Duyvis, 1987). For the acute phase older age, male sex, pain on the center of the chest, and nausea specially contributed to a classification as MI-patient; various somatic symptoms, palpitations, general malaise and paresthesias specially contributed to the classification as an NCCP patient.

The present data suggest that the symptom patterns of AP patients resembles that of MI patients more closely than that of the NCCP group does. Discriminant analysis will further quantify the predictability of the symptom patterns in each patient group.

We are presently engaged in implementing the results of our studies in a computer program. Our aim is to develop a computer based supporting system for medical decision making by nursing staff, possibly in a telephone referral center. When patients present at our hospital, this system should be able to make a preliminary diagnosis. While on the one hand, this could lead to an earlier and more accurate diagnosis, which would be of major importance in the pharmacological treatment of patients aimed at preventing lethal arythmias and at limiting muscle damage caused by myocardial infarction (Koster & Dunning, 1985; Simoons et al., 1985). On the other hand we will be able to diagnose NCCP conditions positively in an earlier stage. This may limit the number of unnecessary visits by this group of patients to the ECCU or the cardiology outpatients departments. This will contribute to the prevention of somatic fixation of somatic complaints. It may also lead to referral to the psychological treatment facilities in the case of cardiac phobic patients. Earlier diagnosis will improve the effects of treatment with behavioral methods.

Acknowledgements
The authors wish to thank R. Kurpershoek, D.J. Duyvis and E. van Daalen for their technical assistance; staff and members of the Department of Clinical and Experimental Cardiology of the Academic Medical Center Amsterdam, the Department of Cardiology, Onze Lieve Vrouwe Gasthuis Amsterdam for their permission to interview the subjects of this study.

REFERENCES

Bennett, J.R. (1983). Chest pain: heart or gullet?. *Medical Journal, 286*, 1231-1232.

Beunderman, R. & Duyvis, D.J. (1983). Myocardial infarction patients during the prodromal and acute phase: a comparison with patients with a diagnosis of "Non Cardiac Chest Pain". *Psychotherapy and Psychosomatics, 40*, 129-136.

Beunderman, R., van Dis, H. & Duyvis, D.J. (1987). Eine Vergleichsstudie somatischer und psychologischer Symptome bei Patienten mit nicht kardial bedingtem Brustschmerz und solchen mit Myokardinfarkt. pp.56-65. In: Nutzinger, D.O., Pfersmann, D., Welan, T. & Zapotoczky, H.G., *Herzphobie*, Stuttgart: Ferdinand Enke verlag.

Blacklock, S.M. (1977). The symptom of chest pain in family practice. *The Journal of Family Practice, 4* (3), 429-432.

Huberty, C.J. (1984). Issues in the use and interpretation of discriminant analysis. *Psychological Bulletin, 95* (1), 156-171.

Koster, R.W. & Dunning, A.J. (1985). Intramuscular lidocaine for the prevention of lethal arrythmias in the prehospitalization phase of acute myocardial infarction. *New England Journal of Medicine, 313*, 1105-1110.

Nutzinger, D.O. & Zapotoczky, H.G. (1985). The influence of depression on the outcome of cardiac phobia (panic disorder). *Psychopathology, 18*, 155-162.

Richter, H.E. & Beckmann, D. (1969). *Herzneurose*. Stuttgart: Thieme.

Simoons, M.L. et al. (1985). Improved survival after early thrombolysis in acute myocardial infarction. *Lancet, 2*, 578-582.

Schutz, W. (1987). Zur Differentialdiagnose der Herzphobie aus der Sicht der Intensivmedizin. pp.33-41. In: Nutzinger, D.O., Pfersmann, D., Welan, T. & Zapotoczky, H.G., *Herzphobie*. Stuttgart: Ferdinand Enke verlag.

Todd, J.W. (1983). Query cardiac pain. *Lancet 1*, 330-332.

Wilcox, R.G., Roland, J.M. & Hampton, J.R. (1981). Prognosis of patients with "chest pain cause ?". *British Medical Journal, 282*, 431-433.

PART VI:

COMMUNITY APPROACHES

THE COACHING PROJECT: TRAINING BY NON-PROFESSIONALS FOR YOUTHS WITH POOR COMMUNITY LIVING SKILLS

I.C.M. Beljaars & M.A. Berger

Paedologisch Instituut, Amsterdam, The Netherlands.

INTRODUCTION

The Coaching project started in 1984 as an extension of the existing youth care scheme. It ran until summer 1987. It is intended for youths who cannot easily benefit from regular treatment procedures, which require a certain level of verbal capacities and introspection. Furthermore, the official youth treatment programmes are limited to office hours. These young people are offered the training of a coach (male or female).

In this article we first present an outline of the theoretical background of the Coaching project. Then some general aspects of the project and the target population are described, followed by a paragraph in which we go into the role of the consultant. As we are talking about a mediation approach, the aim is transmission of the method. We describe the manner in which this is achieved. Finally, some research findings about the effects of coaching are presented, followed by some concluding remarks.

THEORETICAL BACKGROUND

Since 1973 the staff members have been developing and evaluating treatment procedures for young people in trouble. These are boys and girls who are in trouble because of psychosocial problems which can bring about difficulties, as some of them have already had police contacts, or run the risk of future offences. The treatment procedures are based upon the so-called "deficiency model". In this model, problematic behaviour of adolescents is seen as a result of skill deficiencies and the treatment focusses on the enlargement of the skill repertoire. There are several reasons for the choice of this model. The first is a pragmatic one: treatment based on this model has proved to be effective. At the start of the Coaching project follow-up results for 118 youths who had been treated according to this model, were available. On average, considerable progress has been assessed. The greatest progress was found with regard to "relations in the family", "future aspirations", and "problematic behaviour". There was also significant progress with regard to delinquency, although in some of the projects this progress runs parallel with the comparison group (Slot & Jagers, 1986). Bartels (1986) supports the deficiency model from another viewpoint. He studied the characteristics of effective treatment programmes for delinquent youths and demonstrated that all these programmes were aimed at teaching concrete behaviour patterns which enabled the youths to function more successfully in their daily life. Bartollas (1985) concluded after a comparative research: "Effective programs ... help delinquents develop skills that prepare them for adjustment in the community. These range from educational and vocational to interpersonal and problem solving skills". Ross and McKay (1980) showed that the teaching of new skills, instead of placing emphasis on the present inadequate behaviours, is responsible for the effectivity of succesful residential treatment programmes.

The second motivation for the choice of this treatment model is concerned with the supposed causes of antisocial behaviour in youngsters. Research findings show that deficiencies in concrete, daily required social skills are related to the development of this behaviour. Previous research findings have indicated that youths with antisocial behaviour have skill deficiencies (Patterson, 1982; McFall & Dodge, 1982; Freedman, Donahoe, Rosenthal, Schlundt & McFall, 1981). Later on Loeber & Dishion (1985) showed that skill deficiencies, displayed at an early age, are a precursor of antisocial behaviour in adolescence. They state correctly, however, that this is no proof that skill deficiencies form the main factor for antisocial behaviour.

The findings support the deficiency model. When put into practice, however, it is found that a therapist is seldom or never influenced by research findings in making a choice for a treatment programme. This is also valid with regard to results from research of the effect of coaching. People are only going to work with a certain model if the model appeals to them. That is why the third reason is of great importance: namely the deficiency model enables the therapist to present himself/herself to the youth in the mode of teacher and to make a proposal. This has proved to work effectively with youths who do not or cannot formulate a problematic situation for which they need help. The therapist does not wait until the boy or the girl states a problem, but comes up with a proposal to: "See how you can handle this in the most practical way", "To see what other people's interests are, so that you can use those interests to your best advantage". Statements like these stress the personal concern for the boy or girl. The therapist does not suggest to the youth that he has a problem, but gives him/her the idea that "other people" are causing problems. In this way the stalemate, usually experienced by social workers with youths who are said to be unmotivated, is tackled. Provided that the therapist stays active and keeps focusing on the daily life, the youngsters usually become interested in such a programme. Flexibility is also of great importance. When a youth is not interested in a proposal, the therapist has misjudged the situation of the youth or the youth is not yet ready to do something with the proposal. In both cases a quick switch to a different proposal is desirable. Talking about problems and delicts is only avoided in the first phase of the training. Later on, when the training is well under way, these subjects come up for extensive discussion; sometimes the youths themselves start talking about them.

In elaborating and testing the deficiency model, by means of diverse projects (Slot & Jagers, 1986), the active assistance of non-professionals seemed to be a logical step. Treatment appeared to have a greater chance to be effective, if directed at skills dealing with functioning in "daily life" (Heiner et al., 1982). The term used in the United States is: "community-based". The next step was to develop a treatment programme with non-professionals, who can be regarded as representatives of the youth's local community. The youngster also meets his coach in daily life via family or friends, in the neighbourhood, in social life or at work.

In order to attain the enlargement of the skill repertoire, the mediation-approach has been applied in the Coaching project. In behaviour therapy this triadic model is well-known mainly in the combination therapist-parent-child or therapist-teacher-pupil. The behaviour therapists Tharp and Wetzel (1969) made an important contribution to the further development of this model. They state that behaviour can best be changed in the natural environment of the child or the youngster. In the Coaching project we understand the natural environment to be the youths' local community, in which the coach acts as a mediator between the therapist/researcher as consultant and the youth as the target.

AN OVERVIEW OF COACHING

During the course of the Coaching project coaches were recruited, trained and supervised by staff members of our department. Young people were referred by social workers of several institutions for youth assistance.

The coach, who normally trains only one youth at a time, has contact with the youngster about once a week. Sometimes the coach visits the youngster, although they usually meet at the house of the coach. Emphasis is placed on issues that play a role in the daily life of the youngster. The coach gives advice and information, explains how to tackle a problem, thus stimulating him or her to take action. Aside from this more structured training, time is taken for more informal activities like watching television, playing a game, and so on. The aim of the training is the youngsters' independent functioning in daily life. The volunteer acts as coach for a period of six months. Youths usually keep on visiting the coach for a long period afterwards, by then the training contact has developed into a more informal one.

THE TARGET POPULATION

The applicants can be subdivided into three categories. The first category is represented by youths who indeed have some problems with functioning in daily life, but do not have such psychological problems that warrant more intensive treatment. For example, youths who go into lodgings, because they do not want to or cannot stay at home. Normally these youths show moderate skill deficiencies, for example in the area of handling money, independent living and finding a pleasant way to pass their leisure time.

The second category consists of youths who have just completed residential or outpatient care and need additional support and guidance in daily life afterwards.

The third category consists of young people who need a very intensive form of treatment, but who cannot be or are insufficiently covered by the normal treatment care. The reason could be that they became opposed to the official youth care scheme, or that they have a very unstructured life style. A coach can offer these youths a great deal because the coach normally has much more time available for them and therefore is more flexible than an average social worker.

THE ROLE OF THE CONSULTANT

The role of the consultant is of major importance in the Coaching project. Apart from the recruitment and selection of coaches and the contact with youth and referring agents, the consultant is responsible for the transmission of the method, by means of training and supervision of the coaches.

The *training* of the coaches takes up three evenings. During the training a number of methods and techniques are transmitted to the coaches, which they can use in the coaching of the youth. In the first place the consultant teaches them a number of basic concepts:

- Talk with the youngster as much as possible about *observational* matters
- Try to emphasize the *daily life* of the youngster. On the basis of

this the deficiency model is explained to the coaches
- Use *small steps* in teaching skills to the youngster
- Give much unconditional *positive feedback* to the youngster.

In the second place a *behavioural checklist* is introduced to the coaches. This is an observation instrument used in the Coaching project to stimulate talking about daily life and observational matters. With the help of this behavioural checklist the coach gets a clear picture of the functioning of the youngster during the previous week. Items of the checklist are day-time occupation, contact with parents, contact with friends, with a partner, spending of leisure time and handling money. Taking the scores of the checklist as a starting point, the coach and the youngster work on a particular item. In the training, the checklist is explained and trained by means of role playing.

In the third place the coaches are trained to teach a youngster skills: the *paper-and pencil-training*. This technique is used to subdivide skills in small steps, and to teach a youngster how to make a well-considered choice. For example the decision "what kind of sport am I going to do and how will I go about carrying it out?" can be made with the help of paper-and-pencil. In this way, the youngster is stimulated to think for himself/herself and to come into action.

In the fourth place the coach is taught that it is important to *make a proposal* to the youngster about a subject they can work on. In this way the coach is taught an active role: the coach does not wait until the youngster formulates a problematic situation, but comes up with a proposal himself/herself.

These are the most important aspects of the method that the consultant transmits to the coaches during the training. This training is extensively described in a manual (Berger, Dik & Slot, 1987). Coaches are recommended to read it.

The training constitutes the first part of the method transmission. It is continued in the *supervision* of the coaches. Supervision is given by telephone. The consultant calls the coach about once every three weeks to discuss with him/her the progress of the youth's training.

In the supervision the consultant uses the following techniques:

(1) *Observation*. With the behaviour checklist as a starting point, the consultant observes the behaviour of the youngster in an indirect way. The consultant tries to get as much information as possible of the behaviour of the youngster by asking a lot of questions. In this way the consultant is also a *model* for the coach. The consultant also observes the behaviour of the coach in order to assess whether the method is used.

(2) *Behaviour analysis*. The consultant takes a systematic look at the

skills and the skill deficiencies of the youth, what the youth has yet to learn and assesses what the youth has already acquired. In fact, a simple functional analysis is made. The consultant tries to include the ideas of the coach as much as possible in this analysis.

(3) *Behavioural instructions*. The consultant instructs the coach in which way he/she can teach the youngster a skill. The choice of the skill is based on the behavioural analysis.

(4) During the telephone call the consultant gives *positive feedback* to reinforce correct behaviour of the coach.

(5) Finally, the consultant often *relables* the youngsters' behaviour.

By means of this mediation approach, one full-time consultant can reach 60 youths per year via the coaches as mediators. More information about the model has been described in a manual (Berger, Slot & Beljaars, 1987).

RESEARCH FINDINGS

In the Coaching project research has been carried out on several topics; amongst others: the characteristics of the applicants for coaching, the selection process of the coaches, the opinion held about the project by coaches, referring agents and the youths themselves, and the effects of coaching. This paragraph goes into the last subject: the effects of coaching. For the other topics interested readers are referred to Beljaars, Berger & Slot (1987).

To answer the question whether there is an improvement in the psychosocial situation of the youngsters as a result of coaching the pretest-posttest design was used:

A pretest and posttest was carried out with an experimental group and with a comparison group. Assessment took place in the form of a multiple choice questionnaire. This questionnaire is used in several research projects of our institute. In contains the following variables: daily pursuits, job aspirations, inter-family relationships, indications for placement into custody, social skills, delicts, addiction to drugs and alcohol, peer relationships.

The *experimental group* consists of thirty-two youngsters. They have seen each other for at least five times. Referring agents for coaching filled in the questionnaire before coaching started *and* six months after it stopped. The *comparison group* consists of forty-five youngsters, from a family custody association in a medium-sized town. This particular group was chosen because a family custody association was the most important referring agent. The time between filling in both questionnaires was equally long for both experimental and comparison groups, namely thirteen months.

Extensive research with the same multiple choice questionnaire was carried out in the field of Child Care by Jagers & Vlaar (1984). Factor analysis of the findings showed three factors, which explain 50 percent of the variance. In a parallel manner three categories of effect measures were formed for this study. The categories are: problems, peer relationships and engagement with society. Each of them are composed of several subvariables.

The first category, *problems*, contains eight subvariables: overall functioning, relationship with parents, inter-family relationships, behaviour problems at home, variety of delicts, conduct disorders, social skills. The second category, *peer relationships*, is a compilation of duration of going steady and social skills. And finally, the third category, *engagement with society*, contains three variables: duration of a job or schooling, job and academic aspirations and addiction to alcoholic drinks. The results are found in Table 1.

During the pretest the differences found on the three categoriess between the experimental group and the comparison group are not statistically significant. During the posttest there are also no statistically significant differences between the categoriess. When comparing the changes on the three categoriess between both groups, there is a statistical significance on "problems" and "peer relationships". This means that *youngsters who have had a coach develop more favourably* with regard to *problems* and *peer relationships* than those of the comparison group. On "engagement with society" the changes follow the same direction, but they are not statistically significant.

CONCLUSION

In the Coaching Project behavioural training for youths with poor community living skills took place via a mediation-approach. A non-professional from the natural environment of the youth, called a coach, acts as a mediator between the consultant and the youth. Research showed that coaching has a favourable effect on problems an peer relationships. We think that *supervision* is of greates importance. A *continued* method transmission is essential. Therefore, it is necessary to supervise the coach by means of behavioural therapeutic techniques. By precise observations of the behaviour of the coach, reinforcement of desirable behaviour and explicit behavioural instructions, the consultant is able to influence coaching. This was of importance to make sure that the effect was caused by the method and not by all sorts of coincidental circumstances. In the future supervision remains an important factor.

Table 1: **Results on "problems", "peer relationships" and "engagement with society" of the experimental group and the comparison group. (alpha ≤ .05).**

	EXPERIMENTAL GROUP (N=32)		COMPARISON GROUP (N=45)			
	m	sd	m	sd	df	t
PROBLEMS:						
PRETEST	- .91	3.27	-2.20	4.67	75	1.34 ns
POSTTEST	-2.86	3.05	-1.59	5.29	75	-1.22 ns
CHANGE	-1.95	3.65	.60	3.79	75	-2.95 s
PEER RELATIONSHIPS:						
PRETEST	- .40	1.54	- .58	1.52	75	.51 ns
POSTTEST	-1.01	1.66	- .33	1.88	75	-1.64 ns
CHANGE	- .61	1.69	.25	1.67	75	-2.22 s
ENGAGEMENT WITH SOCIETY:						
PRETEST	- .47	1.94	- .34	1.78	75	- .30 ns
POSTTEST	- .57	1.89	.05	2.10	75	-1.33 ns
CHANGE	- .10	1.75	.39	1.63	75	-1.26 ns

Explanation: The lower the score the less problems, the more peer relationships and the more engagement with society.

REFERENCES

Bartels, A.A.J. (1986). Sociale vaardigheidstraining voor probleemjongeren.Lisse,Swets&Zeitlinger.

Bartollas, C. (1985). *Juvenile Delinquency*, New York, Wiley & Sons.

Beljaars, I.C.M., Berger, M.A. & Slot, N.W. (1987). *Coachesproject, Onderzoeksverslag*, Amsterdam, Paedologisch Instituut, dept. GT-projects.

Berger, M.A., Dik, M.I. & Slot, N.W. (1987). *COACHING: handleiding voor coaches*, Amsterdam, Paedologisch Instituut, dept. GT-projects.

Berger, M.A., Slot, N.W. & Beljaars, I.C.M. (1987). *COACHING: handboek voor coördinatoren*. Amsterdam, Paedologisch Instituut, dept. GT-projects.

Freedman, Barbara J., Clyde P. Donahoe, Jr., Lise Rosenthal, David G. Schlundt & Richard M. McFall (1987). A Social-Behavioral Analysis of Skill Deficits in Delinquent and Nondelinquent Adolescent Boys. In: *Journal of Consulting and Clinical Psychology*, Vol. 46, 6, 1448-1462.

Jagers, J.D. & Vlaar, E.B. (1984). *Constructie van een follow-up lijst psychosociale situatie "probleemjongeren"*. Masters thesis, Amsterdam, Paedologisch Instituut, dept. GT-projects. In cooperation with the department of Development Psychology, Paedology and Special Pedagogics, Free University, Amsterdam.

Heiner, J., Bartels, A.A.J., De Kruijff, G. & Slot, N.W. (1982). Hulpverlening aan adolescenten vanuit de ambulante optiek: 'Begin bij alledag', in: M.J. Eijer, D.J. de Levita & J.A.M. Schouten (Eds.), *Adolescent en psychiatrie*, (p.120-128). Deventer, Van Loghum Slaterus.

Loeber, R. & Dishion, T.J. (1983). Early predictors of male delinquency, In: *Psychological Bulletin, 94*, 68-99.

McFall, R.M. & Dodge, K.A. (1982). Early predictors of male interpersonal skills learning. In: Karoly, P. & F.H. Kanfer (Eds.), *Selfmanagement and Behavior Change*, New York, Pergamon.

Patterson, G.R. (1982). *Coercive Family Process*, Eugene OR, Castaglia.

Ross, R.R. & McKay, B. (1980). Behavioral Approaches to Treatment in Corrections: Requiem for a Panacea. In: R.R. Ross & P. Gendreau (red.), *Effective Correctional Treatment*, (p.37-53), Toronto, Butterworths.

Slot, N.W. & Jagers, J.D. (1986). De GT-projecten: 12 jaar onderzoek naar de effectiviteit van ambulante en residentiële vormen van hulpverlening voor "probleemjongeren", in: *Kind en Adolescent*, Research special 3, 192-204.

Tharp, R.G. & Wetzel, R.J. (1969). *Behavior modification in the natural environment*, New York/London, Academic Press.

PSYCHOLOGICAL INTERVENTION FOR THE RELATIVES OF SCHIZOPHRENIC PATIENTS

U. Ehlert

University of Trier, Clinical and Physiological Psychology, Trier, F.R.G.

INTRODUCTION

The application of the behavioral family therapy approach is of growing importance in the treatment of patient's schizophrenic illness (Beels & McFarlane, 1982). Of special interest are family studies based on the concept of expressed emotion (Brown, Birley & Wing, 1972). Expressed emotion refers to the emotional aspects of speech during a half-standardized interview with the relatives of schizophrenic patients. Apart from neuroleptic medication, the frequency and duration of face to face contact with relatives, ratings of the emotional overinvolvement, criticism, and hostility in speech are, at least in English speaking countries, predictive on the course of schizophrenia (Vaughn et al., 1982).

Those studies based on the concept of expressed emotion and conducted with the families of schizophrenic patients show that complex therapy programmes are effective in the prevention of relapses of schizophrenic patients (Anderson, 1986; Leff, Kuipers, Berkowitz, Eberlein-Fries & Sturgeon, 1982: Falloon, Boyd & McGill, 1984). The family therapy programs of those studies consist of some education regarding the illness, problem solving training, communication skills training, marital therapy, or crisis intervention programs.

The efficiency of the complex programs in terms of relapse prophylaxis as well as attitude and behavior changes of the relatives has been shown, however there is no information available about the consequences of applying single interventions or of combining of two of these interventions.

This report presents a therapy study with the relatives of schizophrenic patients during the patients' ambulant psychiatric treatment. The purpose of the study is to determine the specific effects of a family education program and of a problem solving training. The study utilizes diagnostic instruments and procedures derived from the American family therapy studies mentioned above.

METHOD

The intervention to be investigated was carried out as one of the standard services offered by a therapeutic team including one psychologist and one psychiatrist. The psychologist, the author, was responsible for differential diagnosis and the intervention with the relatives; the psychiatrist offered medical services including crisis intervention. Treatment of patients and relatives started in July 1985 and continued until October 1986; nine month follow-up data were finished in July 1987. Before details of the study are presented, the general aims of the investigation should be mentioned:

1. Estimation of the effect of two different elements as parts of a family training program.
2. Assignment and validation of new or translated diagnostic and evaluative instruments. These procedures are developed for the assessment of attitudes and behaviors of relatives towards their schizophrenic patients.
3. Experience with psychological research outside scientific institutes.

The study consists of a pilot study and a main study. The purpose of the pilot study was to test a German version of the Camberwell-Family-Interview (CFI, Vaughn & Leff 1976) and a test run of the entire therapy programm.

The most important aim of the main study was to evaluate the effects of a family education program and problem solving training. These effects were assessed in a three-group-treatment design without a control group. The intervention for treatment group one was composed of a family education program and problem solving training. Treatment group two received only a family education program; the intervention for treatment group three consisted of problem solving training only.
It was hypothesized that treatment improves problem solving behavior, increases knowledge about the illness and the means of relapse prevention, and significantly lowers patients' relapse rates during a nine month follow-up. It was expected that the combination of family education and

problem solving training is likely to be more effective than either training element applied singly.

Subjects

A total of 57 relatives of 35 patients were treated in succession during the investigation. Eight relatives of five patients received the combination of the training elements during the pilot study. The relatives of the remaining 30 patients were subdivided into the three treatment groups of the main study.

Patients

At the beginning of treatment all 35 patients showed the clinical picture of a paranoid schizophrenia (DSM III criteria 295.3). Mean age of patients was 29.9 years. 22 patients were male, 13 were female. 27 patients were singles, four were married and the remaining four were divorced. Of 35 patients eight were employed, 14 were unemployed, five were pensioned, six still received some form of education, and two were working in their own household. 13 of the patients had visited grade school, 10 high school, 12 college. The mean premorbid status of a German version of the Phillips rating scale (Harris, 1975) was 6.9. The patients' initial illness began, on the average, 7.1 years before the intervention. The period of time between the last exacerbation and the beginning of treatment amounted to an average of 2.7 months. For 15 patients compliance to medication was good and for 20 it was problematic.

Relatives

In the total sample of family members 32 relatives were mothers, 11 were fathers, five were spouses, and 19 were siblings. The mean age of relatives was 51.7. Five of the relatives were singles, 39 were married, two were divorced, and 11 were widowed. Of 57 relatives, 25 were employed, two unemployed, and nine were pensioned; 21 were working in their own household. 39 had visited grade school, 12 high school, six college. Nine of all relatives had been treated for a psychiatric illness either recently or in the past.

Treatment

The intervention of this family research study was subdivided into family education (five sessions) and problem solving (five sessions). The participants of each treatment group were split into subgroups of three to four families. Both interventions were highly structured, with each session having a designated theme and relatives receiving work sheets during each meeting and leaflets for home study.

Family education

Family education was composed of three sessions for knowledge transfer and two booster sessions for repetition and relating specific experiences of the relatives. The following topics were taught during the sessions:

(1) Etiology, symptomatology, course of schizophrenia. The main emphasis of knowledge transfer was on the pathological imaginations of patients, their resulting behavior, and perception of this behavior by the relatives. For each theme examples were given.
(2) Treatment of schizophrenia. Primary interest concerned treatment with psychopharmaca, especially neuroleptics.
(3) Relatives' reactions to schizophrenic illness. Individual experiences were discussed.
(4) Relapse prevention through interventions of the patient's relatives. This means the revision of expectations, adjusting to a simple style of communication, creation of barriers to overstimulation, selectively ignoring certain aspects of patient behavior, support of patient's medical compliance, setting limits against an overextension of the family's coping resources, normalizing the family routine, and using professional support.

Problem solving training

Problem solving training was along the lines of D'Zurilla & Goldfried (1971). During the first session relatives were informed about the theoretical assumptions of rational problem solving. The remaining two sessions and the two booster sessions were used to solve special problems of the families. This was done utilizing the following structured procedure: definition of the problem, determination of the goal, generation of solutions, evaluation of solutions, decision for a solution, planning of the solution's real life test.

Assessment

Treatment was evaluated in terms of (1) the course of patient's illness, (2) relatives' perception of the illness and their attitudes and behavior towards the patient, and (3) problem solving behavior of the family.

Course of the patient's illness

Each patient was tested by PSE, DSM III, RDC (Research Diagnostic Criteria) for psychiatric diagnosis.

Relatives' attitudes and behavior towards the patient

Subjective perception of the patient's illness was measured by a half-standardized interview. Relatives' attitudes and behavioral aspects to the patient were estimated by a German version of the Patient Rejection Scale, developed by Kreisman, Simmens & Joy (1979). Family atmosphere was assessed by a 132 items questionnaire.

Problem solving behavior

The experience with interviews held in the same way as the CFI during the pilot study, showed that it is not possible to transfer the English and American findings about the degree of expressed emotion to the relatives of German schizophrenic patients. Therefore a new instrument had to be developed to assess relatives' problem solving abilities and verbal behavior. This was accomplished with a ten minute problem discussion between the relatives and the patient. This discussion was rated on the dimensions of qualitative and quantitative aspects of problem solving competencies and intrafamilial communication behavior.

Knowledge about schizophrenia and rational problem solving behavior was assessed by multiple choice tests.

RESULTS

Essential results of the pilot study as well as the main study concerning relatives' knowledge about the illness and structured problem solving, encrements, findings from the self reports of attitudes towards the patient and family atmosphere, as well as relapse rates of the patients during the nine-month follow-up period will be reported.

Pilot study

The pilot study revealed the following results:

(1) Relatives' knowledge about the illness increased significantly from

pre test to post test as well as to follow-up. This effect was estimated by Friedman's two way ANOVA (Chi-square 14, $p < .01$). The data about problem solving knowledge didn't reach significance but the comparison of means shows a decrease of errors in the multiple choice test.

(2) Overprotective attitudes, measured by the Patient Rejection Scale, significantly decreased from the pre to the post test (T 1.49, $p < .1$). Behavioral appreciation of illness increased significantly (T-2.77, $p < .025$) from the pre to the post test.

(3) Significant changes of family atmosphere were found for outbreak of conflicts, sorrow, overburden, and distress. These four factors decreased (significances reach probabilities ranging from $p < .01$ to $p < .1$). Individual liberty was increased ($p < .01$).

(4) None of the patients showed a relapse during the nine month follow-up period. A relapse is defined as the occurrence of delusional thoughts or readmission to hospital. PSE ratings of the patients from the follow-up data did not show any psychotic symptoms.

Main study

Data analysis of pre tests (t1), post tests (t2), and follow-up tests (t3) of the main study showed the following results:

(1) Group one, which was treated with the combination of the two interventions, showed significant increases of knowledge about the illness and problem solving from pre to post test (Wilcoxon test z-2.201, $P < .25$). Group two, which was treated with family education procedures, showed significant improvement of knowledge about the illness (Wilcoxon test z -2.023 $p < .05$). Significant increases were found for problem solving training and group one which was exposed to both training elements (Wilcoxon tests, pre - post, $p < .01$).

(2) The comparison of subjective reports by the relatives of group one (pre test to post test) showed a significant reduction of their rejective attitudes and of overprotection. They decreased rejection and overprotection but also decreased their appreciation of the illness and acceptance of the patient. None of these effects can be shown for group two. Group three participants showed an increase for all factors of both instruments. Follow-up data of group one show an increase of attitude and behavior levels compared to pre test data. At the follow-up the participants of group two showed increased scores on overprotection, behavioral rejection but also appreciation of the illness. Group three showed increased overprotection and appreciation of illness at follow-up. Best discrimination between the

groups as well as over the duration of the study is accomplished with the factors of overprotection, appreciation of the illness and acceptance of the patient.

(3) At post test family atmosphere for group one was judged to be significantly more negative on 8 out of 12 subscales of the FFB. For the relatives of group two no significant changes of family climate could be shown. The only significant changes for the problem solving group were for their opinions about the quality of problem solving and subjective burden. At the follow-up test group one showed more positive judgments than at post test but less than at pre test time. Group three showed less positive reports about family climate than at the post test. Group three members judged family climate worst.

(4) A total of five patients relapsed, four patients didn't change their schizophrenic symptomatology during the follow-up. Prior to relapse, four of the five relapsed patients discontinued medication against medical advice. There is no significant effect between group membership of the relatives and relapse of patients.

DISCUSSION

Treatment was found to be highly effective in transferring knowledge. The measurements of treatment related knowledge show significant increases for all three groups. These results are stable over nearly one year. Data concerning subjective reports about attitudes and behavior towards the patient as well as family climate at post test show tremendous changes for group one and three contrasted with group two. But those effects, which can be related to treatment are not stable over time. At follow-up the members of all groups changed their subjective reports towards the reports of the pre test results.

No specific relationship between relatives' treatment and patients' relapse rates could be shown, although the rate of relapse and patients with no change of symptomatology (27%) is far below the rate reported for patients only treated by medication.

Results concerning relapse rates are comparable with those of American studies concerning family management. The conditions under which this study took place are somewhat different from those in the published research projects which were mentioned above. Some of the problems of conducting research with psychiatric out-patients are listed in the following summary.

1. The most annoying problem was the recruitment of families for the intervention. It was impossible to cooperate with local psychiatric hospitals or with psychiatrists in private practice. The reasons for

refusal were lack of interest, mistrust in behavior therapy, unwillingness to collaborate with a psychologist, and fear of loss of patients.

2. Relatives differed widely with respect to their motivation for therapy. For example, there were families who had to drive nearly 160 miles to participate but were never absent. Others within walking distance constantly had to be reminded of their appointments. There was no correlation between duration of patient's illness and the motivation of relatives.
3. It was impossible to set all patients on comparable medication. For instance only half of the patients regularly received neuroleptic decanoate injections. The other half of patients refused those injections or showed serious side effects after application. It was tried to assess the optimal dosage but out-patient treatment usually precludes the intensive control necessary for successfully optimizing medication.
4. The decision not to use the CFI as diagnostic instrument for measurement of relatives' expressed emotion deserves special mention: The experiences with the CFI during the pilot study resulted in the question whether the cut off point for critical comments may be transferred from American or English to German populations. Kreisman, Simmens & Joy (1979) found a strong correlation between PRS answers and CFI results. The data of the pilot study did not replicate those correlations. All relatives expressed many comments during the interview which had to be rated as more critical on the CFI than on the PRS. Köttgen and her coworkers (1984) also showed different relapse results in their German diagnostic study about the predictive value of the EE-Index from those studies conducted in English speaking countries. The EE findings definitely must first be validated for German populations before the CFI can be used to diagnostic purpose in German samples.

Taking all arguments into account, the findings of this study show that research outside scientific institutes is possible and that therapeutic work with relatives of schizophrenics leads to positive effects.

REFERENCES

Anderson, C.M. (1986). Psychoeducational family therapy. In: Goldstein, M.J., Hand, I. & Hahlweg, K. (Eds.). *Treatment of schizophrenia.* Berlin: Springer, 145-152.

Beels, C.C. & McFarlane, W.R. (1982). Family treatments of schizophrenia: Background and state of art. *Hospital and Community Psychiatry, 33,*

541-550.
Brown, G.W., Birley, J.T.L. & Wing, J.K. (1972). The influence of family life on the course of schizophrenic disorders: A replication. *British Journal of Psychiatry, 121*, 241-258.
D'Zurilla, T.J. & Goldfried, M.R. (1971). Problem solving and behavior modification. *Journal of Abnormal Psychology, 78*, 107-126.
Falloon, J.R.H., Boyd, J.L. & McGill, C.W. (1984). *Family care of schizophrenia*. New York: Guilford.
Harris, J.G. (1975). An abbreviated form of the Phillips rating scale of premorbid adjustment in schizophrenia. *Journal of Abnormal Psychology, 84*, 129-137.
Köttgen, C., Sönnichsen, I., Mollenhauer, K. & Jurth, R. (1984). Results of the Hamburg Camberwell Family Interview study. I-III. *International Journal of Family Psychiatry, 5*, 61-94.
Kreisman, D.E., Simmens, S.J. & Joy, V.D. (1979). Rejecting the patient: Preliminary validation of a self-report scale. *Schizophrenia Bulletin, 5*, 220-222.
Leff, J., Kuipers, L., Berkowitz, R., Eberlein-Fries, R. & Sturgeon, D. (1982). A controlled trial of social intervention in the families of schizophrenic patients. *British Journal of Psychiatry, 141*, 121-134.
Vaughn, C. & Leff, J. (1976). The measurement of expressed emotion in the families of psychiatric patients. *British Journal of Social and Clinical Psychology, 15*, 157-165.

PSYCHO-SOCIAL MANAGEMENT OF CHRONIC PSYCHIATRIC PATIENTS: SOME NEGATIVE VIRTUES AND LIMITS OF BEHAVIOR MODIFICATION.

J.P. Dauwalder

Social Psychiatric University Clinic, Berne, Switzerland.

INTRODUCTION

During the last 10 years there has been a considerable shift from treating psychiatric patients in large mental institutions toward community based treatments (Freeman et al., 1985). One of the side-effects of this trend is, that the remaining hospital beds are more and more occupied by chronically disturbed patients, who have great deficits in adaptive skills and for whom hospitalization becomes the preferred living alternative (Drake & Sederer, 1986).
The present contribution will highlight some methodological questions and the most frequent sources of failures for the currently applied behavior modification techniques with these patients. Our aim is to show, that nevertheless their use is still justified. We suggest, that mainly the avoidance of unintended or negative effects (negative virtues) should be considered.

METHODOLOGICAL QUESTIONS

Unfortunately a *consistent description* of the specific behaviors that define these "chronic" or "long-stay" patients seldom appears in the literature. The typical criteria used are length of hospitalization (i.e. at least one year for one single admission) or global clinical diagnosis (i.e. chronic schizophrenia). Despite the convincing evidence on the poor overall social functioning, there exist surprisingly little data on the precise nature or the basis of their difficulties (Morrison & Bellack, 1987). Some years ago we did a cross-sectional study on all the chronic psychiatric patients (geriatric and oligophrenic cases excluded) within a geographically defined care-sector (Ciompi, Ague & Dauwalder, 1987). This study clearly revealed a pattern of social and situational variables (i.e. unremunerative occupation, unmarried state, lack of social contacts, higher age, pessimistic expectations but relative satisfaction with the present situation) to be much more characteristic for the description of this population, than any psychopathological variable. Similar inabilities or apparent unwillingness to adapt to life in the community or to manage routine responsabilities have also been described in subsequent reviews by Matson (1980), Wing (1987) or Drake & Sederer (1986). Perhaps the suggestion of Rothbaum, Weisz & Snyder (1982), that such passive and withdrawn behavior may afford accurate prediction of negative outcomes and thereby promote a certain sense of control ("secondary control"), will open ways to more convincing explanations for the specific behaviors of these patients. In our view, one shortcoming of the literature is that many of the studies with chronic patients have provided inadequate information about the samples.

From a clinical viewpoint the process of rehabilitation of chronic patients must be seen as a complex task, with often very slow or only gradual progresses, partial results and frequent repetitive endeavours (Ciompi, Ague & Dauwalder, 1977). In current research however, the most frequently employed *criteria for outcome* or success only concern simple dichotomies such as living inside or outside (or eventually release from) psychiatric institutions. In order to refine these criteria, we introduced two relatively independent hierarchies, one for working and one for housing conditions.

Figure 1: **Levels of rehabilitation.**

WORKING	HOUSING
1. inability to work	1. full hospitalization
2. occupational activities	2. partial hospitalization
3. sheltered working	3. sheltered housing
4. industrial rehabilitation	4. sheltered appartments
5. part-time or diminished working	5. living in household of others
6. normal working	6. normal housing

The application of these criteria in three independent prospective studies indicated quite different rates of failure over a one year period. Failure was defined as moving down the levels and/or maintaining a low level (1, 2, 3 of 4). Taken together these empirical findings revealed important rates of failure for usual rehabilitative endeavours in different settings. In our view, a second shortcoming of the literature might be the frequently employed undifferentiated criteria for success.

Figure 2: **Rates of failure**

failure in working	failure in housing	N	population type	setting	reference
70%	83%	30	chronic schizo-phrenics	psychiatric hospital	Dauwalder et al. (1984)
63%	27%	81	chronic psychiatric	rehabilitation service	Ciompi,Dauwalder & Ague (1979)
42%	25%	889	chronic psychiatric	social psychiatry	Hess,Ciompi Dauwalder (1986)

Finally *institutionalization itself* has been noted as a factor in the dysfunction of chronic patients (Paul & Lentz, 1977; Ciompi, 1980; Wing, 1987; Morrison & Bellack, 1987). In fact a one year period of follow-up evaluation seems rather short for patients, who have been hospitalized during more than 8 years on average. We recently completed an extended follow-up study on a population of 107 chronic patients with a mean follow-up period of 7.6 years after termination of treatment. While only 23% of the patients remained in psychiatric institutions, 90% still needed professional help (Hubschmid & Aebi, 1986). Perhaps the most interesting single finding of these studies was the very high predictive validity of expectatives formulated by patients, relatives and staff (Dauwalder et al., 1984). Not only did the initial expectatives tend to be confirmed, but they also frequently seemed to remain closely linked and mutually maintained by patients, relatives and staff. In our view, a third shortcoming of the literature might be the neglect of "person-by-situational variables" in studies with chronic patients.

BEHAVIOR MODIFICATION TECHNIQUES

Traditional treatment for chronic psychiatric patients heavily relies on antipsychotic drugs. While it might reduce the rate of relapse for some psychotic patients, it nevertheless seems less than ideal for remediating the basic behavioral deficits shown by these patients (Hersen & Bellack, 1976). Therefore it would be of considerable interest to critically review the particular strengths and weaknesses of behavior modification techniques, applied for these patients so far. According to Lindsay (1982) the behavioral approaches used with this group of patients can be split into three basic categories:

- the reinforcement and motivational approach
- the skill acquisition approach, and
- the approach of situational and environmental manipulation.

Token economy

Perhaps the most heavily researched and most frequently cited treatment technique with chronic patients has been token economy (reviews: Hersen & Bellack, 1976; Paul & Lentz, 1977; Kazdin, 1983). Traditional token economy -- as a reinforcement and motivational approach -- has frequently been critisized. A recent survey of 152 institutions revealed that only 10 institutions has such programs, despite their particular cost-effectiveness (Boudewyns et al., 1986). For standardized token economy programs a rate of 10 to 18% of non-responders was found. Whereas Cohen (1973) attributed positive effects less to the incentives than to a better understanding of the staff's expectations and reactions, Kazdin (1983) identified such problems as insufficient training and morale of the staff or lack of continuous supervision to be frequent sources of failures. Matson (1980) found standardized programs to be less efficient than individualized ones. He also critisized the fact that changes often proved to be transient and not always showed sufficient clinical significance. This lack of generalization of treatment effects seems to be the major limit of token economy programs (Kazdin, 1983).
In our experience, the most important limit was given by the fact that these programs could be applied only in a very controlled setting, where equal motivation for staff was very difficult to maintain and where individualization of the programs rapidly exceeded the forces of the staff.

Social skills training

Entire books have been devoted to social skills training (Bellack & Hersen, 1979; Eisler & Frederiksen, 1980; Curran & Monti, 1982). In comparison with the simple behavioral techniques for skills acquisition used by Paul & Lentz (1977) actual techniques have been extended in

different ways. One example is the integration in the training of cognitive, communicative and social skills as proposed by Brenner (1987), where chronic patients should learn to construct more and more complex coping strategies by themselves. One other example is the development of situation specific modules (i.e. for leisure activities, household activities or drug regimens) as proposed by Liberman et al. (1987). Within each module patients first acquire basic skills in a treatment setting, to be applied and maintained in the natural environment afterwards.
However, Bellack (1987) recently reported the very disappointing fact, that 50% of the patients who successfully terminated such social skills training were rehospitalized within a one year follow-up period. Morrison & Bellack (1987) also critisize investigations in this field for their lack of widely accepted criteria of social competence, failure to control environmental factors and lack of longitudinal studies of individual vulnerability factors. Some other major sources of failures might be the insufficient directivity of therapists with chronic patients (Liberman et al., 1987), or insufficient opportunities for in-vivo training or booster sessions (Matson, 1980). A particualr difficulty might be produced by patient's habituation to positive reinforcement within the training groups, which will no longer be available in a natural environment (Liberman et al., 1987).
In our experience, the most important limit was given by the strong tendency for withdrawal and rapid deterioration of acquired skills, as shown by our chronic patients.

Environmental manipulation

The emerging field of situational and/or environmental manipulation seems very promising (reviews: Stein & Test, 1978; Falloon, 1985; Anderson et al., 1986; Strachan, 1986; Falloon, 1987).
Effects of situational manipulations by placing a group of non-selected patients in the community have been carefully evaluated by Test & Stein (1978) and an extensive cost-benefit analysis has been added by Weisbrod et al. (1980). In comparison to a control group these patients showed lower readmission rates, spent less time in institutions an belonged more frequently to social groups. Furthermore they manifested less subjective distress and were more satisfied with their lives.
Recently however the interest of researchers has turned somewhat more towards environmental manipulations.
Hogarty & Anderson (1987) reported the results of a controlled study, showing that the reduction of "high expressed emotions" (see Vaughn & Leff, 1976) by relatives on the one hand, or the combination of a "psychoeducational program" for relatives with social skills training for

the patient on the other hand, drastically reduced the relapse rates (to 0% !) for a one year follow-up period.
Sources of failure with situational and environmental manipulations are not yet well documented in the literature. Inpatients generally have less favorable living and financial conditions and show more relapses, than community residents (Lehman et al., 1986). One could even suggest, that chronic schizophrenia might be an artefact, due to institutional constraints (Ciompi, 1980). The limits of work with relatives should be considered too: effects of perceived blaming or increased family burden seem to be frequent (Angermeyer, 1982). Failure to solidify family support might even lead to suicides (Cotton et al., 1985) or violent behaviors (Lehman & Cancro, 1985). Environmental manipulation can not stand alone, it must be part of comprehensive care (Strachan, 1986). In our experience, the most important limit was given by the frequent lack of coordination between the multiple therapists, staff or other significant agents working with one particular patient.

In conclusion, one would expect any of these single techniques of behavior modification to be quite effective, as compared with traditional forms of treatment for chronic psychiatric patients. Nevertheless there are a lot of limits and sources of failure, which are quite specific to each of these techniques. Single techniques of behavior modification generally provide necessary but yet insufficient conditions for treatment. Therefore, perhaps the most striking result of this short review might be, that a careful combination of different techniques -- as suggested by Paul & Lenz (1977) and Hogarty & Anderson (1987) -- could produce particularly low rates of failure.

VIRTUES

Any intervention has both positive virtues (contributions to intended, beneficial outcomes) and negative virtues (effects that minimize unintended, negative outcomes). If an intervention should have neither positive, nor negative virtues it ought to be abandoned rather rapidly. Also, if an intervention only had positive virtues -- by definition -- no failures would occur. We therefore should analyze the particular virtues of the behavior modification techniques reviewed here in some detail:

As a major *positive virtue* we should remember the relative success of these techniques with clinical problems, that otherwise have been largely untreatable (see: Paul & Lentz, 1977).
And to a greater extent certain *negative virtues* also contribute to the fact, that these techniques continue to be applied so widely:
1. Their relatively simple theoretical framework allows for a sufficient

clinical understanding of the chronic psychiatric patient's actual behavior. This also facilitates the training of others -- even non-professionals -- and the implementation of efficient procedures with a whole staff.

2. Their emphasis on observable behaviors permits reliable definitions of concrete goals and valid goal-attainment-scaling, as well as agreement on differentiated outcome criteria.
3. The well-structured techniques facilitate continuous and step-by-step progression through intermediate and realistic stages for the severely handicapped patients. Such clearly perceptible progress will also provide more assurance to the therapist and staff.
4. The situational specificity, linking identified stimuli and patient behaviors, favors an increased reality testing, even with the most disconnected chronic patients.
5. The low-emotional yet supportive relationship, centered on patient's learning, avoids under- as well as overstimulation for these particularly vulnerable patients. This will probably be the most important of the negative virtues mentioned here.

In conclusion and with the actual state of our knowledge, behavior modification techniques applied in the treatment of chronic psychiatric patients mainly possess negative virtues, which largely justify their use, despite their particular limitations and sources of failures. Furthermore the methodological questions mentioned earlier in this article, might be easily resolved by paying more attention to these negative virtues.

OUTLOOK

Actually, behavior modification techniques offer necessary but yet insufficient conditions for the treatment of chronic psychiatric patients. Their use is mainly justified by their negative virtues. This state of affairs clearly invites for innovative efforts.

Once chronicity is established, it might be very difficult to modify negative expectatives of patients, relatives and even staff, as one of our prospective studies has shown (Dauwalder et al., 1984). Furthermore very high rates of relapse -- up to 40% in one year (Anthony et al., 1978; Hogarty, 1984) -- are usually observed. Thus the *development of better (behavioral) secondary prevention* could be such an innovative effect (Dauwalder, 1984). In analogy to the negative virtues of behavior modification techniques a particular training of preventive behaviors would probably also show some further virtues and avoid some sources of failure, as reviewed here. In accordance with a recent trend for more integrative psychosocial treatments for chronic psychiatric patients

(Wing, 1987; Drake & Sederer, 1986; Ciompi, 1987), our guidelines for such a secondary prevention can be briefly summarized as follows:

1. The main goal is to provide and maintain an optimal psychosocial autonomy for every patient throughout treatment and aftercare.
2. Treatment is offered in a small, warm community based setting by carefully selected staff, with a non-professional attitude and conceptual and relational continuity throughout treatment and aftercare.
3. The relevant social network is stimulated for low-emotional affective-cognitive participation, realistic-positive outcome expectancies and attention to preventive behaviors throughout treatment and aftercare.
4. Systematic training for preventive behaviors, such as coping with high-risk situations or prodromal signs for relapse is provided and maintained throughout treatment and aftercare.

These guidelines are actually applied and evaluated in a research project and the first results are quite encourageing (Ciompi & Bernasconi, 1986).

REFERENCES

Anderson, C., Reiss, D., Hogarty, G. (1986). *Schizophrenia in the Family: A Practitioner's Guide to Psychoeducation and Management*. New York: Guilford Press.

Angermeyer, M. (1982). Der theoriegraue Star im Auge des Psychiaters. *Medizin Mensch Gesellschaft, 7*, 55-60.

Anthony, W., Cohen, M., Vitalo, M. (1987). The Measurement of Rehabilitation Outcome. *Schizophrenia Bulletin, 4*, 365-383.

Bellack, A. (1987). Social Skills Training for the Treatment of Chronic Schizophrenics. In: Strauss, J., Boeker, W, Brenner, H. (Eds.), *Psychosocial Treatment of Schizophrenia*. Toronto: Hans Huber Publishers, P. 118-125.

Bellack, A., Hersen, M. (1979). *Research and Practice in Social Skills Training*. New York: Plenum Press.

Brenner, H. (1987). On the Importance of Cognitive Disorders in Treatment and Rehabilitation. In: Strauss, J., Boeker, W., Brenner, H. (Eds.), *Psychosocial Treatment of Schizophrenia*. Toronto: Hans Huber Publishers, p.136-151.

Boudewyns, P., Fry, T. & Nightingale, E. (1986). Token-economy programs in VA Medical Centers: Where are they today? *Behavior Therapist, 9*, 126-127.

Ciompi, L. (1980). Ist die chronische Schizophrenie ein Artefakt ? ArgumenteundGegenargumente.*Fortschr.Neurol.Psychiat., 48*,237-248.

Ciompi, L. (1987). Toward a Coherent Multidimensional Understanding and Therapy of Schizophrenia: Converging new Concepts. In: Strauss, J., Boeker, W. & Brenner, H. (Eds.), *Psychosocial Treatment of Schizophrenia*. Toronto: Hans Huber Publishers, p.48-62.

Ciompi, L, Ague, C. & Dauwalder, J.P. (1977). Ein Forschungsprogramm über die Rehabilitation psychisch Kranker. I. Konzepte und methodologische Probleme. *Nervenarzt*, 48, 12-18.

Ciompi, L., Ague, C. & Dauwalder, J.P. (1978). Ein Forschungsprogramm über die Rehabilitation psychisch Kranker. II. Querschnittsuntersuchung einer Population von chronischen Spitalpatienten. *Nervenarzt, 49*, 332-338.

Ciompi, L. & Bernasconi, R. (1986). Soteria-Bern: Erste Erfahrungen mit einer neuartigen Milieutherapie für akute Schizophrene. *Psychiatrische Praxis, 13*, 172-176.

Ciompi, L., Dauwalder, J.P. & Ague, C. (1979). Ein Foschungsprogramm über die Rehabilitation psychisch Kranker. III. Längsschnittuntersuchung zum Rehabilitationserfolg und zur Prognostik. *Nervenarzt, 50*, 366-378.

Cohen, R. (1973). Three Years of Experience with a Token-economy in a Psychiatric Ward for extremely inactive Schizophrenic Patients. *Zeitschr.klin.Psychologie, 2*, 243-277.

Cotton, P., Drake, R. & Gates, C. (1985). Critical Treatment Issues in Suicide among Schizophrenics. *Hospital and Community Psychiatry, 36*, 534-536.

Curran, J., Monti, P. (1982). *Social Skills Training: A Practical Handbook for Assessment and Treatment*. New York: Guilford Press.

Dauwalder, J.P. (1984). Les vertus négatives de la prévention comportementale. *Psychiatrie Francophone, 2*, 13-21.

Dauwalder, J.P., Ciompi, L, Hubschmid, T, & Aebi, E. (1984). Ein Forgschungsprogramm über die Rehabilitation psychisch Kranker. IV. Untersuchung zur Rolle von Zukunftserwartungen bei chronisch Schizophrenen. *Nervenarzt, 55*, 257-264.

Drake, R. & Sederer, L. (1986). Inpatient Psychosocial Treatment of Chronic Schizophrenia. *Hospital and Community Psychiatry, 37*, 897-901.

Eisler, R. & Fredericksen, L. (1980). *Perfecting Social Skills: A Guide to Interpersonal Behavior Development*. New York: Plenum Press.

Falloon, I. (1985). *Family Management of Schizophrenia*. Baltimore, John Hopkins University Press.

Falloon, I. (1987). Behavioral Assessment of Family Systems. In: Dauwalder, J., Perrez, M. & Hobi, V. (Eds.). *Controversial Issues in Behavior Modification*. Amsterdam, Swets & Zeitlinger, p.107-118.

Freeman, H., Fryers, T. & Henderson, J. (1985). *Mental Health Services in*

Europe: 10 years on. Geneva, World Health Organization.
Hersen, M. & Bellack, A. (1976). Social skills training for chronic psychiatric patients: rationale, research findings and future directions. *Comprehensive Psychiatry, 17*, 559-580.
Hess, D., Ciompi, L. & Dauwalder, J.P. (1986). Nutzen-Kosten-Evaluation eines sozialpsychiatrischen Dienstes. *Nervenarzt, 57*, 204-213.
Hogarty, G. (1984). Depot Neuroleptics: the relevance of psychosocial factors. *J.Clin.Psychiatry, 45*, 36-42.
Hogarty, G. & Anderson, C. (1987). A Controlled Study of Family Therapy Social Skills Training and Maintenance Chemotherapy in the Aftercare Treatment of Schizophrenic Patients: Preliminary Effects on Relapse and Expressed Emotion at One Year. In: Strauss, J., Boeker, W. & Brenner, H. (Eds.), *Psychosocial Treatment of Schizophrenia*. Toronto, Hans Huber Publishers, 73-86.
Hubschmid, T. & Aebi, E. (1986). Berufliche Wiedereingliederung von psychiatrischen Langzeitpatienten: eine katamnestische Untersuchung. *Social Psychiatry, 21*, 152-157.
Kazdin, A. (1983). Failures of persons to respond to the token economy. In: Foa, E. & Emmelkamp, P., *Failures in Behavior Therapy*. New York: Wiley, p.335-354.
Lehman, A., Possidente, S., Hawker, F. (1986). The Quality of Life of Chronic Patients in a State Hospital and in Community Residences. *Hospital and Community Psychiatry, 37*, 901-907.
Lehman, H: & Cancro, R. (1985). Schizophrenia: Clinical Features. In: Kaplan, H. & Sadock, B. (Eds.): *Comprehensive Textbook of Psychiatry*. Baltimore, Williams & Wilkins.
Liberman, P., Jacobs, H., Boone, S., Foy, D., Donahoe, C., Falloon, I, Blackwell, G. & Wallace, C. (1987). Skills training for the Community Adaptation of Schizophrenics. In: Strauss, J, Boeker, W. & Brenner, H. (Eds), *Psychosocial Treatment of Schizophrenia*. Toronto: Hans Huber Publishers, p.94-109.
Lindsay, W. (1982). Introduction: Methodological Approaches to Behavior Modification with Long-stay Patients. In: Main, C., *Clinical Psychology and Medicine*. New York: Plenum Press, p.271-278.
Matson, J. (1980). Behavior modification procedures for training chronically institutionalized schizophrenics. In: Hersen, M., Eisler, R. & Miller, P., *Progress in Behavior Modification*. New York: Academic Press, vol9, p.167-204.
Morrison, R. & Bellack, A. (1987). Social Functioning of Schizophrenic Patients: Clinical and Research Issues. *Schizophrenia Bulletin, 13*, 715-725.
Paul, G. & Lentz, R. (1977). *Psychosocial Treatment of Chronic Mental Patients*. Cambridge: Harvard Univerity Press.

Rothbaum, F., Weisz, J. & Snyder, S. (1982). Changing the World and Changing the Self: A Two Process Model of Perceived Control. *Journal of Personality and Social Psychology, 42*, 5-37.

Stein, L. & Test, M. (198-78). *Alternatives to Mental Hospital Treatment*. New York: Plenum Press.

Strachan, A. (1986). Family Intervention for the Rehabilitation of Schizophrenia: Toward Protection and Coping. *Schizophrenia Bulletin*, 12, 678-698.

Test, M. & Stein, L. (1978). Training in Community Living: Research Design and Results. In: Stein, L. & Test, M., *Alternatives to Mental Hospital Treatment*. New York: Plenum Press, p.57-74.

Vaughn, C. & Leff, J. (1976). The influence of family and social factors on the course of psychiatric illness. *British Journal of Psychiatry, 129*, 125-137.

Wing, J. (1987). Psychosocial Factors Affecting the Long-term Course of Schizophrenia. In: Strauss, J., Boeker, W. & Brenner, H. (Eds.), *Psychosocial Treatment of Schizophrenia*. Toronto: Hans Huber Publishers, p.13-29.

published in the

ANNUAL SERIES OF EUROPEAN RESEARCH IN BEHAVIOR THERAPY:
ISSN 0921-9439

volume 1
TOPICS IN BEHAVIORAL MEDICINE
J. Vinck, W. Vandereycken, O. Fontaine and P. Eelen (Eds.)

1987. ISBN 90 265 0762 3

volume 2
CONTROVERSIAL ISSUES OF BEHAVIOR MODIFICATION
J.P. Dauwalder, M. Perrez and V. Hobi (Eds.)

1987. ISBN 90 265 0854 9